What I Remember...

Stories from the Heartland

Dr. Wayne C. Christiansen

Heritage Books
2025

HERITAGE BOOKS

AN IMPRINT OF HERITAGE BOOKS, INC.

Books, CDs, and more—Worldwide

For our listing of thousands of titles see our website
at
www.HeritageBooks.com

Published 2025 by
HERITAGE BOOKS, INC.
Publishing Division
5810 Ruatan Street
Berwyn Heights, MD 20740

Heritage Books by the author:

Camouflage

What I Remember... Stories from the Heartland

Cover Photo: Courtesy of Kim Ryan

International Standard Book Number
Paperbound: 978-0-7884-4716-7

DEDICATION

This book is dedicated to the people of my Iowa home,
especially my parents Leo and Patricia, my sisters Lee Ann and Kim,
and my deceased brother and best friend Gary.

FOREWORD

This is a collection of short stories written over many years originally meant for my two daughters, Carly and Kay. I wanted them to know what it was like growing up how, when, and where I did. My family urged me to expand the audience for other readers to glimpse life in small-town Iowa during the 1950s and 1960s.

The stories are based in fact and actual events, but I've taken certain liberties with chronology and dialogue for effect. Because this is a collection of stories, you will notice some redundancy in the descriptions of various locations.

I enjoyed writing them and very much hope you enjoy reading them.

PREFACE

As a boy I spent a great deal of time listening to the conversations of adults. I was an observer who, it turns out, had a very good memory.

Living in small towns in Iowa during the '50s and '60s had its advantages and disadvantages. We were certainly isolated and protected from the world at large.

In a town where everyone knows everyone, it's difficult to keep secrets, hide misbehavior, or act outside certain norms. Friends and family make certain that you are imbued with a sense of honor, respect, and pride for family, hometown, and state. I think this is a good thing.

I had the great fortune of being raised and educated by many wonderful people who taught me lessons I'd need later in life. I will always be grateful.

ACKNOWLEDGMENTS

First and foremost, my love and profound gratitude to my wife, Pat, for her love, encouragement, advice, and support.

Thanks also to my sisters Lee Ann and Kim, who are mentioned prominently in this book and have been my trial audience and guides through the ancient history of our early years together.

I'm blessed or cursed with a remarkable recall of my childhood that fills my siblings with awe and my parents with... unease.

At first glance, you might think being able to remember detailed pieces of one's personal ancient history is desirable, but all memories aren't rosy. There are some unpleasant recollections lurking in the dusty past, too.

I've often wondered why I'm compelled to record and bear witness to my life's trivia. Some memories are startlingly clear, as though videorecorded and then enhanced by the perspective of time. Why couldn't I have the kind of memory that allows retrieval of more useful information, like say... my wife's cell phone number? Knowledge of that sort is far more practical and has greater potential for keeping me out of hot water.

There are various triggers that press the replay button in my head. Among the most powerful are odors. A whiff of wood smoke, for example, stirs memories of campfires with my Boy Scout troop in the woods outside of town. My skill at starting a fire with only one match, sans combustible liquids, and the pride I took in that simple task is rediscovered.

Other stimuli work well, too. Take this evening, for example, as I walked to the mailbox at the end of the driveway. A chilly November wind stirred the dead leaves and sent a puff down the neck of my jacket.

This is what I remember:

Suddenly, I'm fourteen again walking the lonely railroad tracks outside of my small Iowa hometown, my father's .410 shotgun tucked under my arm. The sun has just touched the horizon, turning the sky metallic silver, a color seen only that time of year. Long low clouds are maturing to the startling violet of Elizabeth Taylor's eyes.

Small birds winging to their night's roost dip and whirl at the edge of the approaching darkness. I pause, shift the gun to the crook of my left arm, draw in the chilly air through my nose, and expel it from my mouth in a little cloud.

The rails merge into a long thin V in the thickening distance and the early evening's first stars are appearing in the east.

In the waning light, I scan the steep slope bordering the tracks of the Illinois Central Railroad. The bottom of the embankment is choked with weeds, long grasses, and thickets. Wood posts and wire fences separate railroad property from fields. Never-ending rows of picked corn are littered with lifeless brown stalks, bent and broken from the harvest. Their empty husks make an eerie dry rattle as they're brushed by the breeze.

Before me, the friendly lights of the houses in my little Scandinavian prairie town glow safe and warm. The dark silhouette of St. Olaf Lutheran Church's spire points to Odin and Valhalla.

At the corner of my eye there's a flickering movement in the weeds. I catch my breath and halt mid-step to focus senses. Again, a shadowy movement confirms something is there.

Slowly, I raise the gun to the ready position, chest level with the muzzle up and to the left. The grass on the slope is glazed with frost and I must be careful to not slip and send the alarm. I feel my heart thudding hard. Despite gloves, my hands ache from the cold and I hope I'll be able to cock the gun.

The legal time for hunting expired when the sun met the horizon, a thought I push from my mind in the excitement. Having returned empty-handed the last few times I've gone hunting pheasant; I've vowed that tonight will be different.

As I pick my way through the weeds, my jeans brush against a milkweed pod. The tiny soft white parachutes spill their seeds in downy graceful arcs in the twilight.

Quietly, carefully, I close the distance, my arms and legs tingle in anticipation. Would the bird choose to jump into the air from in front, the side, or behind me? Or would it simply creep away ducking from cover to cover until safe?

Hands throb from my tight grip on the gun and I make myself take three, slow, calming breaths. It's darker now, but I think I'll be able to see enough for a shot.

An explosion of beating wings and the raspy startled croak of a pheasant tells me it's a rooster and fair game. He launches six feet before me, flying left in a swirl of feathers. In one motion I cock the hammer, settle the shotgun firmly into the hollow of my right shoulder, and sight in. Alarmed at how quickly the big bird has made distance, I hastily jerk the trigger.

I barely notice the gun's recoil. I have never fired my gun in twilight before and the sparks and flame leaping from the barrel startle me. I lower the gun to see if the shot found its target. But the bird, now a dark swift shape, continues to glide over the field untouched, fading sight and sound into the gloom.

I take a deep breath, hold it, and let it out through puffed cheeks. I'm disappointed but somehow relieved. For me, it's the tracking and matching wits with prey that holds the challenge, thrill, and the magic.

There are obligations in the unspoken rites of manhood to be fulfilled. All red-blooded young men in our community are expected to exchange hunting stories and to stock their families' freezers. I'm caught up in an adolescent's need for acceptance, but can't help feeling uneasy over some of those expectations.

While cleaning the birds, I'd found the magnificent plumage of a male ring-necked pheasant to be a thing of great beauty. Its gold jeweled eyes set in the red velvet patches of its proud head sent shards of guilt into my heart. It made my hands work quickly to make it a lump of meat to be eaten with my mother's homemade noodles.

So tonight, I shrug my shoulders with a guilty, albeit diminished, sense of failure at missing the bird. *Besides*, I observe, *it was for the best. It was after hunting hours and illegal.*

*

Looking down, I see grass-stained sneakers instead of hunting boots. Gone, too, are the black crossties of the railroad tracks, replaced by the bluestone dust of my driveway. The youthful and eager bounding in my chest is once again the ticking, plodding metronome of an aging heart.

I remember the mailbox and open the little door to retrieve the unwanted notices sent to me by computers.

In the night sky I see a boyhood friend, Orion the hunter, visiting for the winter; he's still pursuing the Seven Sisters as he has for millennia. He's trekked silently through the winter nights of my youth across the unadulterated darkness of the Great Plains. No matter where life's journey has taken me, Orion has been a touchstone with my prairie home. I double-pump my fist to the sky in an old greeting we've shared for many years. "I'm still here," I whisper.

As I walk to the house with its warm-lit welcoming windows I wonder, *Did Orion come to hate the killing, too.*

More often than I care to admit, my wife, two daughters and I ended up watching television together in the evenings. After the homework was finished, the dishes done, and the phones had ceased ringing, the "boob tube" beckoned from the living room.

The TV wasn't used as indiscriminately in our house as it was in the home of my childhood. It was new back then and not yet accused of the dastardly deeds for which it's blamed today. There's no doubt that television programming offered in that more innocent time had gentler subject matter and was far less graphic. The psycho/social changes to our society will be, I'm certain, debated for years to come.

I'm old enough to remember life before television. Radio, by no means young, was still very popular. *The Green Hornet*, *The Shadow*, and *Fibber McGee and Molly* were part of our evenings in my early years.

This is what I remember:

The summers in Iowa were hot, humid, and long. When I was a boy, they seemed endless. The days were full of butter-yellow sunshine punctuated with violent thunderstorms that spawned tornadoes.

The warm summer nights were special, too. There was little relief from the heat in the evenings in the time before air conditioning. A whispering breeze teased the curtains with little effect on the thermometer. Crickets sang their summer songs accompanied by the husky rattle of locusts in the elms. Bats darted like swift shadows in the gathering darkness; the fragrant air was so full of living things you could feel it rub up against you.

"Waaaaynne! Wayne and Gaaary! This is the last time I'm calling you two! Get in here now and warsh up for supper!" My mother's voice had taken on an edge, signaling the end of the Great Stall Game children play with their parents from time to time.

My brother and I were leaning against the front of the house, perched on our homemade wooden stilts. We'd been trying all afternoon to learn how to walk on them. My record stood at five consecutive steps... well, four, if you didn't count the one taken during the fall to the grass.

Gary wasn't doing much better, but his last attempt threatened my record and he seemed to be getting the hang of it. I was desperate to be the first to stroll around the yard looking upon the world from on high. It was only right as I was older.

"Okay, Mom," I shouted, without looking up.

I pushed off from the house with my rump, took two steps, and had to jump clear to avoid the impending fall. I looked up in time to see Gary, still on his stilts, lurching drunkenly toward the peony bushes.

"Go, Gare, go!" I hollered. And Gary did go… past the peonies and down the walk. He hopped down from his stilts and raised them in triumph over his head, one in each hand, with a big grin on his freckled face.

"In... now!" My mother's voice from the screen door startled us. We immediately started our sorry dog looks… eyes down, shoulders slumped, and head bowed.

We made for the door on the run. (Running is difficult when you're playing sorry dog.)

I reached the front steps first, tore open the door, and hurried past the aproned figure of my mother standing with arms folded and her right foot tapping impatiently. For one happy moment I thought I was in the clear until I felt the sting of her hand on the seat of my pants.

I skidded to a stop in front of the kitchen sink and began scrubbing my hands with the twenty-mule-team power of Boraxo soap powder. A moment later, my brother was beside me, scouring away. We glanced at each other, not daring to make eye contact, while Mom delivered a scolding. We waited for it to be over.

At the table, we stuck to our original strategy of sorry dogs, mute with downcast eyes, absently pushing food around our plates. During a lull in the harangue, I asked, "Could I have some more milk, please?" She quieted then and lapsed into silence.

I ventured, "Sorry, Mom. We won't be late for supper again."

"Yeah, Mom," Gary nodded.

"You wouldn't be acting like this if your father were here. Just because he's in Sioux City at barber college doesn't mean you can misbehave." Her voice betrayed the loneliness and unhappiness she tried to hide.

Now I truly was a sorry dog.

I noticed she'd barely touched her food but saw a small smile tugging at the corners of her mouth. "You boys almost lost your chance to go to the movie tonight."

My brother and I looked at each other with widening grins. The word "almost" hadn't been missed.

"Help with the supper dishes and you can go," she said, rising from her chair. "But no more monkey business."

Those of us in the small rural towns of the heartland were left to our own devices for entertainment and pleasant diversions. Once a week in the summer our little town showed free movies on Main Street. The business district (all two blocks of it) was barricaded, detouring cars onto side streets for the projector to focus its magic lantern on the white double doors of the lumberyard.

The three of us walked down the block to find seats. Mom carried a canvass-folding chair while Gary and I found places on the curb. Others brought lawn chairs and cushions or sat on the front steps of the shops.

Hank Paulson, owner of the general store, wrestled an ancient popcorn machine out onto the sidewalk and began preparing the hot buttered popcorn he sold for a nickel a bag. The yummy aroma wafting over the gathering crowd quickly had people queuing up.

I studied the weeds growing between the plentiful cracks in the sidewalk, contemplating my options. The popcorn was tantalizing, but as I only had five cents, I wanted to use it wisely. Just recently, I'd learned to blow bubblegum bubbles. Since each piece of gum cost a penny, I'd get five whole pieces to chew. The popcorn would last only five or six minutes, tops, but I could practice my bubbles all night. The scales tipped in favor of Bazooka Joe while Gary opted for popcorn.

Farmers who'd come to town with their families joined townsfolk. Neighbor greeted neighbor as the sounds of laughter and bits of conversation floated up and down the sidewalk.

"It sure feels like rain to me," someone said.

"Hope it does. My crop's lookin' a little sad. The hay's holdin' up okay, though," said another.

"How's your wife doin', Virgil?"

My grandmother, who'd walked the three blocks from her house, joined my mother, her daughter-in-law. We smiled and waved to each other. I guessed Grandpa was already in the tavern settling the dust of the day. The lure of a cold beer trumped any movie.

When it was dark enough the projector started to whir and we were soon engrossed in *King Kong*.

A farmer seated on a milking stool turned his head and squinted into the distance. I followed his line of sight and saw a flicker of lightning west of town revealing dark, thick clouds. Others, too, looked up from the screaming Fay Wray to assess the threatening weather.

I blew a big pink bubble that Gary immediately popped with his finger sticking bubblegum to my nose and lip.

"Darn you, Gary," I said. "That was gonna be a big one, too." He laughed as I picked gum from my face.

The low rumble of distant thunder was more frequent now. It looked like the storm front was moving in on us and not going north as weather often did.

By the time Kong had climbed the Empire State Building, streaks of lightning were striking the ground, quickly followed by loudening thunder. The faint summer breeze freshened, carrying the scent of rain. Farmers bid hurried goodnights to friends, gathered their children, and headed for their cars and pickup trucks.

As the closing credits rolled on the lumberyard doors, the rain came. There was none of the warning pitter-pattering sprinkle usually heralding rain. Instead, a torrential downpour was unleashed, catching everyone by surprise.

Everything happened at once: Sam Neilson snapped off the projector and began lugging it to safety, men, women, and children scattered for shelter, dogs barked, and people were shouting above the roar of the rain. A lightning bolt zigzagged nearby, and the immediate clap of thunder left me stunned.

I felt my mother's firm grip on my arm and looked up into her worried face, briefly illuminated by yet another flash of lightning. She was saying something I couldn't understand, but I obediently followed as she ushered Gary and me to shelter.

Within seconds we were soaked. There was no time to run home and the chances of being struck by lightning seemed high, so we sought refuge with others in the fire station. Sam Nielsen, who was the fire chief as well as the projectionist, backed the firetruck out to make more room.

The lights flickered but held while we huddled cold and wet, exchanging fears and reassurances. The men took up observation posts in the doorway and Gary and I watched through the jungle of their legs. Main Street was a river, signs swung crazily in the wind, and pieces of debris flew past the open door.

"Boy, somebody's sure catchin' hell," one man said.

Another nodded agreement, "Twister, fer sure."

I looked around for my mother and saw her talking with my soggy grandmother and two other ladies. I thought of cooped wet hens, guarded by roosters.

Mom caught my eye, smiled, and nodded reassuringly. It was frighteningly exciting, but I felt safe in the stout brick building.

In thirty minutes, the worst was over. The smell of ozone hung heavily in the air and the streets' flash floodwaters were receding.

Mom decided it was time to head for home and we started walking briskly through the waning raindrops.

"Oh, my God! I forgot all about the windows!" I heard her wail and began to run.

All the windows in the house had been left wide open to catch a breeze and were certain to have caught the rain instead.

The west-facing windows were the hardest hit. Rugs were soaked and sections of upholstered furniture were turned into giant sponges. The curtains hung like wet dishrags, dripping puddles onto the floor. A broken lamp lay overturned and dampened magazines and newspapers were scattered.

Mom looked as if she were about to cry when Grandma set her jaw, rolled up her sleeves, and announced, "Well, it can't be helped. Let's get it put right," and marched off to fetch cleaning supplies. With a shake of her head, Mom left to join her.

As it turned out, our misfortunes were made trivial by the news of a community a few miles to the east. There, a tornado had taken its sweet time walking through town, destroying half of it, and damaging the rest. Three people were killed, and they were searching for more victims in the wreckage.

Later that night, Gary and I lay waiting for the sandman, nestled in our double bed on the screened porch. The rain had cleared the air leaving it cool, sweet, and fresh. A moth beat against the screen with a blind purpose only it could know.

"Gary?" I whispered. "You still awake?"

He turned to face me in the darkness. "Yeah. Whatcha want?"

"Were you scared tonight?" I asked.

He paused a beat. "Nope. Were you?"

I lied, too. "Me neither."

Yes, I'd been frightened, but somehow, I always felt... no... *knew* that everything was going to be all right. The absolute trust of a child prevented any thoughts of real danger or harm. It was assumed that those who loved us would always be there. Our family, friends, and our town stood perpetual guard over our world.

As I snuggled beneath the covers with heavy eyelids, I basked in a warm glow of profound contentment and security.

*

I consider myself fortunate to carry this memory with me. The world is a very different place now and I'm no longer that carefree child. I've assumed my place as protector of my own children and grandchildren. But the way I felt on that evening so long ago has served as a kind of personal refuge as I've groped my way through the many storms of life.

I'm of the babyboomer generation, the resultant explosion of births in the years immediately following World War II.

Before our arrival, most Iowa small towns had their own school systems complete with teachers, administrators, and schoolboards. But it quickly became clear that it was expensive and inefficient. Taxpayers realized that they could get more for their money by bussing the increased numbers of children from the little towns and farms to larger, more centralized schools.

There's no doubt we small-town boomers benefited from school consolidations but, well... we lost something too.

This is what I remember:

I began my education by entering kindergarten in the same solid, red-bricked, two-story schoolhouse that had schooled my father's family. Then as before, grades kindergarten through twelve received their lessons within its walls. The building included a lunchroom, gymnasium, stage, laboratories, classrooms, and various offices.

Each school day was announced when Nels Nelsen the janitor pulled the rope to ring an old iron bell, the very same bell from the original schoolhouse built by our pioneer founders. The old wooden school, now used for storage, stood on the edge of school property.

Classrooms were spacious and filled with light from tall windows. Instead of lockers, there was a walk-in closet or cloakroom lined with rows of hooks for coats, hats, and scarves. A long shelf above the hooks provided a place to stash my Roy Rogers lunchbox.

The front and back of the room were covered wall-to-wall with blackboards. *Real* blackboards, not the pale-green ones marked with the faint, yellow chalk in the more modern schools. Our chalk was white, the slate black, and the lines sharp, clear, and unambivalent.

The teacher's desk was on a raised wooden platform overlooking the classroom from the side, not the front, as is customary today. This required you to turn your head to see if she was watching and gave her warning of wandering attention. She had a bird's-eye view of everyone and everything in the room... the queen mother, enthroned over her subjects.

Fortunately, our teacher was a benevolent ruler, unlike some of those employed by the consolidated schools. (My rather harsh initial opinion softened later.) Her name was Mrs. Lewis, or just Teacher, and we loved her.

Mrs. Lewis was everyone's grandmother. She wore her long graying hair in a bun at the back of her neck from which protruded one or two antennae-like pencils. Her print dresses were buttoned high and cut mid-calf. Shoes were either brown or black with thick, sturdy low heels. She

9

always wore a necklace, earrings, and a hint of some flowery perfume that attracted bees like iron to a magnet (an occupational hazard when on playground duty). Our lady was big-boned and matronly, graced with an ever-smiling open face, beaming love and acceptance. Her soft brown eyes made you feel as though she adored you and you alone.

On the wall in front of the room was our country's flag, all thirteen stripes and forty-eight stars of her, flanked by pictures of Abraham Lincoln and George Washington. Each day began as we stood beside our desks, right hands over our hearts, and recited the Pledge of Allegiance. Everyone proudly took turns leading the class in this sacred ritual.

The desks' legs were joined one to the other on long, flat, wooden runners. Each desk had unused holes that had once held ink bottles. Between the inkwells, a shallow groove cradled our fat pencils and under the desktop a small shelf was for tablets, workbooks, and other paraphernalia.

Nels could do little if you were too short for your assigned seat. My feet dangled several inches from the floor, requiring me to slide forward to rest them. Nevertheless, I wouldn't have traded my desk for the world, as scratched into the top was the name of my long dead uncle Wayne, my namesake. It had been his desk, and it seemed right that it should be mine now.

Our classroom contained kindergarten, first, and second grades, each grade in its own row. The teacher simply moved to the head of each row to present subject matter to each grade. If there was something from which she thought we'd all benefit, she addressed the entire room. By listening to upper classmates reading from the primer, *Fun with Dick and Jane*, I learned to read before the first grade.

At the end of each day, Mrs. Lewis pulled a chair into the front of the room and read to us from *The Hardy Boys*, *The Bobbsey Twins,* and *Heidi*.

During these story times we sometimes surprised her with something called a fruit roll. It began when one of the older girls spread word that we were to bring a piece of fruit with us the next day. After Mrs. Lewis had settled in her chair, the signal was given for us to roll the fruit down the aisles to her. She always acted surprised and delighted, even though she must have seen us hiding our treasures in our desks. After gathering the fruit, she carefully peeled and sliced it to share as we ate, talked, and laughed together.

For my first fruit roll, I remembered to tell my mother that I needed to bring a piece of fruit to school the next day. She assured me as I left that morning that the extra fruit was in my lunchbox. At lunch, I discovered I had an orange and a banana. As I liked oranges better than bananas, I naturally ate the orange. Later that day, the big moment arrived, and when Mrs. Lewis opened her storybook, the classroom leader announced, "Now!"

Shaking with excitement, I groped for the secret in my desk, leaned into the aisle, took aim, and launched my offering. That's when I discovered the inherent difficulty in rolling a banana. I finally gave up as everyone was gathering by her chair. I picked up my oblong failure and quietly placed it into her lap with the rest. She gave me a knowing wink, one of her adoring smiles, and I felt better.

Most mornings we assembled around an upright piano to sing from our music books. Those who couldn't yet read mumbled along until they learned the lyrics. In the back of the room was a long, waist-high sandbox where we were permitted to play quietly after finishing our lessons. Blue paper served as water and twigs became trees to make masterpieces of civil engineering. No one was left out as each of us contributed to an ever-changing sandbox community.

At the end of the school day, Mrs. Lewis stood outside the doorway as we left. "Good-bye, Teacher," we said, and she'd reply, "Good-bye...," calling each of us by our first names... a gently taught lesson in respect and manners.

The playground was immense. A large grassy area was perfect for games of *Pom Pom Pull Away, Red Rover, Tag, Red Light/Green Light, and Johnny May We Cross Your Wide River.* Playground equipment was reserved for the peewees, and the baseball diamond in the corner of the property for older kids. A tall metal slide, swing set, jungle gym, tetherball pole, teeter totters, a set of giant-strides, and merry-go-round were in constant use before and after classes and at recess.

The unique merry-go-round had been designed and built by my great-grandfather, the village blacksmith. It was constructed of heavy gauge steel salvaged from pieces of machinery with seats arranged in an octagonal ring that was suspended on a central post. The whole thing was welded into an indestructible web of rods, braces, bolts, and whatnot. It creaked and moaned, but once it got going, there was no stopping it. Risking nausea, you hooked your feet, leaned back, and watched the upside-down world blur by.

Three generations played on that wonderful, groaning contraption unlike any other in the world. I suspect it's forgotten, rusting away in some pasture, and missing the laughter of children. I wish I knew where it is so I could pay my respects.

Each Christmas we practiced the songs of the season to sing before an eager audience of family and well-wishers. The whole town enthusiastically turned out.

The year I was in first grade our classroom was to perform a Christmas play. The plot was that Santa Claus was so soundly asleep no one could awaken him for his Christmas Eve deliveries.

I was an elf, and my only line was: "But Christmas wouldn't be Christmas without Santa, and I wanted a train so bad!"

It was a musical with plenty of songs we practiced daily. I had my line down quickly and repeated it so often to anyone who'd listen that my parents begged me to keep it to myself. I knew it so well that I quickly became bored with the play and my small part in it.

The night of the performance, dressed in a green elf costume, I roamed around backstage with the other elves, awaiting our cues. At the proper time we made our entrances and stood around the somnolent Santa to sing him awake.

I was immediately mesmerized by the audience and the footlights. As we sang *Rudolph the Red Nosed Reindeer*, I became intent on finding my parents and grandparents seated on folding chairs on the gym floor.

Suddenly the song ended, and my classmates began robotically rattling off their lines. I dimly listened, all too familiar and bored with a play that, in my opinion, had been rehearsed to death. And then... silence.

I stood rocking on my elf heels with my elf hands clasped confidently behind my back. The audience grew restless and began to titter slightly. As the silence on stage grew, the laughter got louder. I smiled to myself and thought, *boy, some blockhead forgot their part!*

My fellow actors were frozen in place and time, unable to move or speak until the next line was given in its proper sequence. We waited. The audience shuffled. I rocked.

I looked to Mrs. Lewis, stationed with script in hand, in the stage wings. She looked distressed. *What in the world is she doing*? I wondered. I turned my head slightly to search for the blockhead, then back to her and shrugged as if to say: "Gee, I don't know who the blockhead is either." Then I saw THE FINGER! Her index finger seemed gigantic as it pointed. In horror, I realized *THE FINGER was for me! Me!*

Her brow was damp and shining in the overhead lights. Her eyes were big round ovals roofed with eyebrows arching to the middle of her forehead. And there was THE FINGER... pointing. Her lips mouthed the words: "YOU! YOU!"

Yes, I was the blockhead!

My head snapped forward to face the audience and my once-confident hands fell trembling to my sides. I raised my head to address the back of the room as I'd been instructed and at long last, delivered my line. The play moved on...

In the end, no one remembered an elf had not met his cue on time... only me, that is. I have *never* forgotten. All that's ancient history now but preserved in my memory to be recalled for those times when I get too big for my britches.

*

We babyboomers rode the coattails of a different time, the ushers-in of so much commotion. It seems that we've heralded change since we first appeared in the world, a world of instant mass communications shrinking the globe and speeding time. We are the makers of rock-and–roll, the flower children, hippies, yuppies, and Vietnam Vets. We are the weary veterans of the Cold War, having lived our lives under the threat of nuclear annihilation and global poisoning. We've changed everything in our wake and continue to do so at an ever-increasing pace... for better and for worse.

It's a gift to have been able to peek through a crack in the closing door of that time and glimpse a past now forever gone. Those green years still quietly whisper their lessons.

INFLUENZA

This is what I remember:

One winter Sunday in my third year of grade school in 1956 we had an exceptionally heavy snowfall. After the storm passed, Gary and I joined neighborhood kids to enjoy the fresh snow. In a short time, a fox-and-geese course was laid out on our friend's lawn. To avoid spoiling the paths we moved to our yard to build a snow fort.

The snow was the heavy sticky kind, perfect for construction. We rolled snow into balls that gathered mass so quickly it took four of us to push them. Some were left smaller to be able to lift onto the larger ones. After adding an arched doorway and a secret escape tunnel, we cut peepholes into the walls with an old lath. There were even shelves to store a snowball armory in the event of attacks. Craig, the youngest, was assigned the task of making snowballs in preparation for the inevitable snowball fights.

When construction was complete, we plopped onto our backs in patches of fresh snow, moving our arms and legs to make snow angels.

My two sisters and their friends were busy building a snow family. There was the usual snowman and standing proudly by his side were the snowwoman and three snowchildren. They were still working on the family dog.

Later that afternoon Mom called us in to warm up with hot chocolate and marshmallows that were melting into a creamy, sweet topping. It was a chore to remove all the boots, scarves, hats, mittens, and coats to dry before the oven door.

After the warmup we returned outside for the snowball fight.

The fight was glorious! We took turns defending or attacking the fort, capturing and recapturing it again and again. The fun came to a halt when Craig got a snowball square in the face. It caught him in mid-war whoop with his mouth wide open, packing it and his nose with snow and effectively blocking his airway. Making matters worse, it covered his glasses, blinding him. He stood stock still, frozen with panic, mute and blind, looking like the eyeless Little Orphan Annie.

He made grunting sounds as he pushed the snow from his mouth with his tongue causing it to fall from his lips like the snow cone maker at the county fair.

We paused, waiting for him to either die or get better.

When the snow had cleared enough to allow a welcome and overdue gasp of air, he immediately let out a loud wail. "I'm gonna tell my Mom on you guys!" His eyes were little angry blurs behind the fogged lenses.

"Aw, ya big crybaby," his older brother, Larry, taunted. "It was an accident, a lucky throw."

"Yeah, an accident," I echoed. "It's happened to us big kids lots of times," I lied.

"I don't care! I'm… goin'… an' I'm tellin'!" Then he blubbered and stomped off for home.

"Bawl-baby, bawl-baby, bawl-baby," Larry taunted him in the way reserved for big brothers.

In a short time, Craig's mother called him home, putting an end to our play.

I wasn't ready to quit yet. Feeling oddly bursting with energy, we began shoveling the walks with zeal. I was radiating vigor and… *heat*. In short order, Gary and I had the walks cleared, piling the snow shoulder high. When we'd cleared our ancient next-door neighbor's walks, he tapped and waved a thank-you from his kitchen window.

We raced each other to the backdoor to strip off wet clothes for the second time that day.

"My, your face is flushed," my mother observed. "Did you catch cold?"

"No, Mom," I said. "I think I was too warm."

I stood before her in my long johns as she put a soft, cool hand on my forehead. She looked concerned and frowned. "You're burning up!"

A moment later, I was on the couch with a thermometer sticking out of the corner of my mouth. Come to think of it, I *was* feeling a little funny…

"One hundred three point six," she read. "You're going to bed, young man."

I climbed into bed, sinking into the soft coolness of my pillow. I felt as if I were lying at the bottom of a deep pool with the warm water pressing down on me. Moving my eyes was painful so I closed them and quickly fell asleep.

My fevered dreams were anxious struggles with math problems. I tried to read school lessons but was unable to make sense of the words. All the while, a strange teacher kept whacking me on the back of the head with a ruler. "No recess for you, young man," she said, and smacked me again.

Misshapen people with huge bulging eyes gimped toward me, reaching out with palsied hands to transmit their disease. "Get away!" I shouted. "Leave me alone!"

One of them reached for my shoulder, gripping it hard. I screamed and struggled in terror but when I awoke, I saw it was my mother. "Shhhh," she said quietly, "it's just a baaaaad dream, a baaad dreeeeeeam."

Her voice seemed strange and far away. *I must still be dreaming*, I thought, until I noticed the morning sunlight from the bedroom window. It was like shards of glass in my eyes.

"Here, take some St. Joseph's aspirin." She held out several of the bitter, orange-flavored tablets. I chewed and washed them down with a glass of much-welcomed water and slipped back even deeper into the warm pool. Everything was an effort, and every effort hurt.

"Thanks, Mom," I mumbled. "What's wrong with me?"

Her voice faded in and out like the signal from a distant radio station. "You've got the Asian FluUUuuu," she said.

"I got what?"

"The FLU," her suddenly piercing voice made me wince.

"I'll BRING somethiiiinngggg for YOU TO eeeat laterrRR," I heard her say.

I drifted off again, back to the cruel teacher and her punishing ruler.

After a time, I awoke and looked to my brother's side of the double bed we shared. I hadn't remembered *him* lying there before and wondered how he'd gotten there without my knowledge.

I was surprised to see the moon's sparkling reflection on the snow and then it was back to dreamland.

The next morning Nurse Mom arrived with a tray of patent medicines, cool facecloths, and glasses of cold orange juice.

I looked to see if my brother had left for school. He was on his back staring at the ceiling through half-closed eyes and seemed to radiate heat. I thought I could see little wavy lines emanating from his body, like heat waves reflecting from a summer blacktop.

"Gare?" I croaked. "You got the flu, too?"

He opened one unfocused glazed eye and nodded. I suspected he had no idea who'd asked him the question and just wanted to be left alone. I understood completely.

Mom made her rounds taking our temperatures and fussing. "Does YOUR THOAT HURT? HOW'S your TUMMMMY?" Her voice was a brass gong.

"Oh! Gary! YOUR TEMPerature is ONE HUNdred and FOUR!" she reported.

Gary smiled a dreamy proud smile. *Wherever he is, I hope he's enjoying it*, I thought.

A strange hand was lying next to me on my pillow, and I wondered who it belonged to and what it was doing there. The fingers resembled cooked sausages, and I could see a line of dirt under the fingernail of the index finger. I reached to touch it and discovered the hand was mine. There were also weird changes in the bedroom. The doorjamb seemed to be bowing outward, and the walls looked like billowed sails. *Better to sleep, maybe I'll die in my sleep*, I mused.

The next morning, I awoke facing the back of Gary's head. I felt better, not great, but better. I poked him with my finger.

He rolled over to face me and croaked through cracked lips, "Whatcha want?"

"How're you feelin'?" I asked.

"Real achy, but better. You?"

I nodded.

"You look weird," I noted, observing his matted hair and crusted nostrils.

"Yeah, well, you *smell* weird," he said, wrinkling his nose.

Yup, Gary felt better, all right.

"How long we been in this bed?" I asked.

"Beats me," he shrugged.

I had to go to the bathroom and swung my feet to the floor.

When I tried to stand, my legs shook, and my brain swirled in fog. I eased down the stairs clutching the banister and kept moving toward the back of the house where I remembered the bathroom to be. I arrived at a familiar door. It was the bathroom.

I heard my mother rattling around in the kitchen.

"Wayne, is that you?" I heard her call.

"Yeah, Mom," I mumbled. "I went looking for the bathroom and found it. Long as I'm here, can I take a bath?"

"Please do," she said with an apprising look. It appeared that my brother wasn't alone in observing my need for soap and water.

Two days later Gary and I were back in school, and it was my sisters' turn. My poor mother, who'd nursed us all, was worn to a frazzle. I never knew if she or my father ever contracted it.

It was strange back in class with three-fourths of the students and many teachers out ill. The nearly deserted halls echoed eerily as we survivors scuffed through them.

The virus had decimated my classmates. At the time of my return, we were only nine out of thirty-two and now on our third substitute teacher, who didn't look too healthy herself. She bore an uncanny resemblance to the teacher who'd visited my fevered brain… the one with the ruler. Later in the day when she, too, paled and lurched from the room, I wondered if I'd be paying her a visit in *her* delirium.

Those who'd fallen first were among the first to return. We thought of ourselves as veterans who'd beaten the odds, each with a flu story to tell.

It appeared that telling stories was all we were accomplishing. After a week confined to bed nursed by our parents and another week of killing time in nearly empty classrooms, we were, well… bored. Triple-substitute teachers could think of little else to do with our thinned numbers but to say, "Read quietly at your desks."

Recess periods dragged as we wandered aimlessly on the nearly empty playground in search of familiar playmates. We missed our friends, our teachers, and we missed the learning.

A week later it was over, and things gradually returned to their normal state of orderly confusion. The Asian Flu Epidemic had run its course.

*

That flu was the most ill I'd ever been, a record that held up until well into adulthood. No wonder it made such a deep and lasting impression.

This is what I remember:

The low rumble of the piano being rolled down the hall could only mean one thing… it was time for music class.

Guiding the upright piano was our music teacher, Mrs. Boe. We could see her greying hair above the stack of music books on the piano as she carefully maneuvered it through the door. After positioning it in front of the room, she turned to greet thirty-two eager faces.

"Good morning, class," she smiled.

"Good morning, Mrs. Boe," we replied in singsong unison.

The books were distributed to the head of each row and we dutifully took one then passed the rest to those behind us. All that remained was to learn which would be the first song.

"Turn to page twenty-one and find *Old Dan Tucker.*"

We found the familiar illustration at the top of the page telling us it was indeed *Old Dan Tucker* and then prepared to sing.

Mrs. Boe stepped to the piano, played the first notes, raised her right hand, and briskly brought it down signaling us to start. "Sing," she commanded. We knew by now to watch for her cue. Few of us had a clue how to read music, but we knew the tune by now. The first verse had been committed to memory: *Old Dan Tucker was a fine ole man. Washed his face in a fryin' pan. Combed his hair with a wagon wheel and died with a toothache in his heel.* The strange nonsensical lyrics always made us smile at one another.

Her bouncing right hand kept time to the music as she played the piano with the other. (Amazing, now that I think of it.)

Some songs required explanations of the lyrics or background to the musical story. For the song, *Drill, Ye Tarriers, Drill*, we learned that a tarrier was about quarrymen and that "sugar in your tay" about tea. A few of the songs like *The Battle Hymn of the Republic* or *America the Beautiful* inspired us to sing with gusto. Others, like *Frog Went a-Courting*, with its many verses tended to become confused and muddled by the time it was finished.

The hour was a welcomed break from the usual routine. Mrs. Boe was no pushover and maintained discipline with a cold look or a sharp word, projecting a maternal presence that made us want to behave. It helped that we all loved her.

On rare but memorable occasions she accompanied us on her zither. As she stroked the metal strings with finger picks, she reminded me of paintings depicting angels plucking their harps in the clouds.

When the session was over, she collected the song books and was off to the next room with a wave and little smile.

It was not a sing-along every time. Sometimes her husband, the very dignified Mr. Boe, conducted the class. On those occasions, he brought a portable phonograph player.

Before playing the 33 & 1/3 rpm LP records, Mr. Boe set the stage for what we were to hear. The music from *The King and I* was preceded by a brief sketch of the story; an explanation of each song helped us to understand its motivation. At other times, we listened to classical pieces like the *1812 Overture* and were asked what we saw in our minds. There was beautiful music from Broadway plays, movie soundtracks, the Mormon Tabernacle choir, baroque harpsichord, and songs by Woody Guthrie or Pete Seeger.

I listened to the music accompanied by the hiss and pop of the tonearm on the record while gazing out the classroom windows, letting my imagination wander. He didn't seem to care if someone took advantage of the occasion to nap on their desktops. He just wanted us to relax and hear timeless music not found in our everyday lives. It was important to him that we knew this music was out there and to be able to recognize it if we ever heard it again.

As the holiday season neared, everything changed. The music became centered around old familiar Christmas songs that we practiced until they shined. It was preparation for the annual Christmas concert prior to the Christmas/New Year school vacation break.

It was a time before religious musical themes were banned from the public sphere. Our community of around six thousand was a homogeneous one consisting mostly of Scandinavians, Germans, and Irish. All were Christians... or at least professed to be. There were creche scenes in the city park and traditional Christmas music was played over loudspeakers mounted on streetlights on Main Street.

Each year, the town's two grade schools were brought together for a concert in the high school auditorium. Since the Boes taught classes at both schools, we were all on the same page. As the time neared, school buses brought us to the high school to practice getting on and off the stage risers without injury. It was also an occasion for the East Side and West Side kids to check each other out. We knew most of them from summers at the public swimming pool, church, or little league baseball, but we were still curious about each other. There was a not-so-subtle rivalry.

Mr. and Mrs. Boe made certain to include the Special Education kids in the festivities. They were given the opportunity to learn what they could of the songs and participate in the concerts. A spot in the front row was reserved just for them.

Everything was carefully organized with our teachers. We were given printed instructions as to what to wear for the concert and in which rooms at the high school to assemble. Once there, we were given our black surplices, white paper collars, and plastic red ribbon ties. When properly attired, we were lined up in the hall and herded single file to the stage. It was when Leonard Spangler always made the mooing cow sounds for which he was renowned. Even the teachers had to chuckle.

It was quite a moment when the curtain opened, revealing our parents waiting in anticipation in their Sunday best. There was a collective intake of breath from both the audience and choir. The warm stage lights quickly had us sweating beneath our robes and in danger of losing focus.

Mr. Boe, prepared for the shock, assumed position on the conductor's podium and rapped his white baton on the music stand, centering our attentions. Mrs. Boe, seated at a nearby piano, struck the first notes and we were off and singing like little cherubs.

The applause was always generous and effusive from a loving and proud audience. We smiled at each other, basking in our moment of glory. When it was over, we turned in our things and left with our parents to begin Christmas vacation.

Years later, I was back in my old hometown of Eagle Grove to attend community college. One of the courses I took to satisfy the liberal arts curriculum was Music Appreciation. It turned out that the professor was our beloved Mr. Boe, now Doctor Boe, with his PhD. He spotted me, took me aside, and asked if I'd like to participate in a folk singing group he was organizing for the college. I'd been playing guitar and singing in a little rock band back home and was happy to lend my meager talents.

He was able to get us performances at the college, local churches, and nursing homes. I must say, we weren't half bad. Mr. Boe was his usual quiet, confident self and politely let us shine.

*

Looking back, I've come to realize what that wonderful couple provided for generations of children. It wasn't just the music, either. They taught us pieces of our history and heritage. Songs like *Oh My Darling, Clementine* glimpsed life on the frontier, *Sweet Betsy from Pike*, conjured pictures of our pioneer ancestors, and *The Erie Canal* let us peek at that important, enormous endeavor. The folk song *Get Along Home Cindy, Cindy* was just plain fun. From the *Battle Hymn of the Republic,* we learned about the crusade of our Civil War and Stephen Foster's songs gave us glimpses of the Old South.

In those days, both old and young sang together in church, on buses, hayrides, at the drive-in theater, and in our living rooms with the TV program *Sing Along with Mitch*. At Boy Scout camp, we were led in song after every meal and at campfires in the evening.

Music was a soothing balm of shared memories and the glue of our unique American culture. I think we need it now more than ever and fear it's slipping away. We must remember who and what we were, to know who and what we *are*. People like the Boes knew its importance and made it their life's work. God bless them.

They were the "Special Ed" kids, the forever children. Some of my classmates referred to them with unkind names: retards, tards, mentals, or goofies.

We could hear their little group shambling hand-in-hand down the halls, stealing wide-eyed peeks into open classroom doors. Their shepherd, Mrs. Phillips the Special Ed teacher, stood apart from other teachers with her graying, waist-long ponytail and absence of cosmetics and jewelry. She was a kindly, patient soul and well-suited to her job.

"Shhhhh," she whispered, "let's be quiet as little mice, now."

Where they went and what they did when they got there, nobody knew. They were special.

Mrs. Phillips and her charges could pop up at odd moments and in unexpected places. Suddenly there they were, with their shy smiles, gawking unabashedly. We returned their curious stares with nervous giggles, impolite pointing, and whispers.

This is what I remember:

In December each year, the two grade schools in our town held a Christmas concert. Assembled onto bleachers high enough to give you a nosebleed, we sang our hearts out in front of our families. It was the usual bill of fare: *Deck the Halls, Silent Night, Joy to the World*, etc. This was the 1950s, well before such songs were forbidden in public schools.

When the two schools assembled to practice entering and exiting the stage with minimum loss of life, the Special Ed kids were there, too. They took their places in the front row to the left of the music director, some six to eight eager faces. I guessed that they were near the stage wings so they could be whisked off at the first sign of misbehavior. Of course, it never happened. Some sang along the best they could, some mumbled quietly leaving the singing to us, and others were happy to watch the audience.

Their appearances were always a surprise, and I tried to not stare, but I couldn't help it. Who were these kids? Why were they kinda...well... goofy?

They always seemed to be having such a good time. I noticed, too, that they never showed up at math class, but were there for art, music, and gym. I began to wonder what you had to do to need Special Ed. I mean, did you have to do something as complicated as fail a few grades, or did you just sign up? *Maybe*, I wondered, *you needed your parents to request it?*

I tried this notion out on my mother one afternoon while she was ironing clothes.

"Mom? You know those kids at school?"

She looked puzzled. "What kids?"

"You know, the retarded ones," I said.

She studied me keenly. "Yes, what about them?" she said cautiously.

"Well, could a guy, like, *become* one if he wanted to or does it just sorta… happen?"

She looked up from her ironing board. "You haven't been bothering those children, have you?" she demanded.

I shook my head vigorously.

"Well, I hope not!" she said, "You leave those poor kids alone. They have enough problems to contend with without mistreatment from other children."

Problems? I thought. *What problems*? They had it made in the shade. No regular school as far as I could see, no tests, no responsibility… just fun and games. I wanted in.

"See," she continued, "they were just born that way."

She went on to explain a few of the popular theories of the time. Most theories had some element of blame to lay at the feet of the parents. Either they'd had children late in life or the mother was pregnant when some traumatic event, physical or emotional occurred. The long and short of it was that she didn't seem to know, either.

I did learn, though, that they were to be pitied yet kept at a distance. There apparently was some element of danger, the nature of which I'd been unaware.

"Sometimes they don't know their own strength," she explained. "They may not intend to hurt anyone, but there are stories about them accidentally harming people and small animals."

Wait…. small animals?

My initial notions began to change over the next few days as I researched. Pictures in an old medical book identified a pin head, mongoloid, hydrocephalic, and others. They were posed nude front, side, and rear like mug shots in a police rogues' gallery with little black bars covering their eyes.

The various IQ levels had names, some of which I recognized from the playground: idiot, moron, and imbecile. It was an old, thankfully long-abandoned classification system meant to define and pigeonhole the spectrum of mental retardation. The labels remain today but only derisively.

The photographs shocked me; later, after returning to them time and again, shock gave way to pity and then guilt. How could I have believed that Special Education was some sort of vacation? Sure, education could be challenging, but how could it hold a candle to the determination needed to learn something as simple as tying your shoelaces? The daily tasks I took for granted were just so much background for me but to them, each day must be semester finals.

The next time I saw them, they were waiting for a van with Mrs. Phillips in front of the school building. Some were in constant motion and others still as statues. I recognized a boy who rode my school bus every day named Joseph Amour.

Joey was on the pudgy side with fine, light brown hair, and wide-set, almond-shaped brown eyes. His deep dimples and even white teeth were displayed in a perpetual smile.

"Hey, Joey," I called. When he waved in return, his chubby hand looked like a little white hankie. I quickly looked around for other kids; it wouldn't do to be seen being chummy with a goofy. There'd be no end to the ribbing.

The pecking order on the school bus had long been established, with the rear seats taken by the oldest, toughest, and meanest kids. The degree of passivity and self-confidence waned as you moved forward. Joey always sat directly behind the driver.

The driver's name was Ivan Stutz, but we called him Drivin' Ivan. He was a balding, overweight man with a fierce temper who watched for misbehavior in a wide mirror above the windshield.

Due to a bus shortage the ride was overcrowded, requiring us to jam ourselves three and four to a seat. When the established order broke down, it became dog-eat-dog. By the time Ivan delivered us to school each day, he was red-faced with suppressed rage.

Dennis Woolard and his two cronies were three kids we avoided. As survivors of abusive homes, they'd learned to fend for themselves and take what they wanted from others. They weren't nearly as tough as their reputations but most of us were sufficiently cowed to allow them to dominate us. Bullies prey on the weakest and least able to fight back, relying on the tendency of people to mind their own business and avoid being singled out.

On the ride home one Friday afternoon, the confusion on the bus had reached a level never seen before, prompting Ivan to shout threats into the mirror. We could see his crimson face and neck veins standing out like blue pipes. Clear signs that he was furious at what he saw. Kids were pushing and shoving, walking in the isles, throwing books, and other behavior familiar to anyone who's ever ridden a crowded school bus.

Last to board, Joey toddled onto the bus only to find his usual seat taken. He frowned but smiled when he realized he could sit elsewhere. This was no easy task, as no one wanted to share their seat with a goofy.

Gary, our friend Larry, and I were sitting together in the middle of the bus. After a brief discussion, we pushed close to the window and invited him to sit with us.

"Hey, Joey," I shouted above the noise, "Come and sit here." His face brightened like sunshine after a thunderstorm. He made his way, holding on to first one seatback and then another to steady himself. Tucked under his arm was a clipboard stuffed with papers.

As he passed, Dennis stuck his booted foot out into the aisle to trip him and Joey went down in a heap, papers scattering like autumn leaves.

"Har! Har! Har!" Dennis bellowed. "Look at the big fat tard! He can't even walk and hold his papers at the same time!"

Joseph righted himself amidst the laughter. He seemed embarrassed and began gathering the pencil and crayon drawings he'd made. Joe apparently liked to draw stars; other papers had crooked numbers and letters arranged in an order significant only to him.

One of Dennis' buddies snatched a handful and held them over Joey's head.

"Come on, ya fat tard," he taunted. "Come and get 'em 'for I throw 'em out the window!"

Joey's face changed from embarrassment to bewilderment. His lower lip protruded and trembled as he tried valiantly to keep from crying.

Before I could think things through, I was in the aisle. I grabbed the rumpled papers from the hands of his tormentor and shoved them at Joey.

"Here," I said, "take 'em and sit down!" Then, emboldened by anger, I shouted at Dennis, "Leave him alone! He wasn't bothering anybody!"

My sudden outburst surprised me as much as it did Dennis. Recovering quickly, he said with a sly smile, "Yeah? Who's gonna make me?"

"We are!" said nearby voices. It was Larry and my brother, now up from the seat with determined faces and clenched fists.

The situation was defused when Ivan, who'd been trying desperately to maneuver the bus onto the shoulder of the road, succeeded in coming to an abrupt stop. He leapt from his seat, faced the rear of the bus and bellowed, "If you kids don't sit down *now,* I'm gonna come back there and *kick some ass and you can walk home!*" We knew he meant it. We sat.

The rest of the trip was relatively quiet, sobered by Ivan's intimidating anger. No one wanted to test what Drivin' was capable of during one of his fits.

The three of us decided to ensure Joseph's safety on his two-block walk home, so we disembarked with him. We knew it wasn't finished as Dennis and his two pals were sure to follow. They glared their poison as we passed by. The bus had scarcely moved out of sight before they made their move.

"All right, assholes!" Ya got nobody to protect ya now!" Dennis snarled as he closed on the bewildered Joseph and shoved him, once again spilling the starry papers. Tears welled up in Joey's brown eyes and his chin quivered.

Dennis' pals encircled us as we moved close together like sheep surrounded by wolves.

"Back off, weenies!" Dennis snarled as he turned to face us, "or you'll get some of the same!"

My cheeks burned and my body shook with anger. I screamed, trying to bolster my courage, "You're pretty good pickin' on goofies; why don't you try someone who can fight you back!"

Then we were all pushing and shoving against each other as the fight escalated.

When Dennis pushed me, I lost my balance and went sprawling onto the grass. My head snapped back and hit the ground hard enough for me to see little stars of my own with an occasional comet.

Without a sound, Joey, who'd been an observer of the melee, suddenly stepped behind Dennis and encircled his chest with his arms. He locked his hands together and leaned back, lifting Dennis off the ground and then began to squeeze for all he was worth.

"Hey! Let go a me, you tard!" Dennis grunted. It was becoming difficult for him to speak with his lungs rapidly emptying of air. He wiggled and struggled trying to reach behind him. But Joey buried his forehead into the space above Dennis' shoulder blades and hung on.

We were thunderstruck. No one had ever seen Joey so much as raise a finger in self-defense or anger, even though he'd had ample justification.

The fighting halted as we timidly circled Dennis and Joey. No one knew what to do next.

"Leggo a meeee!" wheezed Dennis.

"No more hurt," demanded Joe's muffled but determined voice.

We watched in awe as Dennis' face changed from red to the color of grape Kool-Aid, and his eyes bugged out in a very scary way.

"Yeah, let 'm go, Joey," said my brother. His voice betrayed how worried he was.

"Hey, Joe," I said, resting a hand on his sweaty shoulder, "you better let 'm go now. I think he's had enough."

"Okay," Joey said and tossed Dennis to the grass like a sack of fertilizer. He shrugged his shoulders and began for the second time that day to gather the little stars blowing all over the sidewalk.

As Dennis lay on the ground gasping for air, reflecting on his glimpse of the great beyond, his two companions slowly backed away. Their eyes never left Joseph as they pulled Dennis to his feet and began stumbling down the walk, picking up speed as they went.

Larry, recovering first, shouted, "Don't mess with us again, ya hear!"

After we'd helped gather Joe's things, he smiled as usual as if nothing had happened.

It seemed superfluous at that point, but we finished walking him home. His mother met us at the front door. She was a plump, plain-looking woman, certainly older than our mothers and wore an old-fashioned apron over an out-of-style dress. Nylon stockings sagged at her ankles, revealing veiny white legs. Her eyes smiled when she saw her boy, then quickly narrowed when she saw us.

"Hi, Mrs. Amour. We walked Joey… I mean, Joseph, home 'cause they were teasin' him on the bus," Larry explained.

We briefly related the details of our adventure. As we talked her face changed from worry to that of someone hearing an old story. She bade us to come inside the porch and thanked us for defending her son. We were somewhat embarrassed as it wasn't clear exactly who'd defended whom.

"Joseph is a good boy," she said and flashed a proud mother's smile at him. "He's not much of a little boy anymore, you know. He'll be fifteen next month."

Fifteen! I thought. *That's impossible! I was eleven, how could he be so much older?*

"Most folks don't know what to make of special boys like Joseph," she went on. "It grieves me that there's so much meanness in the world." She sighed, "I don't know what's to become of him after me and his poppa are gone. We ain't no spring chickens, ya know."

That's when it hit me… Joey was going to remain pretty much as he was. He'd grow chronologically older, as would his parents, but when it came time that they needed help, he'd most likely need to be in some institution. I wasn't sure what an institution was exactly, but I was pretty sure it wasn't like home.

A profound sadness settled on me as we walked home, and I felt on the verge of unexplained tears.

*

That afternoon, I grew up a little, I think, as I pondered this question: Don't we owe something to those without the tools for survival, even if that something is only to give them the respect and kindness we expect from one another?

Our Little League Baseball team was having a bad summer. In short...we stunk. We rarely won, often losing by embarrassing margins. In one especially humiliating game the final three batters in the ninth inning intentionally struck out to mercifully end a hopeless game.

We had a couple of fairly good players but most of us played one error-ridden inning after another. The outfielders, usually the poorest ball handlers, basically chased down balls allowed to fly unhindered over their heads. Our pitchers couldn't find the strike zone, serving up lollipops that floated over the middle of the plate. It was a bad combination all the way around.

Most of us spent the day at the swimming pool and then attended practices when the coaches finished work in late afternoon and on Saturdays. We came directly from the pool waterlogged, red-eyed, and fatigued, prompting the coaches to forbid us from swimming on the day of a game. It made sense, but only served to further my somewhat negative feelings about playing ball.

Right field was reserved for the worst players as most right-handed batters hit predominately to left. From that far-flung lonely position, I barely followed what was going on and my attention tended to wander. I had little faith in my fielding skills and quietly hoped nothing would come my way.

When the coaches hit us practice fungoes, I had difficulty judging where it was best to position myself. The ball either flew over my head or landed short. Then there was the fear of missing a catch altogether and having the ball smack me in the face. I wasn't pretty, but I didn't want to mess up what Mother Nature had given me to work with.

I followed the Milwaukee Braves even though I found it boring to watch games on TV. I preferred to play ball with my buddies on our makeshift diamond next to the railroad tracks. The ball was scuffed and grass-stained, the bat nicked and taped, and pieces of scrap wood or someone's jacket was used for bases. There were no umpires; we relied instead on the honor code or whoever protested the loudest. It was unstructured and without adult supervision.

My father was the coach. He'd been a catcher on his high school baseball team and was an insufferable New York Yankee fan. He attended the evening practices and games after closing his barbershop, showing up for practices tired, hungry, and semi-pissed off at the world. He was never abusive, but he wasn't very pleasant to be around.

To not show favoritism he rarely complimented me but readily praised my teammates. It was okay, as I seldom made a good play, but it still irked me.

There were, though, moments when I shined.

One night I was in my usual place in right field, swatting mosquitoes. To keep ourselves involved in the game, we taunted the batters, "Hey batter, batter. Hey batter, batter, batter. You can't hit, batter!"

Suddenly, in the far distance of home plate, I saw the ball fly off the bat with the *crack* sound arriving a split second later. The ball soared into the night sky, a tiny white orb rapidly gaining altitude and distance... headed right for me.

I ran to where I thought it would land, holding my glove in front of my chest, as I'd been taught. There was a moment of panic when I lost the ball in the lights. Before I could recover, the ball landed neatly into my glove with that satisfying "pop" when caught properly, deep in the pocket.

My triumph was marred when I overthrew the first baseman due to the sudden flush of adrenaline. No one could see me grinning like a goof as I resumed my outpost. I guess even a blind squirrel finds an acorn now and then.

One unforgettable evening game comes to mind...

This is what I remember:

It was a rare close game. We were tied six to six and things were looking up in the bottom of the ninth.

Freshly arrived on first base, I had a chance to catch my breath. The first base coach told me, "Nice hit, Wayne. Now, get a good lead-off and be ready to run." *Duh, yeah coach, no kidding.*

Only moments ago, I was in the batter's box looking at a 3-and-1 count when I connected with a pitch, low and outside. It was a "worm killer" ground ball that puttered between first and second to die in the outfield grass.

The kid following me at bat smacked a dying quail single into left field, and I advanced to second.

The next batter hit a bouncing ball directly to the first baseman for an easy out. We two base runners had astutely taken long leadoffs and were able to advance. I was now on third and the runner behind me on second.

My mind wandered, thinking about an upcoming fishing trip with my uncles. To my credit, though, I remained aware I needed to get to home plate.

The next batter popped out to the pitcher. Now there were two outs with two on.

Our next hitter got a walk. When he dropped his bat and began the trot to first base, our dugout went crazy.

Ensconced on third, having lost track of the game, I somehow believed that the bases were loaded, and I was therefore being forced home. I could already imagine the welcome I'd receive from my teammates and coaches as I touched the plate to win the game.

I started a casual, happy stroll for home. Halfway down the third base line, I was startled when I saw my father running from the dugout waving his arms and screaming, "What are you doing? Go back! Go back!"

The catcher seemed to move in slow motion as he pulled off his mask and began to run at me with the ball in his free hand. The third base coach was apoplectic, "Get back, Wayne! Get back!"

I turned for the safety of third base just as the catcher plowed into me for the tag.

Game over.

My teammates wouldn't even look at me. Dad bluntly asked, "What the hell were you thinkin', kid?" Only then did I begin to understand my mistake and inherent stupidity.

I hung my head, grabbed my ball glove, and numbly walked to the car.

Despite the humiliating loss, the coaches took the team to the A&W Root Beer stand for an after-game root beer. Those were the days before seatbelt laws and liability worries plaguing volunteers today and we piled into their station wagons for the short trip across town.

Pop decided to turn the event into a funny story for my mother who'd stayed home with my sisters. He rubbed my head and smiled, letting me know it was all right and mattered little in the end.

I was grateful beyond words.

*

The following summer, I didn't return to baseball and spent my time goofing off at the public pool where I had my eye on a beautiful lifeguard. She was much older than I... but that's another story.

THE DEEP END

One summer I overreached and ended up over my head.

This is what I remember:

Between the ages of eight and twelve, I was a denizen of the town's swimming pool. It was the only time in my life when I had the opportunity because at twelve, I was mowing lawns and working in the fields. Prior to age eight, my parents kept us on a short leash, bound to our neighborhood.

Our community was proud of its swimming pool. It was on our side of town and within easy walking or biking distance.

Built in the late 1930s, it contained offices, water treatment plant, clothing storage, and showers. The building, a concrete structure graced with curved winged facades, resembled a weird castle. It was certainly a far cry from the ugly, unimaginative bunker squatting there today.

The pool was painted pale blue, which had the effect of deepening the color of the water to that of glacial ice. The main focal points were its three diving boards: a low, medium, and a high board called the Tower. There was room at the top of the Tower for six people to linger and admire the view or build courage for the plunge. If you didn't know what you were doing, you were in for a spanking if you jumped, or a headache if you dived.

The shallow end was for small fry and marginal swimmers; the deep end was for the older and bolder. Naturally, we all yearned for admission to the deeper depths. To be part of the action there, you had to present yourself at the exalted throne of an on-duty lifeguard. Under their direct observation, you swam across the pool and back without resting or stopping. We called it "going across and back."

A string of buoys separating the deep end from the shallow end was called the Ropes.

Lifeguards were mostly senior high or college students and responsible for maintaining the water quality, cleaning the grounds, and keeping order. Any bather found in violation of the safety rules was brought up short by the metal whistles hanging from their necks. They had the authority to kick anyone out of the pool for an hour, a day, or the entire summer. There was no appeal.

Every hour, the lifeguards stood up on their towers and blew a long whistle note, signaling rest period. All swimmers had to immediately exit the pool and rest for fifteen minutes. As the end of the period approached, we lined the pool's edges, poised to be the first into the water. Woe to anyone jumping the gun prior to the whistle. The guards loved to dramatically prolong those last moments, whistles at the ready, luring the too eager to commit themselves. Infractions resulted in a ten-minute ban from the pool, an eternity for a ten-year-old.

Everyone joked that the rest periods gave the lifeguards a break and the chance to look for drowned bathers, floating unnoticed in the crowded pool. We spent the time lying on the hot concrete walkways warming our shivering, water-shriveled bodies, while the teenagers sat on blankets in the grassy areas around the pool and flirted.

A loudspeaker broadcast announcements and music. It was top ten rock-and-roll of the 50s and the soundtrack to our summers.

Season tickets were a must and every year we faced the same problem… how to get the money?

For the first few days of the season, my brother and I were able to sneak in by blending with the rush of kids passing the ticket window. The trick was to be at the pool's opening each day when the largest bolus of kids rushed through. As it would take too long for everyone to individually present their passes, we escaped notice. We were careful to wear our bathing suits, avoiding the risk of discovery by needing to get a clothing basket. Anonymity was the key.

In the end, we had to dip into our birthday money, virtually wiping out our hoarded savings. I did the math: at $1.25 a haircut, Dad could have paid for a season ticket in half an hour. Of course, I had no idea what it took to keep a family of six, a barbershop, and an eight-beer-a-day habit going.

I spent the first couple of years at the pool playing with my friends in the shallow water, but as time went on the lure of the Deep End grew stronger. I stood on my tiptoes near the Ropes to watch the happy splashes of those having passed their swimming tests. I was a dog paddler, good for a few yards at best but not ready for the big time.

One of the lifeguards, a high school junior named Rachael Ash with light brown hair, shapely tanned body, and a very pretty face, caught my eye. I couldn't help watching her whenever she was on duty. Every movement she made was poetry; every note she blew from her silver whistle, a symphony. I made certain to be near when she ascended her chair to watch the muscles of her legs work. In short, I was a stalker, and… I was in over my head.

One afternoon I decided to go for it and sneaked into the Deep End. In the beginning all went well and I enjoyed jumping from the low board then quickly paddling to the ladder.

Apparently, my flailing as I splashed to the pool's edge caught the attention of the head lifeguard, Jim Dooley, an unsmiling, muscular, four-year veteran of the pool. I heard his sharp whistle, *"TWEET."* I saw him point at me. When he motioned for me, I knew I was in trouble.

I approached the lifeguard chair and looked up at his throne.

"Yes, lifeguard," I said innocently, "What did I do?"

"Did you pass your swimmers' test to be in this end of the pool?"

"Ye-ye-yes, I did," I lied.

"Well, let's see you do it again," he demanded, "right here and now."

In that moment I reviewed my options: hightail it for home, feign a sudden illness, or give it a go. I opted for the latter. *Maybe I was a better swimmer than I thought?* I mused. So, I jumped in and paddled off on my journey.

By the time I was across the pool I was alarmingly fatigued but encouraged. *So far so good*, I thought. The pool was very busy that day and the water badly churned up. I'd managed to get halfway back when a choppy wave smacked me right in the face just as I was taking a breath. In a moment of choking panic, I reached instinctively for the Ropes and realized immediately… I'd failed my test.

"You! Kid! Get out of the water, now!" Jim shouted.

I hauled my skinny, exhausted body out of the pool and stood before the guard, shaking from cold and humiliation.

He didn't make it easy. "If I *ever* catch you in the Deep End again, I'll throw you outta here for good. Is that clear?" he said.

To make matters worse, I saw Rachael, my summer obsession, watching.

What could I do? My throat seized up and I felt the sting of tears. Now I really was embarrassed.

I broke and ran for the exit, found my bike, and peddled for home. I swore I'd never go to the pool again. I'd show 'em. There'd be one less kid at their stupid pool. I sulked for the rest of the day, reading comic books in my room.

My father cut the hair of most of the young males in town, including the male lifeguards. They seemed to enjoy his constant teasing banter. He knew them by name, their parents, and what interested them.

When he came home for supper that evening, the first thing he said at the dinner table was, "Heard you got kicked out of the pool today, Sunshine." He glared at me, daring me to make eye contact.

I looked down at my plate and nodded my head.

"I thought, seein' as how you spend all your time at the pool that you'd be a pretty good swimmer by now, but I guess you was just goofin' off, huh?"

"I can swim, Dad," I protested.

"That's not what I heard, buddy boy," he said, his voice rising. "What I heard is that you can't swim enough to even pass your test. I heard you left cryin' like a little baby."

I knew by now when to keep my mouth shut when he was on a mission. My brother nervously shuffled his feet under the table, my sisters watched in silence, and my mother said softly, "Can't this wait until after supper?"

He ignored her and plowed on. "Here's what you're gonna do, Sunshine. Tomorrow you're going to meet Jim Dooley at one o'clock at the pool for swimming lessons. You will do this every day until you know how to swim and swim well. I'm paying for the lessons, so you'd better be there."

With that, he stabbed a potato with his fork and stuck it into his mouth. End of discussion.

We ate our supper in silence, and I went to bed early. It had been a long and ugly day.

The next afternoon, after waiting the pre-requisite hour after eating lunch (an eternity), I put on my swimming trunks, a T-shirt, flip-flops, grabbed a towel, and jumped on my bike.

I found Jim in the lifeguard lounge and gave him a sheepish smile. He acknowledged me by raising his chin slightly, snubbed out his cigarette, and met me in the doorway.

"Change of plans," he said, "You're going to take lessons from Rachael. I got other stuff to do today."

I gulped. "Rachael?"

"She'll meet you in the shallow end after the next rest period."

For the first time in a long time, I didn't hang around Rachael's chair. I sat morosely on the edge of the pool in the shallow end kicking my feet in the water, waiting for her to finish her hour on duty.

What a catastrophe! Rachael, witness to my humiliation, the object of my pre-adolescent fantasies, was going to teach me to swim. There was no going back now, nothing to do but endure.

"Are you Wayne?" I heard Rachael's soft voice behind me.

I half-turned, my feet in the water, and squinted up into the beautiful face of Rachael... my Rachael.

She had her hair pinned up. A few loose strands made blond by the sun floated in the summer breeze. Her two-piece bathing suit tastefully revealed just enough to announce without screaming, that here was a mighty fine-looking woman. She was deeply tanned everywhere I allowed myself to look. Her smile was July and her eyes blue as an October sky.

I couldn't find enough breath to speak, so I just nodded stupidly.

"Okay, then. Why don't we get started, shall we?" she asked.

I watched her ease into the pool and take a quick breath from the sudden shock of the cool water.

"Maybe it would be better if you got in the water with me? Whaddya say?" she said with a smile. She made little eddies in the water as she playfully swirled the surface with her fingers.

I got in.

In an hour she'd shown me the breaststroke, sidestroke, backstroke, and the crawl. She had me practice while supporting me with her hands beneath my chest and belly as I thrashed away.

This wasn't so bad, I thought. She hadn't said a thing about my latest escapade, and I came to believe she was truly enjoying the time with me.

The next day, I arrived early to meet "my date," as I thought of her. I practiced for an hour before to show her how quickly I was progressing.

When she called out a stroke she wanted to see, I happily obeyed.

"Well," she exclaimed, "you're doing very well. I think you just needed someone to show you how, was all."

I grinned and nodded like a dope.

For the next three days, I practiced the strokes Rachael had taught me and spent my nights dreaming of us lying on a blanket in the sun, as I made her laugh and laugh. She told me what a wonderfully amusing, handsome young man I was and how she couldn't wait for me to grow older.

On our last day, she told me I was to take my swimming test in front of Jim Dooley. I was confident and maybe even a little cocky.

I completed the 'cross and back without incident. It was anticlimactic, really.

When I climbed triumphantly out of the pool, Jim said, "Okay. You can go to the Deep End but behave yourself."

Rachael had watched, too. I saw her leaning against the kiddie pool's chain-linked fence. I wanted desperately to impress her. Thinking that I had adequately done so, I puffed out my chest and asked, "What do you think about that, Rachael?"

She didn't smile. Instead, she gave me a hard look, leaned closely and said, "What you did when you tried to sneak into the Deep End was stupid, dishonest, and dangerous. Then, when you got caught, you ran off in a childish pout. What kind of man do you think you'll be, acting like that?"

She continued, "You should have learned to swim long before this, and you didn't because all you wanted to do is fool around with the other kids. Sure, I'm all for having fun, but you must put in the time and effort to be more than you are."

Then she patted me on the head like a puppy and walked away twirling her whistle.

I hung my head. Her words cut me, and I rubbed salt into the wounds knowing she was right.

I turned and made for the Deep End.

Five years later, my brother and I took a Red Cross lifesaving course at the same pool. All the old lifeguards had moved on, and a new crew had the silver whistles.

To pass the course, we were required to swim a mile without rest, demonstrating the various strokes I'd learned from Rachael. In addition, we had to jump into the pool fully clothed, strip down, retrieve a heavy weight from the bottom of the pool, and swim back. We took turns rescuing each other while the "victim" struggled in feigned panic.

It was a challenge, but we passed with flying colors and qualified to be lifeguards.

It never happened. There was better money to be made in the fields where the "real work" was done. When we moved away, that was that. But I'd proven something to myself, my father, and of course Rachael, although she never knew it. I heard she'd graduated from college and was now a teacher. I'm betting a darned good one, too. I'll never forget Rachael and everything she taught me that summer.

*

How is it a boy becomes a man? It isn't just a matter of age, although that's part of it. I think it's mostly through one painful, sometimes embarrassing lesson after another, then finding a way to learn how to make sense of it. Success doesn't hold a candle to failure in its ability to teach, and the trick is to just keep trying.

I'm still working on that.

For a time in my life I was a lost soul, a wimpy version of myself. I still wince when I think of it and know the scars are permanent.

This is what I remember:

Before joining my classmates (all seven) in the Rutland, Iowa, kindergarten class of 1953, I was known as a rough and tumble kind of guy. I rode my tricycle at breakneck speed on the sidewalk. I had rock-throwing fights with the mean kid across the street, didn't wash for supper without being told, and hated baths. Maimie, the ancient woman who lived in the house behind us, was constantly complaining to my mother that I teased her chickens until they refused to lay eggs. I could outrun, outjump, and out holler any kid my age. Friends looked to me to decide how and where to find adventure for the day.

My aunts and uncles marveled at my agility and coordination. During lulls in conversation at family gatherings, I positioned myself on the floor in the center of the room, laid on my belly, and arched my back to rest the back of my head on my feet.

"Wow! Look at Wayne! How does he do that?"

"He's so flexible." My mother would proudly say.

I could handle pain, too. A trip to the doctor for my childhood immunizations was an opportunity to show my toughness when I proudly rolled up my sleeve for him to do his worst. I never allowed a tear or a flinch as the needle flashed.

"Looks like you've got a brave little man here," said the doc.

My mother just smiled and added, "And he's so flexible!"

When my father came home from barber college, he used me for practice. I sat on a stool in the kitchen wrapped in a towel as he combed and clipped my poor head ragged. I remained unbroken and endured with little complaint.

Midway through grade school I got the "wimps." I couldn't figure it out; the change was so gradual. The first signs appeared in second grade, when my family moved from our tiny village of one hundred fifty people to a town of over six thousand. It was where my father opened his first barbershop.

A single room in my old school contained three grades: kindergarten, first, and second. Each grade was arranged in rows of five to seven children. The teacher only needed to walk to the head of each row to conduct lessons for each class. I learned to read and write my letters early by eavesdropping.

At my new school, the woman principal, a squat, frog-like creature, unceremoniously brought me to a classroom with thirty-five students. I assumed that the row assigned me was second grade, mistakenly thinking the remaining rows were other grades.

Girls giggled and everyone stared impolitely. I looked shyly into my lap, suddenly aware of the iron-on patches with curling edges my mother had applied to cover holes in the knees of my jeans. I felt my ears burning. *Surely no one else had patches on their jeans! That was why they were laughing,* I reasoned.

From far away, I heard my name and looked up to see the teacher standing beside my desk. From the expression on her face, I realized she'd grown impatient trying to get my attention. The class snickered.

My lower lip began to tremble, tears filled my eyes, and my throat constricted painfully. I suddenly lost control and bolted for her left leg. Reaching up with both arms, I clung to her waist, burying my face into the folds of her dress somewhere in the region of her upper thigh. I cried like a baby, humiliating myself in front of classmates I'd yet to meet.

She tried to pry me off, but I clung to her like a scared cat. She attempted walking me to the door but had to drag her foot, as my weight prevented her from lifting it. At last, fatigue set in, and I came up for air. I looked up to meet her eyes and thankfully found tenderness and compassion.

She smiled. "Feel better?" she asked.

I nodded and eased my grip, leaving a teary wet spot and a silvery streak of snot on her dress. She wiped my face with an embroidered handkerchief retrieved from her sleeve. The scent of her perfume enveloped me.

"Thank you...Teacher," I sniffed. I'd yet to learn her name.

She was about forty-five with light blond graying hair, a beaded necklace with matching earrings, and gold-rimmed glasses framing china-blue eyes. I thought she was beautiful.

I stumbled to my seat, forcing my eyes straight ahead. The girl behind me whispered, "Cry baby!" I learned the girl's name was Martha, who years later developed a crush on me.

That was the beginning. It seemed from that day the mold was set and the die cast, although I didn't know it then. From then out, I drifted through the next few years like a sleepwalker, a timid lost soul in a foreign land with lackluster report cards and flimsy social skills. As I grew older, reaching fifth and sixth grades, the boys moved from the playground to the softball diamond.

We were allowed two recess periods per day, one in the morning and one at lunchtime. When the bell rang signaling recess, the girls ran for the jump ropes and we boys for the bat and ball. There was no time to choose up sides, so we played a game called work-up.

Those who in some mystical way had been established at the top of the pecking order were first at bat. The rest took up the other positions on the field in descending order, as befitted our status as ballplayers: catcher, first base, then second, etc. Having long ago adopted the view of others, I automatically shuffled off to right field, joining the lowest of the low to pick dandelions and contemplate cloud formations.

As batters were put out, everyone moved up to occupy higher positions. Right field moved to center, then to left field, then third base and so on until finally… batter.

Of course, it was rigged. The best players were the most difficult to put out, prolonging their reigns at bat. Recess invariably ended before ever reaching the coveted batter's box.

Each day I played the game, content to be involved but spurred on by the dangling carrot of a shot at glory. As I grazed in the grass of Loser Land in deep right field, I envisioned my turn at the plate.

I swing the bat shoulder level several times at one-third speed, getting the feel of the ash. At home plate I dig into the dust with my high-top PF Flyers.

Gritting my teeth, I stare down the pitcher with my confident steely eyes and grin.

I look the first pitch over, letting it pass to gauge the kind of "stuff" the pitcher has. If the next pitch looks good, I give it a ride clean out to the street into homerun territory. There are gasps of admiration from the other boys as I trot triumphantly around the bases.

Getting up to bat was made even more difficult due to my questionable fielding skills. After finally advancing to a base position, I seldom caught the ball when thrown to me and my throws were wild, influenced by excess adrenaline.

There was a shortcut to the batter's box: if a player caught a flyball, the batter and the fielder simply exchanged places.

It may be said that every dog has his day, and every wimp has a way. So, there I was in the outfield, lost in my own world, when I heard the pop of the ball on the bat. There was no time to think, only react. I threw up my hands and when I brought them down, behold… I'd caught the ball!

I felt giddy and lightheaded. The batter cursed as he came to take my position in Wimpville. I retrieved the bat and choked up on the handle to speed my swing. My knees trembled as the spotlight was at last on me.

According to plan, I was to take the first pitch. *Plan? What plan?* I swung at the first throw so fiercely it spun me completely around. The catcher chuckled. "Ya couldn't a hit that one if you was on a stepladder," he said scornfully.

The message was clear. I didn't belong there.

The second pitch was a foul tip for strike two. The next one bounced in the dirt in front of the plate, a sucker's ball. I wisely let it go, finally exercising some control.

I stepped out of the batter's box to regain my composure. Gripping the bat at both ends, I raised it over my head and bent forward at the waist, knees straight, and touched the bat to the ground.

Gee, I thought, *I'm still flexible.*

I glanced around the infield and saw boredom on the basemen's faces. They knew I was doomed. "No sweat here," they seemed to say.

Hah, I said to myself, *I'll show 'em something today*!

I stepped to the plate and thumped it hard with the end of the bat. I took my three level swings at one-third speed, ground my sneakers into the dirt, and set my jaw. I was ready.

The pitcher went into his wind-up and tossed the ball. It loomed like a harvest moon on its journey to the strike zone. I stepped into the pitch and swung hard. The contact with the bat sent a jolt up my arms. I'd hit the ball! I looked up on my way to first base to admire it as it got smaller and smaller against the blue sky. Then it began its descent to earth. The boy whose ball I'd caught didn't need to take a single step as it fell into his waiting hands. He chuckled as we exchanged places.

Moments later, standing in my old familiar place, it seemed as though I'd never left and was just daydreaming. *Is that all there is?* I wondered.

That was the question I pondered as I walked into the schoolhouse after the recess bell. In a sick realization, I came to see the rest of my life stretching before me in some endless game of work-up, with few chances at bat and screwing up the rare opportunities that might come my way. Wayne the Wimp, King of the Weenies.

*

My wimp period came to an end as it had appeared... gradually. It helped when my parents had me fitted with eyeglasses. Catching and hitting balls or learning lessons from the chalkboard was some trick if you could see little better than Stevie Wonder.

I never developed the skills to be much good at baseball but instead found the sport that best suited me... wrestling. My academics improved, too, when I discovered *how* to learn and regained lost confidence. Years later, I was relieved to find my wimp title no longer fit.

I remain to this day a steadfast defender of wimps everywhere.

HARD BALL

This is what I remember:

"Hey, hey batter, batter! Here we go! Easy out. Easy out," Larry Torgerson chanted. He punched his fist into his baseball glove with one foot on the plywood scrap marking first base. The summer sun shined hard on our makeshift baseball diamond on the grassy expanse near the railroad tracks.

I was playing combination second base, shortstop, and center field. Gary covered third and left field.

We pounded our gloves and razzed the batter, Billy Spangler.

Larry's little brother, Craig, did his best to stop the pitches of the neighborhood tomboy, Sandy Kasanja.

"C'mon, Sandy," I urged, "put one past him. He can't hit."

Sandy bore down on Billy like a barn cat after a field mouse, studying the strike zone and contemplating her next pitch. The count stood even up at two strikes and two balls. We had no umpire so borderline pitches were ruled by whoever shouted or protested the loudest. She adjusted her ball cap and spit into the grass like a pro. I admired her poise and confidence. What an arm!

Her wind-up was slow and deliberate, meant to rattle Billy. It looked like it was working, too, as he gulped visibly but held his ground. The last pitch, a dust off, had come close to a beanball and had rattled him. Sandy denied throwing at his head intentionally, blaming it on a tiring arm. This of course was a set up for the pitch to come.

It was a fastball, low and inside. Billy swung, sort of half ducking, and clipped the ball into a hot grounder directly at me. The ball hit a gopher mound, bounced, and smacked me on the shin.

"Ow, ow, ow!" I hollered as I hopped around holding my leg.

"Get the ball, for Pete's sake!" shouted an unsympathetic Sandy.

Billy rounded first and was hotfooting it to second, sending dust into the air.

It took a moment to find the ball in the tall grass and when I did, I bare-handed it and cocked my arm to throw.

Gary slid over to cover second and Sandy moved to third. "Here! Here!" he shouted.

It was going to be close.

I fired the scruffy, grass-stained ball; he caught it and swooped to make the tag on Billy's leg as he slid into the blue jacket that was second base.

"Yer out!" Sandy whooped and leaped into the air.

"Am not!" Billy protested with hands defiantly on his hips.

"Aw, c'mon, you were out by a mile," I joined. I had no idea if he was safe or not as from my angle, I hadn't really seen the play. I didn't believe it was lying; instead, I preferred to think of it as the unwritten rule of baseball: do what it takes for your side to win.

Billy gave up in disgust, angrily jumped on his bike, and peddled off to find more agreeable company. That signaled the end of our impromptu ballgame... game called on account of cheating.

We bid each other goodbye and started home.

"Jeez, that Sandy can play, huh?" I observed as we picked our way across the neighborhood backyards.

"Boy, I'll say!" Gary agreed. "She's better 'n most boys I know."

"Nope. Just better 'n you!" I said, punching him in the shoulder. It was probably a bit too hard as he put on his angry face and jabbed me back.

We often fought this way until one of us "gave" or Gary started bawling. Crying was something that came easily for him, which really irritated our father.

"Ya big bawl-baby," he mocked.

It embarrassed Gary, but perversely made me feel superior. I rarely had the opportunity to feel superior to him and held a secret pleasure knowing that I could take pain with nary a tear.

We decided to forgo trading punches and raced for home with the loser taking out the trash after supper. Pausing outside the back porch to catch our breath, Gary suggested, "Let's play some catch. Ya' wanna?"

We were in Little League baseball again for the third year and on the same losing team. He played left field and I, right. No stars here.

Our father had been an athlete in high school, lettering in baseball, basketball, and track. I suppose to set an example, he frequently told stories of his sports career. As a gutsy catcher, we were informed, he'd been the backbone of his team. We came to believe that he'd been on the way to the majors if it hadn't been for WWII.

Dad tried to instill a love of the game and a desire to be the best we could be. The "best," I learned, was a bottomless pit of unmet expectations with him as the sole judge of what was or was not your best.

Facing each other on the lawn among the lengthening shadows of late afternoon, we tossed the ball back and forth. We played for almost an hour, throwing pop flies and ground balls, mixing up the throws.

There's something comforting in the sound of a baseball hitting a leather glove. It sounds so right and feels so reassuring when caught properly, deep in the pocket of the mitt. *THWACK* is the sound. I also loved the smell of the oiled leather lingering on my glove hand hours later. When I closed my eyes and put my nose into the glove, it smelled like summer.

If one of us threw too hard, a complaint was lodged with the offender. The next throw was always softer as it was all too easy to return the ball in the manner received, tit for tat. The result was a catch game called "pepper" or "burn out." The first one to quit due to a sore hand was the loser, a game we rarely played by mutual agreement.

We were ready to call it a day when Dad drove up from his workday. He parked the car and started up the walk.

"Hi, Dad," we called, hoping for a good mood.

"Hello, boys. Playin' some catch, huh? Wait, I'll get my glove and play with you before supper."

We exchanged sober glances. Neither of us liked to play catch with him as he constantly criticized, corrected, and belittled our humble abilities. I thought that we must have been somewhat of an embarrassment, him being such a terrific ballplayer and all.

In short order he returned with his glove.

"Okay, boys, let's see whatcha got," he said as he backed into position.

He began throwing balls, alternating between us.

"Aw, c'mon, Wayne, throw the ball like you mean it, not like some sissy!" he taunted.

I fired the ball at him with a little pepper, making his glove pop.

"That's the stuff," he said, and returned the ball with a little pepper of his own. *THWACK*.

"Ouch!" I complained and pulled my hand out of my glove to examine my reddened palm.

"Aaah, that ball ain't gonna hurt you," he said gruffly.

It was my brother's turn.

When Gary attempted to throw hard, he tended to be wild, so Dad had to leap and stretch for the ball. I got apprehensive when I saw his angry pissed-off-look.

"Get in front of the ball, Son. Don't back away. Catch it like this." He demonstrated by catching my throw squarely in front of his chest.

The next ball tipped Gary's glove, hitting him on the collarbone. *THUNK!* I watched as he bent to pick up the ball and saw tears forming.

Oh Gary, please don't cry, I thought. *It'll just make it worse.*

I was right.

"Well, that's about it for me," I said, heading for the back door. "I promised to help set the table." I tried to be very matter of fact with hopes of ending the session.

"Yep, there goes Wayne the quitter," my father taunted.

The words stung but I bore them. I didn't like being the butt of my father's scorn, but I chose it over being manipulated. I entered the screen door and stood back a way to watch.

My brother had too much pride to follow my lead. It depends on your point of view, I guess; I either had less pride or more smarts.

Dad was getting warmed up now and set on demonstrating how to "not be afraid of the ball." His method was flawed but simple: he threw hard, commanding Gary to catch the ball without moving.

THWACK. THWACK. THUMP. THUNCK. Sometimes the ball hit the glove and sometimes it hit Gary. He was crying openly now, catching and throwing, catching and throwing.

The more he cried, the angrier and more determined my father became. He was throwing even harder now. *THWACK!*

I could hear him bawling as he gamely stood his ground, fielding the balls and returning them as fast and as hard as he could. I didn't know how he could see through the tears.

Mom joined me at the screen door. The cavalry had arrived!

"What's going on here?"

"Dad's teachin' Gary how to play catch," I observed.

"Leo, stop that!" She demanded, stepping out onto the stoop. "You're hurting him."

"Back inside, woman!" he ordered, intoxicated with power, purpose, and a few afterwork beers. "This is just for us MEN!" he said, pointing to my brother with his glove. I noted the exclusion of yours truly.

"Well, take it easy then" she said.

Oh no! I thought. *She's backing down!*

"I told you. I'm handling this. This isn't for you," he said.

I realized I was shaking, not with fear, but in anger. How could my father do this to my brother? How could Mom back down? Why didn't I do something? But we were under his spell, impotent, and silent.

Concerned neighbors appeared on their front steps and shouted for him to stop. "For God's sake, leave the poor kid alone!"

A small group of neighborhood children gathered on the front sidewalk to watch the late afternoon horror show. *THWACK. THWACK. THUNK.* On it went.

"Mind your own business," my father sneered. I saw them shake their heads and turn back to their TV sets.

It finally stopped when my father's arm tired. "Let's go get some supper, kid," he said.

Gary bolted for the house, his eyes swollen red slits. He threw open the door and ran inside.

I felt unimaginably wretched and confused. In a few minutes we'd all be sitting at the table in a thick, heavy silence avoiding each other's eyes, pretending nothing had happened. We were guilty of cowardice, abandoning an eleven-year-old-boy to the cruelty of a frustrated, ex-high school jock.

*

As in most families, a little rain must fall and so, too, ours. I know my father was trying to do what he thought was right. Seeing a flaw that he felt obliged to correct, he went after it with a vengeance, like pushing a tack into a corkboard with a sledgehammer. He was not a physically abusive man, but he'd clearly stepped out of bounds that afternoon and didn't know how to reverse course without embarrassment. Backing down was admitting a mistake, and he could never do that.

I've forgiven him, but I don't know if my brother ever did. We never spoke of it, although I'm certain he remembered it.

I quit baseball and never played again except on our makeshift diamond by the tracks. I liked the game and still do, but it just didn't seem worth the effort.

My brother became the athlete of the family and continued to play in Little League for the rest of the summer. In high school he played football, basketball, track, and golf, but never, ever, played baseball.

Some of life's lessons come unexpectedly. It seems to me that our father had set out to teach a lesson about being a man that day, but it was my brother who was the teacher, and the lesson was for our father.

Did you ever have a friend with some little quirk you thought you could ignore, but it continued to grow and become irksome? I did, and his name was Roger Becker.

I liked Roger. We often played together, rarely disagreeing. He always had an idea how to spend an afternoon that perfectly fit our mood, the weather, and the other cosmic factors guiding children in decisions. But Roger, I learned, could drive me crazy.

That was the situation in which I found myself during my eleventh summer.

This is what I remember:

"Waaayne, your little friend Roger is here," my mother called. She had the irritating and embarrassing habit parents have of calling your pals a "little friend."

"OK, Mom," I shouted down the stairs. I'd already heard the familiar rattling crash of Roger's bike falling from its kickstand onto the sidewalk. It never stayed where he put it.

I could see his tangle of black hair through the screened door. The porcupine-like bristles stuck out every which way, independent and undirected.

"Hi, Becker," I said as I pushed the door open and stood aside. "C'mon in."

Roger wore his typical summer attire. While most of us in the fifth grade preferred T-shirts, blue jeans, and sneakers, he chose short-sleeved Hawaiian-style shirts and baggy shorts. His shirts were often buttoned wrong, and he wore argyle socks with sandals. Today we might call him funky, but back then he was just plain *weird*.

Most of my classmates considered him too weird for words but it only served to draw me to him. Roger was, well… different, and I liked that.

"Wanna watch The Gale Storm Show?" I asked.

"Sure, it's too windy to haul rocks," he quipped.

"Oh, yeah, I get it. Ha. Ha," I said flatly. Roger was witty as well as weird.

He stepped inside the door, tripped on the doorsill, and caught himself on the wall, leaving grimy fingerprints.

We plopped down in front of the Motorola, propping our heads with couch pillows. Roger fluffed his pillow over and over, adjusting it until he had it just the way he fancied it. As he assumed a comfortable position, I saw stuffing from a fresh tear along the seam of the pillow spill out. I sighed and surreptitiously gathered the white fluff and pocketed it. A quick side-trip to the trash would hide the evidence and save Roger the embarrassment of having torn it.

We enjoyed the show, basking in the pleasure of knowing we had nothing better to do. The whole summer stretched before us and there was no sense in rushing things.

After watching our program, we stood and tossed the pillows back onto the couch. There was more stuffing, only this time Roger saw it and judging by his puzzled look, I knew he hadn't a clue how it got there.

I leaned to pick up the pieces at the same moment Roger decided to pitch in. We bumped heads hard enough for me to see stars.

"Ow, Roger," I said as I checked for blood. "Watch it, will ya?" One often said that to Roger Becker.

He shrugged and rubbed his forehead, "Sorry, excuse me fer livin'."

"Hey, ya wanna play with the Army Guys?" he suggested.

I brightened. "Yeah!"

The Army Guys were a collection of small plastic soldiers molded into various combat poses. We had names for them based upon the weapons in their little plastic fists. There was Machine Gun Mike, Bazooka Joe (also a bubblegum comic character), Hand Grenade Kelly, Bayonet Bill, etc.

We split them up equally, built fortifications out of blankets, Lincoln Logs, Building Blocs, and whatever else was available, and then went to war.

About twenty minutes into the battle, Roger got the idea of bringing the Air Force into the action. He grabbed a plastic jet fighter from the bedroom shelf that I'd assembled from a kit. Simulating machine-gun-like noises, he began strafing my men.

"No fair," I protested. "Hey, that's not fair."

"Here, you take one," he said, tossing me the model Soviet MIG I'd made last Christmas. Unprepared for his throw, I fumbled and dropped the plane, breaking off the landing gear.

"Oops! Sorry 'bout that," Roger said, continuing his strafing run.

"Roger, I don't think we should play with these planes any…" I could have saved my breath. The right wing of the plane broke off in his sticky hands.

"Way to go, Becker," I said crossly.

"Oh, gee, I'm sorry," he said with a face so full of remorse that I immediately felt regret for being so testy.

"That's all right. I can glue it good as new," I reassured him.

"Hey," he brightened, "let's fix 'em up right now!"

Happy to give my friend the chance to make amends, I consented. Within five minutes he'd emptied half a tube of glue, smearing it on the desk, the models, and his Hawaiian shirt. He'd even managed to get some in his hair.

We left the crooked repairs to dry, but I knew they were destined for the trash. I was hoping that later I might be able to pry them from the desktop.

"Maybe we should do something outside, Becker?" I suggested.

"Hey," he said, "let's make skateboards! I saw how to do it in a magazine."

I thought a moment and couldn't think of anything too risky, so we moved to my father's cluttered garage.

After locating some wood scraps, it was time to cut them to length.

"You hold and I'll saw," Roger directed.

It was against my better judgment, but I agreed and held the piece of wood for him. With his tongue out of the corner of his mouth, he marked the board with a pencil. Eyes narrowed into a determined squint; he began sawing. *WHOOPA. WHOOPA. WHOOPA.*

He was making slow progress, and my fingers ached. "Geez, Becker, can'tcha go any faster?" I whined.

"I'm doin' the best I can," he said, and blew sawdust into my eyes.

A tearful moment later we were back at it. *WHOOPA. WHOOPA.*

When at last the end piece dropped to the floor, I realized why it had taken him so long; he'd sawed clean through a corner of Dad's workbench.

"Uh, oh," Roger said, "I did a boo-boo."

Oh, crap! I thought. It would take time for Dad to notice, but when he did... I made a mental note to tell him after supper and get it over with.

We moved on.

Next, we nailed old roller skates to the wood. Roger narrowly escaped serious eye injury when he clipped a nail head with the hammer and sent it flying.

"Hey, that was a close one," he said distractedly and continued hammering.

I shook my head in wonder and said two quick prayers... one for me and one for Roger the Wrecker. My hopes were dashed when he hit his thumb with the hammer.

On completion, we inspected our work. Roger's skateboard had so many bent nails sticking out of it that it looked like a Roman war chariot. The wood was splintered and chewed as if attacked by a hungry beaver. A blind man could have done better.

We launched them on the front walk.

Roger's ran like a dream. He streaked past me with no effort while I pumped and pushed only to coast a few miserable feet before grinding to a halt.

"It's all in the engineering," he grinned as he weaved unsteadily to my side. He lost his balance and fell sideways, bringing me with him to the sidewalk, skinning my elbows.

"Whatcha ya say we call it quits for the day, Rog?" I begged as I inspected the damage.

At first, he looked hurt, but rallying quickly said, "Hey, sure. I'll see ya tomorrow."

"Yeah," I agreed and limped off for the Merthiolate and Band-Aids.

The rest of the summer went pretty much like that. I escaped with only minor injuries, but Roger got five stitches in his chin from a bicycle accident.

There was, however, one nasty near-drowning incident at the "Ole Swim 'n Hole" in mid-July. It had to do with Roger, a length of rope, and a tractor tire inner tube. He made a quick recovery and was out of the hospital in a couple of days.

His reputation spread throughout my family. Now when Roger came to play, my mother suggested that we play outside or, "Maybe you could play at the Becker's house today?" she'd say.

When he did get inside the house, my brother jumped up and ran to our bedroom to hide precious objects. He'd long since lost any confidence in my ability to prevent Roger from destroying his personal property. He was especially wary after Roger had allowed several of his favorite cat's-eye marbles to roll into a heating vent.

After the workbench incident my father forbade us from going near the garage "or anything that even looks like it's mine."

I was growing weary of my weird little friend and running out of places to play. Roger was blissfully unaware and seemed pleased to get together as often as we could.

What was I going to do? I wondered. *At this rate I might not survive the summer*.

Events seem to have a way of sorting themselves out if you just wait long enough.

Roger and I were returning from a day at the swimming pool, exhausted and waterlogged. The lifeguards had kicked everyone out as they'd seen lightning from an approaching thunderstorm.

Sure enough, halfway home it began to pour. We didn't mind as we were in our bathing suits. I was following Roger, a habit I'd developed to keep him in sight.

The heavy rain blinded me as we pedaled along the flooded gutter. When I blinked to clear my eyes, Roger was at a full stop, looking into someone's front lawn at God knew what.

I slammed on the brakes and went into a skid. "Look out, Becker, you're in the way!"

I collided with the rear fender of his beat-up-broken-down-wreck-of-a-bike, tipped over, and hit my head against the curb. My poor brain rattled around in my skull like a B.B. in a soup can and out went the lights.

In what seemed like only a moment later, my consciousness floated to the surface like a bubble through oil. I found myself in the back seat of a car as a man in a brown suit peered into my eyes with a penlight. He had a concerned look on his face and blinked in surprise when I abruptly sat up sputtering, "Whoa! What? Who?"

"Now just take it easy, son," said the man in a velvety smooth voice. "I'm Dr. Munroe and you've been hurt. I want to make sure you're alright." Then he smiled an unnerving false smile.

"I want my Mom," I said, fighting the urge to cry.

"You'll see your mother soon enough," he said as he listened to my heart with a cold, black stethoscope that smelled of rubbing alcohol. It made my stomach turn.

I became aware there were others present: Roger's mother, Roger himself, and another woman I didn't know were watching from the front seat. All wore the same worried expression no kid wants to see on an adult's face.

"I think he'll be all right now," mumbled the doctor. "I'll phone his mother from my office. Will you folks drive him home?"

Mrs. Becker nodded. I noticed her abundant gray hair and wondered how many of them were attributed to her only son.

Doc Monroe gave directions to my parents in the care of a patient with a cerebral concussion, and they assumed the responsibility with a vengeance.

The instructions were to awaken me every two hours to make certain I was only sleeping and not drifting into a coma due to bleeding inside my noggin.

I'd been sound asleep when my parents first awakened me. Dad accomplished this by switching on the naked light bulb in my room. The light was painful even through my eyelids, which I instinctively closed tight as a clam.

"WAKE UP, WAYNE," he shouted through the fog. "OPEN YOUR EYES AND LOOK AT ME!"

I tried but couldn't get them open. I mumbled a protest but might as well have talked to the Man in The Moon.

"I SAID, OPEN YOUR EYES!"

"Oh, my God!" I heard my mother's frightened voice. "Is he alright?"

Finally, I was able to open my eyes and squint up at my hovering parents. They seemed concerned and unsure.

Gradually, my eyes became adjusted to the light, and I was able to fully open them, which my father promptly rewarded by shining his fishing flashlight into them to check my pupils.

"Ow, Dad," I protested. "I'm okay. I'm okay, I tell ya!"

That seemed to satisfy them, and they retreated to gather strength for the coma checks to come.

We met like that for the rest of the night until we were all exhausted. By dawn, I would have welcomed a nice peaceful coma.

After the last check of the night, I heard my mother say, "I don't want that Roger Becker playing around here anymore. He's dangerous!"

I quietly smiled. It was out of my hands now… the problem had been solved.

Some years later after we'd moved to another town, I heard about an explosion in the chemistry lab at my old school. There'd never been such an accident in the history of the school, and never was again. No one was badly injured, but the boy responsible was quoted as saying, "Gee, I guess I made a boo-boo."

*

Despite my curiosity, I've fought the urge to reconnect with my old friend. There'd been opportunities, but somehow, I always found a reason not to. Maybe it's for the best reason of all… self-preservation.

I confess. My favorite holiday isn't Christmas, it's Independence Day.

My love for this day has its roots in small-town Iowa where it was celebrated with joy, optimism, and heart.

This is what I remember:

The Midwest's growing season is in high gear by early July. The corn is "high as an elephant's eye by the 4th of July," the hay ready for cutting, and the world green as a peapod.

It was hot, worsened by the fact that most homes and cars were not air-conditioned back then. That luxury was years in the future. We kids didn't mind as there were sprinklers to run through, a public swimming pool, and the ole swimmin' hole to splash around in. It was normal to be hot in July, so why complain? It got you nowhere. It was best to enjoy it and recall the long winter past when we'd have given anything for a day or two of July weather.

The year I turned eleven, I graduated to a Fourth of July experience previously denied... firecrackers. Starting with the legal stuff like caps, sparklers, snakes, and poppers, I'd finally moved on to explosives.

They were illegal in Iowa and I had no way of buying them, relying instead on friends traveling to the Dakotas where such dangerous pleasures were accepted. One of my friends, Mike Jenson, had an uncle who was a long-haul trucker. During his stops in fireworks legal states, he bought boxes of them to sell. Mike was my main source and I started buttering him up days in advance.

I approached him one afternoon. "Hey, Mike, wanna grab a pop? My treat."

He consented and we walked to the corner store. As I opened the front door for him, I asked casually, "Say, your uncle back from South Dakota yet?"

Mike let me buy him a Coke and a candy bar before he answered. "Yeah, and he's got a whole lotta great stuff!"

I tried to be indifferent. "Glad to hear it. What'd he get?"

"The usual, you know, lady fingers, firecrackers, Roman candles, cherry bombs, but this year he's gonna let me have some M80s!"

My pulse quickened. "Did you say, *M80s*?"

An M80, for those unfamiliar, is basically a small stick of dynamite. A cardboard cylinder, the diameter of your thumb and about an inch and a half long, is packed with gunpowder primed with a short fuse. It could blow off your fingers no problem, but what a *BANG!*

"You heard me," he said. "M, by God, 80s! Said he'd get me a few but, I can't sell 'em or give 'em away. He doesn't want any trouble 'case somebody gets killed."

This was a setback, but I pushed on.

"So… can I get a few crackers from you this year?" I asked, taking a nonchalant swig from my Pepsi.

"Yeah, I guess so," he said and pulled out a stubby pencil and a creased piece of paper. He squinted, wrote my name, and cocked me a quizzical look, waiting.

"Put me down for five packs of Black Cats, a string of Lady Fingers, and a couple 'a cherry bombs," I said. "No chance on the M80s, ya say?"

"Nope. No can do," he said as he wrote up my order. "But if ya let me come over, we can blow up some stuff together."

So that's the deal, I thought. I get to watch *him* having fun blowing things apart. Better than nothing, I figured and agreed. We decided to meet on the morning of the Fourth.

Mike wasn't someone I hung around with much. He was in my younger brother's class at school and a bit of a whiner. Likeable enough, he just wasn't one of the guys. He preferred to stick close to home instead of playing ball, riding bikes, or going to the swimming pool. Consequently, his clothes remained un-patched and un-stained, his skin pasty white, and his arms and legs skinny. I guess you'd call him a "Momma's Boy," not really a sissy, just, well… whiney.

He whined when he was hungry, tired, or had to walk anywhere. He whined when it rained, when it was too hot, too cold, or if we called him Mikey. Naturally, we called him Mikey, but never near the Fourth of July. It wouldn't do to tick Mikey off, dependent on his firecrackers the way we were.

The days passed as they do in a child's summer.

Independence Day was sunny, hot, and humid. Mike awakened us by lighting off a string of firecrackers in our yard at 8 a.m.

My father, who'd closed his barbershop for the holiday and was sleeping in, shouted from the bedroom. "Get that kid the hell outta here before I drop kick him into next Sunday!" I knew from his tone that I needed to act fast.

I threw on my clothes and made a beeline for the back door. Breakfast could wait.

"Mike! Gettin' an early start on the day, huh?" I said as I stepped out into the bright morning sun.

"I brought your firecrackers and thought you might wanna start. I couldn't sleep very well 'cause it's so hot." *Gee*, I thought, *it's only 8 o'clock and he's already whining.*

I paid him and he handed me a paper bag containing my loot. I dumped everything onto the sidewalk and knelt to take inventory. Everything was there as ordered. All I had to do now was figure out how to get hold of an M80.

I invited him in for cereal and orange juice and Gary arrived to join us at the table to make plans. Mike complained the OJ was too bitter and that his mommy always added sugar. Gary and I shared a conspirator's smile and an eye roll.

We mined for the things we needed for our explosive experiments in the trash barrel in the alley behind our house. Metal cans were most desired, as experience had taught us to avoid glass bottles. (Even eleven-year-olds have their limits of stupidity.)

A short walk to the railroad tracks and we were on safe ground. From there we had a clear view for prowling cops and as there weren't any nearby houses there'd be no complaining neighbors.

The first order of business was creation of a crude rocket: we punched a hole in the bottom of an aluminum can with a nail and then pushed a Black Cat firecracker halfway into the hole. Next, the open end of the can was set in a shallow basin with two inches of water. Our hands shook with anticipation as we took turns lighting the fuses for each launch. When the firecracker went off, the can shot wonderfully into the air.

We decided that the firecrackers must be from the "Orient" after seeing the Chinese letters on the exploded, shredded bits of paper resembling chickadee tracks.

The Demolition Phase was next... The idea was to see how much damage could be inflicted upon various objects. To that end, we looked for ways to beef up the power. One method was to twist the fuses of two firecrackers together; but the best method, though, was to simply use a cherry bomb. After each explosion, we made a careful inspection of the damage to see the cans bulging and torn in impressive and satisfying ways.

The fun, you see, was the preparation of the charge, the anticipation, the anxious moment of lighting the fuse, and finally... detonation.

Throughout the morning, I waited patiently for Mike to produce an M80. Unable to wait any longer, I looked with feigned interest at a passing cloud and said, as if to myself, "I wonder what an M80'd do to a can packed with rocks?"

Right on cue, Gary asked, "Hey, Mike, you got M80s, dontcha?"

Mikey thought about it, then theatrically drew the explosive from out of his back pocket for us to admire. It looked as serious as a tombstone. We took turns reverently hefting and stroking it while Mike looked on importantly, doling out viewing time.

We filled a soup can with pebbles, packing them around the M80. Mike had the honor of placing it in the can with the stiff green fuse protruding.

For better visibility, we set the can onto the steel rail. Kneeling in a tight circle to block the wind, Mike struck a kitchen match and slowly moved the golden flame to the fuse. The sinister hiss and sparks told us it was time to take cover, and we ran into the tall grass with our heads just above the weeds to watch.

The explosion was louder than we'd ever imagined. Pieces of rock and aluminum were flung in every direction and debris peppered us as it fell back to earth.

At the blast site we found shredded hunks of the can and a scorched spot on the rail. It was glorious!

"Holy crap! Did you see that?" I shouted.

"Man, what a job on that can!" Gary exclaimed.

"Let's do it again," Mike said as he eagerly reached for another.

All agreed that the flying rocks resembled the hand grenades we'd seen in countless war movies. We were out of cans, so the next M80 was buried under a small mound of pebbles on a railroad tie.

We were rewarded with a wonderfully loud explosion and another stone shower. Again, we escaped injury, although Mike whined about getting grass stains on the knees of his jeans.

The fire station's noon siren sounded, and we left for home. Mike announced he was going to eat, take a nap, and would be at his house if anyone was interested.

It had been a wonderfully destructive morning, but it was time to move on.

Back home, we watched Dad solemnly hang up the Stars and Stripes to join most of the other houses on the street.

After lunch, Gary and I took stock. We had six boxes of sparklers (three red and three green), one box of snakes, twelve rolls of caps, the ladyfingers firecrackers, and a string of Black Cats. It was understood that the sparklers were to be shared with our sisters once it was dark enough.

Our cap guns had long ago been broken, leaving us wondering how to make use of the leftover rolls of caps. Gary recalled a friend who'd told him how to explode an entire roll with one blow, so we decided to ration the firecrackers and make do with the caps for a while.

We set individual rolls of caps on the hot sidewalk and then smashed them with a brick for a satisfying explosion. The gunpowder's ignition blackened our fingers and made our ears ring.

Not everyone enjoyed the loud explosions. Our cocker spaniel, Spotty, had long since found a place to sit out the Fourth under my parents' bed while my sisters watched from the swing set with their fingers in their ears.

Supplies were running low, so we took to lighting off the Black Cats one at a time. The game now was to light and throw a firecracker for a mid-air explosion. I was pretty good at it and got cocky, until a fast-burning fuse went off mid-throw, raising throbbing blood blisters on my index finger and thumb. I was careful not to let anyone see my injuries to avoid parental confiscation.

Toward evening, my parents finally got into the swing of things and began organizing for the evening cookout. Gary and Dad left to buy charcoal and lighter fluid for the grill, and I rode my bike to the store for

54

hotdogs and hamburger. My sisters dumped ice into a cooler and loaded it with soda, beer for dad, and a ripe watermelon.

It was 90 degrees in the late afternoon, and I was sweating by the time I parked my bike next to the porch. In need of a cool-down, we put on our swimming suits and turned on the garden hose. After filling buckets, squirt guns, and water balloons, we chased each other around the yard, taking turns charging whoever had possession of the hose.

Dad got the charcoal going and was poking at the briquettes with a stick in one hand, a beer in the other, and a cigarette in his mouth. Pop was a grilling aficionado. He knew to wait until the coals were at peak after they'd turned from black to red and then white-hot. He kept his trusty turkey baster in a can of water nearby to extinguish flame flare-ups from grease drippings.

Mom brought out a platter of hotdog and hamburger buns, then bustled back inside for the potato salad and baked beans.

Shadows were reaching into the yard and our stomachs rumbled from the aroma of the cooking food. It brought Spotty out of hiding, until the first *pop* of a distant firecracker sent her scooting back into the house.

We devoured our dinner with gusto from red-white-and-blue plastic plates. Juice dripped from the knife as Dad cut into the watermelon, revealing the red center dotted with flat, black seeds. I never liked the taste of watermelon and opted for the cake adorned with a sparkler.

The sky was darkening, and we knew it was now or never if we were to see a fireworks display. It was time to start working on our father.

"Are we going to go see the fireworks tonight, Daddy?" Lee Ann asked sweetly.

"Yeah, Dad, can we? Please?" Gary pleaded.

"We'll see," was all he said, but we knew we were going by the way he said it.

While we waited for Dad to extinguish the coals, we lit our sparklers to make colored designs in the evening air. My sisters were thrilled now that they, too, had a chance to participate in the celebration.

A slight pall was cast over the festivities when I succeeded in throwing my burning sparkler onto the roof of the house. Dad made a comment about my brains being somewhere that is anatomically impossible and grabbed the garden hose. He had it out in short order with only a small scorch mark on the shingles.

"Okay, let's go see some fireworks," he announced. We cheered and ran for the station wagon.

"Are we going to the fireworks at the fairground?" Gary asked.

"I'm not goin' to fight traffic at the fairground," he said as he started the car. Traffic for my father, who'd been born and raised in a small town, was anything more than ten cars. The fairground was sure to have at least a hundred people, so that option was out.

"Where are we going, then?" demanded my mother.

"Hold your horses," he said. "You'll see soon enough."

We drove into the dusk on the southwest side of town and onto a gravel country road. At last, he pulled over on a small hilltop and shut off the engine.

Are you kidding me? I thought as I looked out at the surrounding darkening fields.

"Oh, look it! Lightning bugs," Lee Ann said, pointing out her window.

The ditches and the soybean fields were filled with thousands of tiny, slowly winking, green lights. They looked like twinkling, earth-bound stars. The more you looked, the more you saw.

"Can we go catch some, Mom?" we begged.

"Sure," she said, "just don't lose sight of the car."

"We won't!" we assured her and the four of us climbed out into the soft, warm night.

Soon we were running in the long grass of the ditch and among the rows of soybeans chasing fireflies. We found a discarded glass jar and quickly filled it with the blinking insects whose mating rituals we'd interrupted. I kept the top of the jar covered with my hand to keep them inside.

When Dad flashed the headlights of the car, we headed back with our insect-powered lantern lighting the way.

"You're not bringing those into the car," Mom told us.

We saw the wisdom in that and let them climb out of the jar and back into the night.

Suddenly, in the distance, we saw a rising fountain of color and then another and another. It was the fireworks display from one of the neighboring towns. Every year, even the smallest of Iowa towns found ways to raise money for their own displays. It was a matter of civic pride, with volunteer fire departments in charge of setting them off.

"Oh, look, there's another one over there!" Mom said, indicating a red glow farther west.

"Hey, there's our town's display!" I said, pointing east.

From our location, we could clearly see four different fireworks displays simultaneously. The aerial bombs flashed with the thunder of their detonations arriving seconds later. The distant bursting rockets showered the sky horizon with colorful flashes in patterns unimagined. Some were shimmering waterfalls, some a whirling confusion of color, and others giant chrysanthemums blooming before our eyes.

We oohed and aahed our appreciation in unison.

Then it was over, and as the mosquitoes had found us, it was time to go.

On the ride home, we all agreed that it had been a great Independence Day and sang Happy Birthday to our wonderful country.

I looked out of the car window and wished on the brightest star I could find that I would remember this day forever.

*

I got my wish.

Back row: Gary, Dad, Mom, me
Front row: Kim, Lee Ann

Grandparents
Victoria and Agner
Christiansen

Grandma Bonita Edwards
with me and Gary

Rutland schoolroom, K-2nd Grade, 1953
Me, first row, 5th seat

My Little League baseball team
Coach Leo (Dad), brother Gary, front row, second from left
me, second from right

The Illinois Central Railroad had laid down tracks a block from our house many years ago to move grain, farm machinery, coal, and other cargo across the Iowa prairies.

In the night, snug under our quilts, the rumbling trains shook our house, lulling us to sleep and rocking our beds in a gentle sway and jiggle. On evenings near bedtime when we heard the far-off whistle of an approaching train, my brother and I raced to our beds to burrow like moles under the covers. The house shook and the windows rattled as the boxcars click-clacked off the miles. The vibrations moved objects from shelves and pictures from walls. It was the price we paid for being rocked to sleep by thundering night trains.

This is what I remember:

Of all the places we liked to play, the railroad tracks were our favorite. The wide, grassy slopes on each side of the railbed were havens for field mice, rabbits, gophers, pheasants, and meadowlarks; in winter, we tracked them in the snow and in summer chased them relentlessly. It was where we fought battles with dirt-clod hand grenades and scrap lumber rifles, and where we faced hostile Indians, hordes of Huns, and jungles crawling with enemy Japanese soldiers.

Railroad crossties were heavy timbers treated with creosote or tar. The spaces between them were tamped with rock and the cinders from the bygone era of coal-fed steam engines. Caution was in order, as a fall onto those sharp-edged clinkers could shred your knees and hands. The year the railroad decided to replace rotting ties, section-workers stacked them along the tracks for burning later. The old beams became lonely outposts on the edge of the Great Frontier or the shelled-out ruins of a war-torn European village.

We were fascinated by the tracks. From Western movies we learned that if you put your ear on the rails, you could hear a train before you could see it (not true). My brother Gary and I used them on our route to school in a never-ending contest to see who could walk a rail the longest without stepping off.

The immense weight of a train flattened pennies in the most amazing way. We kept a sample of them on hand to impress nonbelievers.

A passing train was reason to suspend all activities while we ran to the edge of the tracks to gather small stones and wait in ambush. With the locomotive safely by, we pelted the boxcars with rocks, then hid when the last car, the red caboose, came in sight. The last car was where railroad crews slept, ate, and whiled away the miles sitting on the car's platform, smoking cigarettes in their striped caps and overalls.

Occasionally we saw hobos hitching rides in empty boxcars. They stood in the doorway and waved or shook their fists as met their mood. They were proud of the name hobo, fiercely defending the distinction between themselves and the garden-variety bum. Bums, they assured us, were losers who refused to work and survived by begging or stealing. Hobos, on the other hand, were folks with families and means, who for the sake of adventure took to the road when the urge struck them.

Each year Britt, Iowa, holds the National Hobo Convention. They elect a hobo king and queen, and tourists line up to eat Mulligan Stew. The hobos, or "bos", for short, originally prepared this concoction in large pots, adding meat, vegetables, potatoes, water, seasoning, and whatnot. It's a recipe from the old "hobo jungles," a name given their temporary camps along the tracks where they congregated to share the edibles collected that day.

My grandmother told me stories about hobos who stopped at her house during the Great Depression, requesting a chore for a bit of food. Then they marked the house in some way so that others might find the same generosity.

They had colorful road names like Steam Shovel Charlie, Boxcar Betty, and Mulligan Mike. Although Mom admonished us to stay away, we couldn't resist talking with the more friendly ones who spent a hot day beneath the elms of Central Park. Sometimes they could be persuaded to sing a song, tell a story, or recite poems of the rails.

The trains that moved past our neighborhood were loud, but that's not to say they were fast. On the contrary, they were usually slow and lumbering, depending upon their load and condition of the tracks. We quickly realized we could easily keep up with them. I'm not sure who started it, but around the age of eleven, we began to play the game of "dare" with the trains. At first it was enough to touch the boxcars, but soon that progressed to hopping onto the side ladder for a short ride. We'd been told not to, but of course, that just made it even more enticing.

Late one Saturday afternoon in mid spring, Gary and I were trying to get our kites into the air near the tracks. When we heard an approaching train, we quickly wound up our kite strings and stashed them in the weeds.

The engineer sounded the whistle in a long deafening blast that ripped the air as the train shuddered by. The earth trembled and shook as the steel wheels click-clacked along. We stood our ground waiting for the right car.

Then we saw it... the open door of an empty boxcar. I pointed and shouted, "Here comes one!"

We waited as the car neared, helped each other up into the doorway, and tumbled inside. Moments later, we were standing triumphantly on the wooden floor of a rocking boxcar watching the houses glide by. We clapped each other on the back and laughed in shared congratulations. We were hobos on an adventure.

"Let's get off at the grain elevator, okay?" Gary shouted over the noise.

I nodded. But as we approached the elevator, we saw a group of men standing at a siding watching the train and decided that jumping off in plain view was a bad idea. Small towns have their disadvantages; one of the men would be sure to recognize us and more than likely knew our father, the town barber. We decided to wait to abandon ship at the edge of town.

It sounded like a good plan...

As the train neared the town limits, the engineer opened the throttle and before we could react, we were going too fast to jump. The sudden change in speed nearly knocked us off our feet. I felt a knot tighten in my stomach and panic arose in my chest. Gary looked stricken. Each of us waited for the other to say something comforting or share a plan. We clung to each other in fear, disbelief, and embarrassment at our stupidity.

We found some dirty gunnysacks to sit on and plopped down, exhausted, on the rumbling floor. The passing countryside became a mesmerizing blur as the distant towns slipped by. The engineer announced each railroad crossing with his mournful whistle. The farms, fields, fences, and telephone poles of Iowa became unfamiliar as we were whisked away to meet an unknown fate.

The daylight began to fade and the shadows inside our swaying prison grew darker and deeper. The spring nights were still cool, and we pulled the coarse, stinking sacks around our arms.

"Boy, is Dad gonna be mad," Gary said at last, giving voice to a growing dread.

"Yeah, that's for sure," I agreed. At this point I'd have welcomed a good scolding just to be home again.

"I'm hungry, Wayne," he whined.

"Well, me too. Whatcha want me to do about it?" I snapped.

I was immediately sorry when I saw his face fall. He was scared and looking to me, his older brother, for comfort. I didn't have to make things worse.

"Sorry, Gare, don't worry. The trainmen must have to stop and eat, too. Right?"

Digging into my pockets I found thirteen cents, a piece of kite string, and two sticks of Wrigley's Double Mint gum. We opened the wrappers, savoring the gum in our hungry mouths.

He cheered a bit and smiled sheepishly. "I didn't mean to be no crybaby."

"It's okay," I said, "I'm kinda scared, too." I hoped I sounded braver than I felt.

I thought how frantic our mother must be. She would have called us for supper many times by now, with anger giving way to concern, then fear. I pictured supper growing cold on the table and my two little sisters wondering what was happening. Dad would be searching for us and phoning neighbors. They'd say, "Why, no, they haven't been around here all day. What's the trouble?"

My eyes suddenly widened with the thought that he'd probably call Tom Larkin the town cop to report us missing. I pictured people searching with flashlights and finding our kites, thinking that bums had kidnapped us.

I didn't feel so hungry anymore.

It was just dark when the train finally slowed, and at long last huffed to a halt by a weathered depot. The faded sign on the station read, Albert Lea, Minnesota.

"Holy cow!" I said, "We're in Minnesota!"

We'd been fishing in Minnesota many times with our uncles. Our town was only a few hours away by car.

We jumped from the train, scurried off the platform, and hid in the shadows to plan our next move.

It made no sense wandering around a strange town in the dark, so we walked into the depot. A telegraph key sitting on an oak table was tapping, attended by a heavy-set, balding man. When the clicks stopped, he tapped a signal that the message had been received.

He looked up, grunted himself to a standing position, and approached the counter. "What can I do fer you boys?" His voice was a rusty hinge, and the tangled bird's nests of his eyebrows bobbed up and down as he spoke.

"Mister," I said, "we messed up real bad and got stranded on this train, an' we couldn't get off, an' we kept getting farther an' farther from home, an' we're hungry, an', an'…" I'd run out of words and was afraid to start blubbering. Gary nodded vigorously in agreement near my elbow.

When he learned of our town of origin, the man whistled low. "Looks like you two are in some heavy-duty trouble."

Our eyes found the floor.

"I can tell you," he continued, "if you was mine, you wouldn't be able to sit on yer butts for a week from the blisterin' I'd give ya!"

I nodded. I could see his point.

We used his phone to call our overjoyed parents. The county sheriff had been only minutes away from being notified.

The stationmaster, Ralph Oleson, spoke briefly to my father, assuring him that we were safe and sound, and gave directions to find us.

"Bet you boys could use a little somethin' to eat, huh?" he squeaked.

We nodded.

He took us to a small cafe three blocks from the station. We rode in his vintage black Buick that shed paint and rust like hair from a mangy dog.

"Hello there, Ralph," the waitress said as we entered. "Who ya got with ya tonight?"

Ralph smiled and jerked a thumb at us. "Ah, just a couple a hobos come in on the six-thirty freight from Iowa."

We sat at the counter with Ralph and ordered hamburgers, French fries, and malts. While we ate, he told our story to the customers drinking coffee and gossiping. Soon, we were the celebrities of the hour.

"Imagine pullin' a stunt like that," one gent said, "Why, I'd skin 'em alive."

"What you Iowa boys use for brains down there, anyways?" another chided. People laughed and we blushed.

We suffered in silence but managed to wolf down every bite.

Hours later, our father arrived. I'd been wondering what he'd say or do and every notion I had about it made me squirm. We were unprepared for what he did.

The stationmaster refused to be repaid for our suppers. Ralph winked and grinned as we left the station. "Y'all come back now. Ya hear?" he said in a fake southern drawl.

My father uttered not a single word during the entire trip home. Far worse than any spanking or scolding, we sat in dreadful, heavy silence for three hours. I had a lump in my throat as big as a golf ball and barbed wire cinched my gut.

Once home, Mom hugged us with tears of relief, then asked, what we were using for brains... a familiar question by now.

"Get to bed," were the only words my father said. He suddenly looked very weary.

"We're awful sorry, Mom and Dad," Gary said, his voice cracking with emotion.

"'Sorry' just doesn't quite do it, does it now, Son?" my father said quietly and shot us a look that could have etched a diamond.

That night, safely in our beds, there were no freight trains to rock us to sleep. We listened instead to the soft murmuring of the thankful prayers of our parents.

Americans love their automobiles. Soon after the end of WWII and the re-emergence of the auto industry, the race was on to make cars with the latest technology and designs. What the country wanted may be summed up in three words: big, fast, powerful.

Each manufacturer had its own design style; in the 50s and 60s you could distinguish a Ford from a Chevy or an Oldsmobile from a Cadillac just by looking at it. Now, with rare exceptions, cars look pretty much the same and most are from foreign manufacturers. I'm not a car geek or gearhead, but it depresses me to see the cookie-cutter cars lined row upon row in parking lots. Maybe I'm getting old, but lately I seem to rely more and more on my key fob to find my car hiding among the sameness. All you need is a tour through an auto museum to see how quickly things have evolved.

Think of the many things you can do without leaving your car. You're able to do your banking, fill prescriptions, and pick up fast-food, coffee, soft drinks and ice cream. It's convenient, as you needn't find a place to park, exert yourself, or brave the weather. All snug in your car, you are king or queen of your very own portable space. Woe be to anyone who threatens that space, as perceived infractions may be met with rage.

Before drive-throughs there was the drive-in theater. They're mostly a curiosity now or a nostalgic trip into the past, but back in the 50s and 60s they were very popular.

This is what I remember:

It was a family thing. On warm summer nights my parents took my brother, sisters, and me to the drive-in to watch a double feature in the comfort of our car.

Finding just the right location was critical. First, you must not be too distant or too close to the screen. Second, finding a location somewhere in the center was important. Third, it was preferred to park a handy distance to the snack bar and restrooms, but not so near as to be bothered by the steady stream of customers. Finally, you needed to be near a working speaker. Two speakers hung from a post and had to be hooked onto the car door or window. One car had the speaker on one side of the post and the neighboring car used the one on the opposite side.

My father was a pro at finding the right parking space. Arriving early while it was still light, he'd cruise up and down the little graveled lanes... searching.

There were playgrounds near the screen for kids to play until twilight. Sometimes we dressed in pajamas, anticipating that we'd be asleep and ready for bed when returning home.

Dad loved the junk they served at the snack bar. Popcorn, hotdogs, French fries, burgers, candy, and every sugary drink imaginable were for sale. I was usually called upon to help carry it all in little cardboard trays. The smell of hot food in the closed space of our station wagon made everything taste that much better. It was a special treat, and we loved it.

As showtime approached, impatient drivers honked their horns, urging the projectionist to fire up his magic lantern. Latecomers who were supposed to observe good drive-in manners and drive with parking lights only were loudly chastised if they neglected to turn their headlights off. On-screen messages warned drivers to keep their foot off the brake pedal or it would make those behind them "see red."

During the sing-along at the start of every show, we were encouraged to "follow the bouncing ball" as it bounded along at the bottom of the screen, touching each word in time with the music. I recall "Alexander's Rag Time Band" was a big favorite. On special nights we were treated to a short fireworks display after the features.

It was summer and the warm nights required us to roll the windows down for fresh air. Naturally this invited mosquitoes, so Mom kept a bottle of insect repellent in the glove compartment.

Usually by the end of the first feature we kids were asleep. I remember the ride home as the summer night slipped by the windows, the motor hummed, and the wheels rumbled.

One evening our family was enjoying a drive-in double feature. The first movie was family fare and soon after it was finished my sisters and brother had conked out. The second feature was the more adult film, *Butterfield 8*. I wasn't exactly certain what was going on but was intently interested in watching Elizabeth Taylor on the big screen in her slinky underwear. Our parents kept peeking over their shoulders to assure that we were asleep. Whenever they looked, I shut my eyes, pretending to slumber.

I clearly remember hearing Elizabeth's co-star and later husband, Eddie Fisher, saying the line that he was tired of seeing her "boozed up, burned out, and ugly." As far as I was concerned, I had no problem whatsoever seeing her in *any* condition.

Years later, drive-ins ran movies catering to us baby boomers who were now driving. The "beach movies" were a huge attraction featuring young bikini-clad girls and handsome muscular men romping around on California seashores. The plots were paper thin and the acting bad, but it didn't matter, as most dating couples weren't paying much attention to the screen anyway.

Double-dating rules of etiquette dictated that the front seat couple had to mind their own business and vice versa for the back seat couple. That's when drive-ins got the nickname "passion pits," of which our parents remained blissfully unaware.

When my wife Pat and I were courting we went to a local drive-in at the Ponta Delgada in Tiverton, RI, for a walk down memory lane and relive the experience we'd had as children. Before the feature began, I left to get a few items at the snack bar. By the time I was ready to return, the movie had begun, and the lights were out. The problem was, I couldn't remember exactly where we'd parked. I had an idea of the general location but nothing specific. Cardboard tray in hand, I crunched up and down the graveled lanes. I was beginning to panic. *Which row were we in, anyway?*

As I passed the same area for the third time, I heard the incredulous voice of a young woman, "Here he comes again!" followed by loud guffaws from the car. How embarrassing! To make matters worse, when I found the car and told Pat, she couldn't stop laughing. Decades later it still makes her laugh.

The price of admission was initially like that of a movie theater, with a charge for each person. It became impossible to control when kids smuggled in friends in the trunks of their cars. The solution was to charge per car, so the cars arrived packed like sardine cans. When underage kids who couldn't care less about the movie smuggled in beer, it could get rowdy as they partied on each other's car hoods.

The death knell for drive-in movies was the invention of VCR home movies. Why spend money on gas and admission when you could watch any movie you wished from your sofa?

*

Many years later, Pat and I took our young daughters to one of the remaining drive-in theaters near us. Instead of the audio from a speaker on the car's window, we listened via our radio. The playground was still there but rusting and weedy. My arthritic neck ached from watching the movie from the car seat and the girls were bored... so, that was that.

I have fond memories of drive-in movies, but truth be told, I much prefer my couch.

It was my very first live football game, and I was utterly bored.

I'd been invited to attend the high school game by Emmitt, a friend of my father's. A big fan of all sports, he always had an athletic event on the radio or his TV.

Watching or listening to sports was not big in our house. As kids, my brother and I dabbled in little league baseball for a few summers, but sitting down to watch an entire ballgame was not on the agenda. There were more interesting things to do, like watching the grass grow or studying the accumulation of moss on tree trunks.

Pop was keen to have me involved in sports to "round me out." So, the invite to the football game was readily accepted on my behalf.

This is what I remember:

It was a cool Friday evening in late October at the high school gridiron. I started out in the bleachers next to Emmitt, but within fifteen minutes or so, I began thinking I'd made a mistake. My thoughts turned to escape.

I had very little idea as to what was going on. It appeared that two bunches of very large guys were smashing into each other, trying to knock each other down. People got very excited when the thundering herd got near one end of the field or the other. Periodically, someone kicked the ball to someone else and it started again.

All was not lost, though, as I quickly discovered the cheerleaders in their short, pleated skirts, tight white sweaters, and cute little earmuffs jumping up and down along the sidelines. I was young but starting to pay attention to such things.

The band was fun, too. I liked the lively music, and the precision marching was a bonus I'd not expected.

After a time, I begged off, ostensibly to buy popcorn and hot chocolate from the Band Booster's booth behind the home bleachers. On the way, I ran into a classmate wandering around under the bleacher seats.

"Hey, Roger, what're you doing?" I asked.

He raised his head briefly. "Lookin' for money, that's what," he said. He bent down to pick something up, examined it, and tossed it aside in disgust. Obviously, it wasn't money.

I joined him searching for loose change under the legs, feet, and backsides of the spectators. At my feet was an assortment of empty cups, popcorn bags, and candy wrappers. It killed time, but I didn't find anything of note. Even that was turning out to be a bust.

Roger informed me that the best time to find money would be the next morning before they picked up the trash and when the light was better. It was a long ride on my bicycle across town that morning, but I made it. He was right. I found an unopened pack of Juicy Fruit Gum and thirty-seven cents.

The following year, now in 7th grade, I went to junior high in a school building mobbed with baby boomers. Gone were the halcyon days of the two recess periods of elementary school. Instead, we now attended weekly physical education classes called gym.

My parents had to fork over $3.50 they couldn't afford for "gym clothes." The uniform consisted of a pair of black shorts and a gold-colored T-shirt with the school's name printed on it.

The physical education teacher was one of the junior high coaches. He always wore gray sweatpants, a gray sweatshirt with the faded logo of his alma mater, and a silver whistle around his thick neck. He seemed to have a perpetual pissed-off look, hinting that he wished he were somewhere else, doing something else.

On the first day, he set about assigning lockers and combination padlocks from an omnipresent clipboard. He informed us that we needed to keep a pair of gym shoes at school and must buy an athletic supporter.

I had no idea what he was talking about and asked him, "Coach, what's that other thing you want?"

"A jockstrap. You gotta have a jockstrap," he snapped.

"Why?" I asked.

He sighed at my stupidity. "You don't wanna go running around with only one ball between your legs, do ya?"

I remained confused, but he didn't look like he was in the mood for more questions. I turned to one of the other guys who explained, "It's so your nuts don't get busted."

"Oh," I said, but still didn't understand how such a thing could happen and why it was even a consideration. I mean... *busted nuts?!*

"Come with me after school and I'll show ya," he said. "I got an older brother, and he knows all about that stuff."

Later at the downtown clothing store, with impressive self-assuredness, he approached a salesman. "I want a Bike... medium," he said. He gave me a quick glance, jerked a thumb at me, and instructed the clerk to get me "a Bike... small."

I didn't know enough to be insulted, so I nodded my head idiotically. Why would I be buying a stupid bicycle in a clothing store? Hadn't we come to get an athletic supporter? Still confused...

After reading from the box that "Bike" was the brand name, I figured it out. I was relieved, as I already had a perfectly good bike and didn't need another.

At the next gym class, I dutifully brought it with me to the locker room. I watched in amazement as naked, peri-pubescent boys stood in front of their lockers, attempting for the first time to don a jockstrap. There were so many straps to contend with! A kid next to me staggered and fell after hopping around like a jackrabbit with both legs in the same strappy space. Another somehow managed to put it on backward. It was a mistake I was thankful to have seen before my own attempt.

The physically and mentally aberrant Strange Steve put it on his head, covering his big pimpled nose. "My nose is so big it needs extra support," he explained.

It felt weird with everything stuffed into a little pouch swinging between my legs. Worse still, part of it rode up into my butt crack, making me feel like I had a load in my shorts.

The coach had been blowing his whistle until the veins popped out on his forehead by the time we were all out on the gymnasium floor, picking straps out of our butts.

"Get out here, boys," he ordered. "We got stuff to do!"

What he meant by "stuff" was for us to line up in front of various pieces of gym equipment. Some of it was left over from the Woodrow Wilson administration (The early 1900s for the historically impaired.) The parallel bars were made of cast iron and oak, stained with the sweat of generations. A set of rings and a thick climbing rope were suspended from the ceiling and a pommel horse covered with leather had horsehair stuffing escaping from a tear. Scattered on the gym floor were stained, rock-hard matts offering perfunctory protection. The only piece of equipment that was relatively new was a pull-up bar screwed into a doorway.

This was the era of President Kennedy's Physical Fitness Initiative. The impossible task for physical education teachers was to record how many chin-ups, pushups, sit-ups, etc. we could do, then check for progress periodically. By the time we'd made the rounds at each task, the class was over. Then it was off to the showers.

Everyone was required to take a complete shower after each gym class. This, too, was a new experience. We weren't used to communal showers, and it soon became clear that you had to avoid looking at each other's nether regions at all costs, so I focused intently on the tiled shower wall directly in front of me.

We dried ourselves with towels from a stack near the showers' entrance. The towels were promptly converted into instruments of torture to snap the bare bottoms of the unwary. It was a real feat opening a combination lock while simultaneously keeping an eye on your backside.

I learned to lag to let the crowd thin before embarking upon the undress, shower, and dress ritual. This made me late for the next class, where I arrived with dripping wet hair.

Once the statistics were finally recorded to the government's satisfaction, we had the actual gym class. When the weather forced us inside during the Northern Iowa winters, we were introduced to the trampoline. It was wheeled out into the center of the gym and surrounded by the class, who were supposed to keep jumpers from a nasty fall. At roughly chest high, it left your head exposed to the out-of-control bodies of the overly zealous. It was a crapshoot as to whether someone was up to the job or not. The urge for self-preservation sometimes trumped saving someone from a bad landing, as the would-be "catcher" just stepped out of the line of fire.

Naturally, everyone wanted an opportunity on the "tramp" until an unfortunate incident: Fern, a tall lanky fellow, was enjoying his turn at bouncing when he was suddenly launched forward and landed astride one of the heavy suspension springs. The spring separated slightly during his landing and immediately resumed its contracted state, pinching and trapping his family jewels in the coils.

His Bike did little to nothing in the way of protection and he howled like a timber wolf. Coach was able to free him but not before we were all permanently traumatized. After that, our turns on the tramp became a timid, reluctant exercise.

During the warmer months, we were sent out into the elements to play flag football, where we dutifully tucked white strips of cloth into the elastic waistbands of our gym shorts. You were considered tackled if your flag was pulled off. The coach thought it was funny when some of the running backs tied their flags to their jockstraps, but I didn't think it was funny and thought it cheating.

I was beginning to be aware of the symbiotic relationship between kids on the athletic fast-track and their coaches. Those with advanced hand-eye coordination and athletic musculature were termed "jocks" for obvious reasons. They were the only ones allowed to run plays and score points while the rest of the rabble were left to be trampled to a pulp.

As I said previously, I hadn't spent much time or effort understanding the finer points of football. It occurred to me that instead of knocking someone down (quite unlikely for me) all I had to do was to pull their flag out of their pants. When I did just that, the kid I "tackled" was incensed. "What're you tacklin' me for, you stupid idiot? I don't have the ball! I'm not even near the ball!"

Once again, I was confused.

So, I embarked upon another strategy. I decided to maintain a nonthreatening, motionless pose of nonchalance at the line of scrimmage. The offensive back, thinking I was an easy portal, naturally ran in my direction, whereupon I quickly stepped aside and grabbed his flag for the tackle. After repeating this maneuver, he got wise and had his blockers grind me into the ground. The skin on my knees and elbows had barely grown back before the end of school in May.

Coach came up with a game of his own, mostly for his own sadistic amusement, that he called Mexican Basketball. The rules were that there were no rules. The class was divided equally into two teams, roughly twelve per team. The kid with the basketball wasn't required to dribble; he just lit out for the basket as fast as he could go. He usually didn't make it far, and quickly attracted defenders like lint on a wad of chewing gum. Anyone in possession of the ball was kicked, slapped, and punched until he gave it up to another masochist. There was blood.

Oddly, the game became quite popular as it seems the desire for anarchy runs strong and deep in adolescent boys. It was certainly more fun than the mindless collection of statistics that was eventually and wisely ignored.

*

Many of my friends were jocks and their athletic scholarships afforded them college educations not otherwise available. Certainly, the benefits of learning to work as a team toward a common goal are invaluable, as well as the fostering of perseverance and drive.

No, I was not and never would be a jock for a variety of reasons. I discovered other ways to build character and, as it turns out, they were a heck of a lot easier on my body.

I admired, envied, and even despised them at times. Some have maintained a stay-fit lifestyle that has kept them healthy and productive. All too many, though, are permanently crippled with ruined joints, bruised brains, and spinal injuries. The price of fame is dear.

Gym class is a thing of the past now and I'll leave it for you to decide if that's wise or not. One thing is certain though: I will never get on another trampoline.

METAMORPHOSIS

This is what I remember:

Strange things happen when the hormonal tides of early adolescence begin rising.

For my sixth-grade class, those awesome chemicals were only beginning to course through our veins. As the youngest in my class, my own tide was somewhat delayed but rising just the same.

The effects were first apparent among the girls. Instead of the usual jump-rope games, they began collecting in groups, spending their recess time on the playground giggling and talking.

We boys continued to play much as before but puzzled by the effect we had as we passed by the whispering females.

What's with them? we wondered.

We shrugged and ignored it, hoping it was a passing phase. But avoiding them proved ineffective, as runners were sent from the groups to ask if we "liked" so and so. No matter the response, it always resulted in ear-piercing squeals.

As for me, I wasn't exactly sure what, if anything, I was supposed to be doing about girls. Now don't get me wrong, there were several of the opposite sex over whom I'd mooned and moped.

In fifth grade I brought a Milky Way candy bar to school for my secret crush, Arlis, but before I could present it to her, the chocolate had melted and rather than see it go to waste, I ate it myself. Days later, after again mustering my courage, I bought her a fresh one and delivered the goods.

She accepted it with a surprised smile that made my heart do flips, then she turned to Jim Larson in the desk behind her and said, "Look what Wayne gave me. Isn't he sweet?"

The look of jealous hate from Jim left no doubt that I had competition for her affections. I considered him to be one of my best friends and bowed out right then and there.

Having since sworn off girls, I was startled when one afternoon a runner from one of the cliques appeared to say, "Martha Hart likes you and wants to know if you like her," and then stood by waiting for a response.

I glanced at the group she'd been sent from and saw the plump, round figure of Martha Hart. She was pretending to be engrossed in conversation, but I knew she was watching.

I'd known Martha since my first days at school and considered her a friend. Not only that, but my parents were buying our house from her parents, giving me cause for our paths to meet outside of school.

At times, our payments to the Harts lagged. Barbering, being the business it is, plus my father's poor money management skills, left us in a state of frequent financial embarrassment. When we fell behind, my parents sent me on my bike to deliver a partial payment with the promise that the balance would be forthcoming. This tactic was very effective, as it made me a go-between that insulated the Harts and my parents from a confrontation.

During those visits to the Hart's nice new home, Martha greeted me at the window with a wave and a shy smile. It seemed Martha had decided that we were destined for each other.

The thought left me, well… lukewarm. Not cold, mind you, just… tepid.

Facing the runner I started to say, "Yeah, I like Martha. She's a nice girl and I…"

If I'd gotten to finish my sentence it would have ended: "…like her just as I like most of the girls in our class, no less, no more." But I didn't get the chance. The runner shrieked and leapt into the air, her saddle shoes lifting a full foot off the ground. In a flash she was off to give a reconnaissance report.

They looked like a football team in huddle, standing in a tight circle, leaning forward with their heads nearly touching. Suddenly, they were all jumping up and down, clapping their hands, and hugging Martha. I knew what that meant… she was being *congratulated*!

Martha blushed beet red and stared cow-eyed at me.

I blanched and made a beeline for the farthest corner of the playground to hole up and wait for recess to end. *What was I going to do?*

The next few weeks were hell. Whenever I neared a group of girls, they pointed at me and giggled. "Hi, Martha," one would say in a taunting voice and the snickering would begin. At odd times I'd catch her mooning at me from across the classroom.

A particularly admirable trait of girls is how they always seem to rally around the not-so-attractive one in their group. They bolster their spirits and support them in their search for the "right guy." Apparently, I'd been singled out as Martha's Mr. Right. After all, I was the perfect match, as apparently no one else wanted me and I was reputed to be "kinda cute."

On the bus to and from gym classes at the high school, the girls sang a rope-skipping song, pairing boys with girls. It went: "First comes love, then comes marriage, then comes Martha an' Wayne with a baby carriage."

It was unbelievably embarrassing. Even more aggravating, my buddies began to tease me about my "girlfriend." My parents even got into the act.

Just when I thought things couldn't get worse… they did. Diane Finkle, one of the girls in my class, was having a birthday party at her farm east of town. As kids, we'd attended each other's parties in a mix of girls and boys, but as we grew older the parties had become unisex. This was to be the first time since then to bring us together again.

I was flattered I'd been invited, and after my parents were assured that the party would be properly chaperoned, I gratefully accepted.

The week of the party, the classroom buzzed over plans for the event. The birthday girl assured us there'd be dancing with plenty to eat and drink. I was interested mostly in the eating part.

It was late spring and although cool, the evening held the promise of approaching summer. A south wind carried the scent of freshly plowed earth. Bees buzzed around the newly bloomed tulips and robins were carrying bits of grass to build nests.

The birds and bees were busy awakening in some of us, too.

The night of the party was warm and clear with bright stars and a thin crescent moon. One of the mothers offered to chauffeur a group of us boys from town.

Diane's family farmhouse was a white two-story with a wrap-around front porch. Music flowed out of the door and windows, welcoming us poor lambs to the slaughter.

When we arrived, we puffed out our chests, plastered on smiles, and strutted up the front walk. Diane and her mother greeted us on the porch and ushered us into the parlor. We stepped into an elaborately decorated room lit with lamps, subdued by yards of hanging crepe paper and silk scarves. Balloons bobbed as we moved en masse to the center of the floor. We seemed weirdly stuck together by some invisible force, making it necessary to travel in unison wherever we went.

Most of the girls, we discovered, had arrived a full half-hour early to "help out." This gave them the advantage of staking out territory and getting the lay of the land. They'd already found the most advantageous positions near the phonograph, food, and darkest corners.

I was having trouble recognizing everyone. Some of them looked familiar but I wasn't sure in the dim light. *What's going on*? I wondered. *Isn't this a class party? Who are these people?*

But they *were* our people. Fancy clothes, new hairdos, touches of makeup, and padded bras had transformed the girls into strangers. We gawked at them, and they giggled at us.

We boys made tracks for the snacks, stalling to sort things out. Then I saw my buddies… I mean, really *saw* them. They, too, were dressed strangely in pressed slacks, crisp shirts, and Sunday shoes. Under their slicked hair were the familiar faces of my old friends, but on those faces, aside from ripening pimples, was one of two looks: badly concealed terror or open excitement. I checked my look in the bathroom mirror… it was the first type.

I splashed cold water on my face and returned to the party.

The boys occupied one side of the room and the girls the other, creating a sort of No Man's Land. No one seemed sure what to do next. Were we supposed to talk to each other, dance, or wait for runners?

My pal Jim, from the excited-look group, made his move. With studied nonchalance, he stalked his prey, closed in, and offered Arlis a cup of punch. She smiled and nodded. Moments later, they'd set their cups down and started dancing to *Tan Shoes and Pink Shoelaces*.

That broke the ice. We weren't stupid; we just needed someone to show us what to do.

I pretended to sip my punch while scanning the crowd to see who was available. I spotted Martha watching me from a folding chair. I winced and shifted my attention to the hostess, Diane. *Ah,* I thought, *here's safe territory.* She was the perfect choice for my first dance foray. No one could accuse me of neglecting Martha or making a move on Diane. It was, after all, her birthday party.

I crossed the room and sidled up to her. "Can I get you some punch?" I asked.

She smiled wearily and held up a nearly full cup in her hand. I blushed, not having bothered to see if she needed one.

I recovered quickly. "Ya wanna dance?" I asked. She consented and we shuffled to the center of the room.

I'd studied everyone else's dance moves, and figured I could fake a slow dance but have trouble with anything else. The timing to ensure that the tune was of slow tempo had not been easy, but we made it in time for the last sixty seconds of *Love Me Tender*.

After thanking Diane for the opportunity to badly abuse her feet, she whispered, "You're welcome, but don't you think you should dance with Martha?"

I stole a quick glance at Martha sitting alone and bulging the seams of her party dress. She looked so... forlorn. I felt like a jerk. *If it wasn't for this stupid girlfriend stuff,* I told myself, *I wouldn't even think twice about dancing with Martha; I'd just do it.* I was at a loss as to what to do. The next record was a fast one, so I retreated to the porch where some of my friends were seeking refuge.

"Wow! Did you see Arlis?" Jim said. "She looks great! Do ya think she's wearin' a bra?"

There ensued a brief debate as to the likelihood that Arlis was or was not wearing a bra. The final vote was ayes 4 and nays 2. The ayes had it.

"How'd you learn to dance?" I asked Jim. I'd been admiring his moves.

He beamed proudly, "Been watchin' American Bandstand."

I'd occasionally watched Dick Clark's Saturday afternoon show. It seemed silly to waste an hour watching a bunch of teenagers in baggy pants and flared skirts hopping and bopping in Philadelphia. I wasn't even sure where Philadelphia was, let alone care a whit how they danced there... till now.

"Just watch the ole master," he told me.

So, I did. He didn't have many moves in his repertoire, but the ones he knew were impressive.

After Diane had blown out the candles on her birthday cake, Mrs. Finkle left to clean the kitchen. That's when the lights went out...

I heard giggling and snickering, and then someone switched on a single light on the pole-lamp and focused it on the center of the room.

Diane stepped out into the patch of light, cleared her throat, and announced, "Now we will have a special spotlight dance for two of our good friends and everyone's favorite couple… Martha and Wayne."

She led everyone in applause as I, in full panic, contemplated running the two miles back to town. Friendly hands pushed me to the center of the floor. I felt like I was wearing giant clown shoes. My vision dimmed. I got lightheaded and shook my head to clear it.

Waiting center stage was Martha, her eyes shining, hands clasped behind her back. I was surprised that she could reach around to her back, but she'd done it.

She held out her arms for me and I found two safe places to put my hands: her left armpit and her right shoulder… both were damp. She stepped in close for the kill as the music started, and we began rocking stiffly to the beat.

Rivulets of perspiration tickled as they rolled down my back, and I suppressed the urge to stop and scratch.

I glanced at Martha's face and into those brown, hopeful doe-eyes brimming with happiness and triumph. My face was paralyzed in a rictus as I gritted my teeth and clung to her moist bulges.

Mercifully, the record spun to an end and she blew me a kiss as I backed away for the exit.

That dance took the wind out of my sails for good and I spent the remainder of the evening on the porch steps listening to the Finkle's cows mooing in their pens. They seemed to taunt me. MOOOAARTHA. MOOOAARTHA.

Martha continued to pursue me, and I continued to duck and run for the next two years. Our involuntary pairing finally ended when Diane Finkle and I briefly became "an item." It was an arrangement that suited us both. She had a reasonably acceptable someone with whom to attend the occasional party and I had an excuse to let Martha down easy.

Eight years passed.

While attending classes at a community college not far from my hometown, I was cashing a check at the bank. A very fetching cashier stepped to the teller window to serve me.

She had long blond hair, beautiful soft brown eyes, a lovely face, and a very nicely put together body. An appreciative smile and my raised eyebrows gave away my thoughts, but the smile quickly changed to an open-mouthed gape. The lovely creature before me was none other than Martha Hart.

She'd recognized me immediately and was enjoying watching me discover her. Her warm smile was genuine, reflecting how pleased she was that I appreciated the changes time had made.

"Martha!" I gushed. "You... you look terrific!"

She blushed, and just for a moment I saw the girl I once knew. "Thank you," she said, but there were no blown kisses this time. I was pleased to find her the same sweet person I'd known.

We exchanged pleasantries, bid good-bye, and never saw each other again.

*

Isn't life strange? We come and go like butterflies over a summer pasture, pushed by the slightest breeze or whiff of pheromone. We flutter and flit, trying to decide what to make of each other one moment and the next... we're gone. Why then are we surprised to later find our original notions of each other were baseless?

Martha Hart, wherever you are... I'm sorry I didn't see past the caterpillar to the lovely butterfly you always were.

By the time I was ten, I'd concluded that school was just not my cup of tea. It had become increasingly difficult and imposed itself heavily into playtime. Each year and another rung up the educational ladder only served to verify those conclusions. I'd developed a plan reflecting my belief that school was just something to endure and would one day be over for good. All I had to do was wait.

My plan was to be pleasant, polite, and cooperative so that everyone would overlook or excuse my sub-par performance. *What the heck,* I thought, *I know how to read, write, add, subtract, and find Iowa on a map. What else is there? I mean, who needs to know how to multiply, do long division, or learn the chief export of Brazil?*

Sure, my parents wanted me to attend college, but that would be out of the question once everyone got a load of what a dim bulb I was. My plan, I believed, was applied genius.

This is what I remember:

Most school lessons were easy for me. I could do passably well with scant effort, with one exception… arithmetic. For some reason my brain just didn't seem wired with the proper circuits to grasp its concepts with the ease I'd grown to expect.

Math demanded a four-letter word that made me recoil… WORK.

My teachers said, "Wayne, you're going to have to WORK on your arithmetic a little harder." But I shied away from anything resembling WORK like a deer from a forest fire.

My parents sternly warned me that I must, "Buckle down and WORK if you ever expect to get anywhere."

Mathematics seemed terribly important to everyone but me. I, on the other hand, was convinced that it was highly overrated, and held the belief that if I just kept plodding along, eventually my teachers and parents would give up and we could all just forget the whole ugly mess.

My distaste for arithmetic was so intense that I refused to commit to memory even the spelling of the word. I didn't want to have it floating around in my brain with good stuff, like the date of my birthday or how many days until school vacation.

That I constantly misspelled the word arithmetic caught my teacher's attention. She taught me how to use first letter of each word in the sentence, "A rat in the house may eat the ice cream." Problem solved. One might well point out that it was far more complicated than simply memorizing it, but as I said, I had my reasons.

I fooled around like this for some time until the end of sixth grade. My regular teacher had been an easy target for my strategy of pleasant politeness.

To my dismay, a late-year reorganization of faculty assignments relieved her of her math class. Miss Baines, the school's principal, replaced her. Her reputation made Attila the Hun seem like St. Francis of Assisi.

Miss Baines was overweight, yes, but it was only a disguise. Beneath the adipose tissue lurked a muscular body capable of separating heads from the shoulders of disobedient children with one quick chop of her beefy hand.

One minute the class clown was entertaining the troops in the back of the room, and CHOP… the next minute his head was rolling down the aisle like an over-ripe melon.

She enjoyed her power and strutted the halls like a drill instructor, freezing those suspected of misbehavior with icy blasts from her piggy eyes. We aptly referred to her as "Miss Pains." Even more chilling than her frown was her smile. Certainly, Adolph Hitler possessed such a grimace as he conjured his terrible plans.

She set the tone when she waddled to the front of the room, grabbed the teacher's chair, and spun it into position next to her desk. Lifting one leg she planted her foot on the seat and leaned forward, resting a Popeye-sized forearm on her knee. Her steely, ball bearing-like eyes darted around the room as she waited for silence...a silence that reduced the bravest to guacamole.

"I am to be your aRITHmetic inSTRUCtor for the reMAINder of the term." She pounced on parts of her words for a chilling effect.

Oh, God, gasped a frightened mouse from a dark corner of my brain.

"No," she continued as if reading my mind, "You are NOT having a bad dream. As a matter of FACT, I am looking FORWARD to teaching once again, as math-a-MATics is my favorite SUBject."

Oh, my God, the mouse squeaked again.

"I think that SOME OF YOU have been getting by PRETTY eeeasily around here and it's HIGH TIME we change that," she continued. "It is time to settle down for some real WORK." She punched her ham-sized fist into the palm of her other hand with a loud smack to emphasize WORK, making us jump in our seats.

"Now for some math problems, to find out what is what," she said with a wicked smile and turned to the chalkboard.

The next forty minutes seemed an eternity as she wrote problem after problem in thick heavy chalk strokes on the green chalkboard. Our minds reeled as she pointed her stubby fat fingers at one and then the other of us, probing for weakness. With rare exceptions, we were pathetic.

At the end of the period, she stood in front of the classroom, legs apart, hands on her hips. "We begin WORK tomorrow!"

After she'd left, I looked around the room at the shocked faces of my classmates. We were in deep dog doodoo!

The next week was a week from hell. Tough enough on those who knew their multiplication tables and whatnot, but an endless torture for those like me, who'd loafed along for the past two years.

My performance in class was dismal. I stood at the chalkboard, chalk in hand, staring in profound bewilderment at the incomprehensible scribbles representing mathematical questions.

"Do you have ANY idea as to WHAT you're doing, Wayne?" she demanded.

"I… I thought I did," I stammered.

"Take your seat!" she commanded, her voice full of loathing and disgust.

One evening after gathering the nerve to impose on his newspaper reading, I asked my father for advice about Miss Baines. He told me that her purpose was to teach and if I didn't understand something, I should go to her for help.

This made sense to me, so the next day I gave it a shot. During a quiet period to work math problems at our desks, I ginned up my courage and made my way, book in hand, to her desk.

"Well," she glared, "what is it?"

I gulped and tried one of my dimpled smiles. It had no effect whatsoever and faded like a frost in September.

"Number seven," I said, "I don't get it."

A crafty smile twisted her lips. "What don't you GET?"

"Well, how do I start? Do I multiply or divide?"

I was leaning forward on the edge of her desk, facing the class. Without the slightest warning she doubled up her fist and pounded it twice into the seat of my pants… *POW, POW!* The impacts lifted me slightly into the air.

"WAKE UP THOSE BRAINS OF YOURS AND START THINKING!" she shouted.

My mouth opened and my eyes widened. *Had everyone seen this?* I looked up quickly at my classmates. Some seemed amused, some quizzical, and still others looked on with pity. Most were relieved it was someone other than themselves suffering public humiliation.

"Y… y… yes, Miss Baines," I said, closing my book and backing away. "I… I see it now."

I saw nothing. I slunk to my desk and pretended to be engrossed in the fascinating world of mathematics. My panicked eyes scanned the pages without comprehending the neatly printed rows of dots and jiggles.

That night my insomnia began. My dreams were filled with the glaring Miss Baines. Endless rows of numbers whirled and danced in nonsensical patterns. The dreams so disturbed me that I grew fearful of sleep and came to dread bedtime.

I began stalling my parents, finding excuses to stay up late. My appetite left me. I seemed to have no room in my stomach, as it was now colonized with fluttering moths. I could feel their winged stirrings deep in my belly as I prepared to leave for school each day.

Sunday nights were the worst. An uneasy dread started in the late afternoon and built to a crescendo after supper. I smiled little, laughed even less, and thought endlessly of my unsolvable situation. My plan for peaceful passivity was a flop, and I didn't have a backup.

One Sunday night, after everyone had gone to bed, I crept downstairs to the television for diversion from a sleep that would not, could not, come.

Around 2:30 a.m. my father, aroused by a full bladder, walked through the living room en route to the bathroom.

"What in the world are you doing up at this time of night, kid?" he asked in surprise.

"Can't sleep," I said.

"Why not," he asked.

"Thinkin' too much," I said cryptically.

"Thinkin' 'bout what?" he asked, as he sat down and lit a cigarette.

Soon the whole story came tumbling out. I was so relieved to unload my burden that I found myself speaking faster and faster, pausing only to catch my breath.

My father sat smoking, listening, then crushed out his cigarette, and padded off in bare feet for the bathroom. After all, who can think on a distended bladder.

When he returned, he resumed his place on the couch and announced, "Tomorrow mornin', you and I are going to pay a visit to Miss Baines." He put a reassuring hand on my knee, "Don't you worry, Son, I won't embarrass you."

"Now get to bed," he said wearily.

I slept soundly for the first time in weeks.

The next day we drove together in silence to school.

Miss Baines' secretary asked politely if we had an appointment. My father regarded her with coolness, "Don't figure I need one to talk to her about my boy." He nodded in my direction.

Her face closed abruptly, and she bustled off in search of the principal. Secretaries know trouble when they see it.

I was nervous as a dog at the vet, shifting from one leg to the other. *Was she going to be angry with me for ratting on her,* I wondered?

Miss Baines came strutting into the office, sporting a cool business-like attitude. "Yes, Mr. Christiansen, what can I do for you today?" she said crisply.

"Well, for starters, MISS BAINES," he said with the growl of a rabid dog, "You can get off my son's back and do what you're paid to do... TEACH."

The professional smile melted into an expression I'd not seen on her before... puzzlement.

"What on earth do you mean?" she asked, beckoning us to chairs.

We sat.

"Before I tell you what I mean," Dad continued, "let me just say: don't you EVER strike my son again because he doesn't know something." He held up his index finger briefly at the word, ever. "When I went to school, no one got a licking for not knowin' something or askin' for help. Don't make that mistake again." The finger rose again. He was starting to scare me a little.

"Are we clear on that?"

Miss Baines nodded.

"Okay. Now let's talk about what's goin' on here and figure out what to do about it," he said.

A half hour later they were laughing and talking like old pals. It was a knack he had of making friends out of adversaries. She seemed warm and friendly and even managed an almost human smile. I thought, *Maybe I had Miss Baines all wrong?*

They shook hands as we left the office, and Dad walked me to the front door. I looked into his bloodshot eyes that bespoke of the sleepless night he'd assumed for me, and I loved him for that.

"Son, you and I both know you've been goofin' off for far too long now and it's gotta end. Miss Baines knows now that her way isn't the best to get a kid like you motivated, but at least she's trying. There won't be any more of that from her, I think.

"You and I are going to go over your times tables until you know 'em backwards and forwards. That's your trouble, kid, you just never learned 'em... and now you will."

He touched my shoulder briefly, turned, and walked to our beat-up Plymouth station wagon.

I went to my classroom with wings on my feet. However, as time drew near for class, my uneasiness returned. To my great relief, Miss Baines' attitude toward me softened noticeably. Now, when called upon, her manner was brisk but polite. When I had difficulty with a problem, she carefully explained the solution and then posed others to verify my understanding.

In the passing weeks, I grew more confident in asking for help. She and I managed all of this without any acknowledgement of our earlier problem.

My father and I rarely spoke without a quiz on the multiplication tables. We held our question-and-answer periods in the car, before bed, in his barbershop, and on fishing trips to the river on Sundays.

And lo, it came to pass, I learned to multiply backwards and forwards, and soon long division began to make sense, and a great rejoicing was heard throughout the land.

83

Dad and I occasionally spoke of that time. The experience had brought us closer. He'd stuck up for me and I'd decided to listen and learn.

I learned more than the multiplication tables that difficult year. I found that bullies come in all shapes, sizes, genders, and ages, that I could tackle any problem with the right approach, and having my father in my corner wasn't such a bad thing.

Each year at the end of summer, the Wright County Fair arrived in the night, unseen and unheard. Like some giant assembly toy, the rides and booths were unpacked and put together under the tall elms of Greenwood Park. It was the official end of school vacation, heralding the resumption of classes the following week... our last hurrah.

County fairs in rural Iowa are no small deal. Church groups and organizations like the Lion's Club set up concession booths among the amusements to raise money. 4H clubs enter critters from chickens to cattle specifically raised for competition. Arrangements of vegetables and flowers, handmade quilts, embroidery, and artwork all had a chance at a blue ribbon.

Nightly entertainment featured local talent or a celebrity headline act. Crowds filled the bleachers along the edge of the racetrack to see stars from the Lawrence Welk TV Show. My favorite was the year the Lone Ranger, Clayton Moore himself, made an appearance in full costume.

This is what I remember:

We kids knew the exact dates of the fair. The morning of opening day, we rode our bikes to watch the goings on where the smells of sawdust, corn dogs, and French fries were already in the air. It was the intoxicating scent of the county fair.

I'd been saving my money for months as part the Great Fair Plan. The Plan called for careful budgeting of my daily spending through disciplined fiscal responsibility. It was a sorry sight indeed to see a kid shuffling around the fairgrounds with their hands shoved into empty pockets, wistfully pining for the unreachable. I was that kid last year and vowed never to repeat it.

First on the to-do list was a visit to a trailer with an assortment of arcade games. For ten cents you could shoot down Nazi airplanes projected onto a tiny screen. Mechanical outlaw cowboys popped up from behind cacti or rocks and were knocked down with a BB or beam of light. The machines vibrated and made sounds simulating gunfire, making it sound as if war had broken out.

In a matter of minutes, I went through my first day's spending allotment, and it wasn't even noon. *Whoa*! I thought, *I'd better slow down here and pace myself.* Then I thought, *ah, just one more thing*, and left to throw balls at the cat dolls on shelves. I eyed the prizes hung around the canvas booth and picked out the one that would be mine... a pair of fuzzy dice to hang from the rearview mirror of the family car.

Fifteen minutes later, I was clean through the next day's allotment. So much for fiscal frugality.

I tore myself away from the games of chance and went to inspect the midway. I walked by the swings, the Ferris wheel, and the kiddie rides, saving the best for last… the Spitfire.

For the past two years, this notorious ride had both attracted and repelled me. I chickened out each year and decided that this year I'd ride it.

The Spitfire was named for the famous British fighter plane of WWII but bore little resemblance to one. Instead, it looked like something a deranged sadist with a welder and a heap of scrap metal had pieced together in some weedy junkyard.

The cockpit was a steel cage with a chicken wire windshield. The vestigial stubby wings and tail were added as an afterthought to help identify it as an airplane. You entered via steps at the bottom of the fuselage. Once inside, you strapped yourself onto a bench with a thick leather belt and hung on to bars welded onto the dashboard.

The eight planes were attached fore and aft, allowing them to spin. They climbed for part of the circuit, dived for another, and briefly leveled before ascending again.

When it was in action, I could hear screams of terror and see objects falling from the riders' pockets. It made my stomach do flip-flops. I shuddered and moved off to the safety of the merry-go-round.

Gary and I biked home for a free lunch, and I immediately began begging my mother for some paid chore, but it was no dice.

"So, what happened to your Big Plan?" she asked.

"I blew it," I mumbled.

"I guess you'd better slow down, then, huh?" she said.

"I'm workin' on it," I said, around a mouthful of a peanut butter sandwich.

Back on our bikes, Gary and I returned to the fairgrounds. The exhibit buildings were a cost-free diversion where various businesses set up advertising booths. A popular one was the lumberyard that handed out free yardsticks printed with their logo. There were demonstrations of how well aluminum gutters worked or the wonders of a miracle food chopper.

The livestock pens were a veritable Noah's Ark.

I stopped to talk with a few 4H guys I knew from school who were camped out with sleeping bags on cots near the stalls. From there they bathed, brushed, and manicured their animals for the judging arena. The top winners of the livestock contests were sent on to the State Fair in Des Moines for a chance at yet more honors and bragging rights.

A neighborhood pal, Stevie, was a year older than me with a very creative imagination. You never knew what he'd think of next. One of the things at the fair he most enjoyed was the Spitfire. That by itself caused me to hold him in the highest esteem.

Stevie was wise to the usual money traps at the fair, preferring to exclusively devote himself to rides. He knew about my challenges with the Spitfire and promised to be at my side when and if I decided to dare it.

I'd learned to use some discipline while patrolling the game booths and curtailed my original recklessness. I did, however, have some luck at the nickel toss. At this booth, stacks of cheap dishes were set on a platform surrounded by a barrier that kept participants at a distance. The idea was to land your gently-lobbed nickel onto a dish. If successful, it was yours. For years, our mother kept a collection of these odd, mismatched dishes in a far cabinet of her kitchen.

When I reached into my pocket for money, I realized in horror I was now in the situation I'd vowed to avoid. Once again, I was that lost soul, wondering the fairgrounds under the elms… flat broke.

Gary had a brilliant idea: we went searching beneath the bleachers for money that may have fallen from the pockets of the audiences. We even looked under the Spitfire while it was closed for lack of riders. In time, we found enough money for the traditional treats of snow cones and cotton candy.

Our parents wouldn't allow us at the fairgrounds unattended at night for fear of pickpockets. It didn't help when I pointed out that I had nothing in my pockets but lint and told, "Don't be a wise guy."

Through the open windows of our bedroom, we could hear the distant music of the fairgrounds beckoning.

Saturday night was the last night of the fair, and our parents had agreed to take us all to the fairgrounds after Dad closed the barbershop.

Pathetically penniless, I tagged along with my parents, brother, and two little sisters. I watched as my father paid for my sisters to ride in circles on ponies, little boats, and kiddie cars.

Dad knew lots of people and was constantly greeting and being greeted.

"Well, hello there, Sid. The wife let you out for the night, huh?" he teased.

"I see you got yours on your arm to keep you out of trouble," Sid replied.

They laughed and I rolled my eyes. Pure torture! It went on like that. I was utterly bored, but kept my mouth shut having been told, "this is the girls' turn at the fair."

Unable to tolerate our long faces any longer, Pop reached into his wallet and handed each of us a dollar bill. "Here," he said, "go have fun, but don't ask me for more."

Gary and I grinned at each other, thanked him profusely, and ran off to find Stevie. We found him dismounting the swings.

"Let's ride the Ferris wheel," he said.

"Okay, Stevie," I agreed, "just don't rock the seat at the top the way you do."

Stevie made clucking chicken sounds as we waited our turn. After the carny had tipped the car for us to board and locked the safety bar, we were off.

The Ferris wheel was in a narrow opening among the trees with its apex near some branches. When we paused at the top for more riders to load, I was horrified when Stevie half stood to grab at leaves. Even worse, he began to vigorously rock our seat.

"Stevie, for the love of God, *stop!*" I screamed, as I clutched the bar and braced my feet, but he just laughed and chicken-clucked again.

Safely back on the ground, the merry-go-round seemed a peaceful refuge, but I knew what was coming... the Spitfire. I could hear it whispering from the dark edge of the midway, *What's the matter, kid? Are ya chicken? Cluck. Cluck.*

"C'mon," Stevie cajoled. "This is the year. Let's do it!"

I examined the dented, paint-chipped planes with their screaming inhabitants spinning overhead. My brother shrugged and said, "Why not?"

When it was our turn, the carny pulled the steps down with a clang and we climbed in. It smelled faintly of sweat and vomit. Great...

I pulled the strap tightly around my waist and took a deep breath.

On the plane's steep climb I thought, *hey, this isn't so bad...* and then we went into the dive.

Stevie shouted, "Roll!" and shifted his weight so that the plane began to spin.

That's when I thought, *I going to die, but I'm going to enjoy doing it.*

"Roll," shouted Stevie and we rolled like a barrel of monkeys. Gary and I laughed so hard, tears spilled from our eyes and our ribs ached. We shouted for the carny to do his worse and I swear he gave us a longer ride at top speed.

Afterwards, we strutted arm and arm like three sailors out on the town, laughing as we relived the ride over and over.

The crowd was thinning, and it was time to go, so we gave Stevie a ride home. I called to him, "Thanks, Stevie!" and he waved from his front door.

After church that Sunday, Gary and I returned to the fairgrounds and found it empty and silent... just trampled grass and a few bits of litter blowing around. The fair had folded up and left in the night, just as it had arrived.

*

That was the last year for the Spitfire; it was replaced by the Octopus. There was a rumor that two kids were badly injured at a county fair in Kansas on a ride that sounded a lot like the Spitfire. Of course, there's no way to prove it, but it did make me proud, knowing I'd overcome my fear and lived to tell that I'd ridden the Spitfire, the ride from hell.

WHITE WATER

This is what I remember:

I was at the kitchen sink, a damp dishtowel in one hand and a dinner plate in the other, helping my mother with the dishes. Suddenly, it slipped from my hand and fell in slow motion to the floor. I turned and bumped a stack of dried dishes and they too, crashed into bits. Pieces of crockery flew in explosions of brittle porcelain.

Mom shook my arm, "Wayne! Wayne, wake up*!" It didn't make sense. Why would she be telling me to wake up?*

The kitchen dissolved and, like a movie fade-in, materialized into a familiar room. Instead of my mother, it was my grandmother shouting and shaking my arm. "Wake up, Wayne! Wake up, Gary!" The room was a bedroom in her little house.

Pieces of shattered windowpanes flew, made more frightening by the racket of breaking glass. *Was I still dreaming?*

Another crash sent shards of glass onto the bed. Through the broken window, I could see a dark, fierce sky and the wind tearing through the trees in the early morning light. The ground was white with hailstones, bouncing like popping corn. They beat against the house in barrages, as if a dump truck was dumping a load of gravel. Another crash threw still more glass.

"Get under the covers, boys," Grandma ordered. Gary and I knew by her voice that she was dead serious. Like me, he'd awakened in confusion. We ducked our heads under the flannel sheets and waited for an all-clear.

A few minutes later, the noise abruptly ceased, and the swift clouds were swept away to rain destruction elsewhere.

"Can we come out now, Grandma?" Gary begged.

She consented, but only after we promised not to set foot on the floor until she'd swept up the glass.

I heard the back door slam and Grandpa entered the room. He stopped at the foot of the bed, holding hailstones the size of softballs in each hand.

"Look at these, boys!" He grinned his toothless grin, blue eyes twinkling. "You'll never see the likes of this again in your whole lives!"

By the time we were allowed to arise and dress, the sun was out, and we were disappointed to see that most of the hail had melted.

An inspection of the damage revealed every window on the west and north sides of the house was broken. The shingled roof was ruined, and the siding pitted. We couldn't count all the dents in Grandpa's black Oldsmobile. There wouldn't be much of a vegetable crop that summer, as his well-tended garden had been beaten into a sad, pathetic pulp.

Later that morning, the four of us toured the Iowa countryside to see the damage. Corn stalks once "as high as an elephant's eye" were stripped to green sticks with their shredded leaves covering the wet ground.

From the vantage of a hilltop, we saw a mile-wide path of stripped trees that lined the river, marking the storm's track.

Heavy rains to the north quickly filled the rivers, creating flash floods. The lazy little creek running along the edge of my grandparents' property was now a torrent, carrying branches and other debris toward the Des Moines River. Year by year, soil from Iowa flowed into the Mississippi River, contributing to the Louisiana delta.

For young boys, there's an inherent temptation in things dangerous and forbidden. The town's hydroelectric dam represented that for us. It was a source of power, adventure, and stories to tell our friends.

A two-story brick building atop the dam housed the turbines. Adjacent to the building were two large floodgates that allowed spring floodwater to escape. A cable car suspended from thick steel cables running the length of the dam connected the building to the opposite shore.

Whenever the turbines were activated, a loud horn sounded, warning that the water level upstream would be falling and rising downstream. Townsfolk referred to the turbines as "The Wheels."

Boatmen fishing near the dam were careful, as the sudden pull of the water could draw them into the dam. Rumor was the wheels could suck you under in a moment and spit you out in fish-food-sized chunks on the other side. Dad told us that when he was young, it was a mark of bravery (or stupidity) and swimming prowess to dive into the water just above the dam while the turbines were running and swim away.

An old wooden rowboat built by our Uncle Virgil was stored upside down under a huge maple at the creek's edge. It was ours to use during the annual two-week visit with our grandparents. It leaked badly, but slowly enough to stay afloat if you kept up with the bailing.

Gary and I used it for fishing and visiting places inaccessible by foot. The rowing and poling up and down the winding creek (pronounced "crick" in Iowa) made us yearn for a motor. We wanted to shoot a white-water-rapids or raise a mighty wake that slapped the riverbank.

Gary and I knew the swiftness of the now-flooded stream wouldn't last long and decided to take advantage of the opportunity. We were certain that launching our boat into the stream would make for a wild ride. The problem was how to get it upstream and then be able to repeat the trip. We had no motor, and rowing was out of the question, due to the fast current.

The solution was to pull the boat upstream using the thick overhanging branches and brush growing along the bank. It was slow, hard work, but we eventually tugged our way to a large granite boulder and could go no farther.

"Okay, Gare, let 'er go!" I shouted above the rushing water.

Immediately, the boat began gathering speed moving downstream… backwards. We hadn't considered how we were to steer. I made a mental note to use an oar as a rudder on the next trip (if there was one).

The boat swung sideways as we passed the maple and smashed dead center into a submerged rock, nearly capsizing us. The nose of the boat banged into a protruding tree root with enough force to throw us onto the wet deck, but we clung to the gunnels for dear life, laughing hysterically. Overhanging brush whipped and stung our faces. We howled and whooped as we spun, bumped, and bashed our way downstream toward the river. It was our dream of a white-water boat trip come true.

When the creek widened, the velocity of the current diminished and finally dumped us out onto the muddy river just above the dam. The river, too, was swollen, but moving slower than the narrower creek.

We emerged from the dense shade to a bright clear day. Judging from the movement of the water and absence of the turbine's whine, we knew The Wheels were not operating.

Fully exhilarated, we were determined to continue our adventure and answer the siren's call of the dam.

"Let's just go for a look," Gary suggested.

"Yeah, okay," I agreed; the effects of the flash flood were sure to be a sight. It was my turn to row, and I cautiously approached the sleeping giant, wary of a sudden awakening.

Gary, poised as lookout at the bow of the boat, encouraged me to row closer to the maw of The Wheels. Tingling with the thrill of danger, I rowed until we gently bumped the vertical grates protecting the entrance from debris. It was just a touch to say we'd done it, and I pulled away immediately, like a kid teasing a beehive.

We continued parallel with the turbine house to the spillway. We were close enough now to hear the roar of the water flowing over the dam. A mist arose from the falling water, and pieces of mud-brown foam floated in the air.

"Let's see where Gramps went over the dam," I said and Gary, always up for anything, nodded.

While working for the electric company many years before, Grandpa had miraculously survived a fall from a maintenance cable car and was swept over the dam with tons of spring ice.

From my position in the middle seat facing the stern, I couldn't see much but was aware of the rising sound of the cascade.

Suddenly, Gary shouted, "Go back, Wayne! We gotta get outta here!" I glanced over my shoulder and saw the color in his face had drained away, making his freckles look like painted dots.

"What's the matter?" I hollered over the roaring water.

"Water's goin' over the top a good three feet high and moving fast!" he shouted. "It's gonna pull us over!"

That's when I realized I'd been slowly losing ground, despite a good hard pull on the oars. I felt my heart quicken and muscles tighten in preparation for "fight or flight." In this case it was going to be flight.

I pivoted the boat away from the dam and rowed with all my might against the current. I grunted, pulled, and strained as Gary shouted encouragement. We held our own but only managed less than a couple of yards of progress.

"I'm poopin' out, Gare!" I gasped.

"Want me to take over?" he shouted.

I calculated how long it would take to change positions, and figured there would not be time. We were in trouble. Things had gotten serious in the blink of an eye.

"Move over!" Gary screamed. "I'll take an oar and you the take the other. We'll do it together!"

I knew I was reaching my limit. What did we have to lose besides our lives?

Gary hovered over the center rowing seat, waiting for me to give the word. I slid far to the right and shouted, "Go!"

He took position beside me, grabbed his oar, planted his feet, and we began sculling for all we were worth.

For a moment, we slipped nearer the brink of disaster. I could see the sunlight penetrate the graceful arch of brown water as it passed over the thirty-foot plunge. It was mesmerizing. I glanced downstream and wondered where we'd end up in the river below. *Maybe we'd be as lucky as Grandpa and live?*

I noticed for the first time that we were ankle deep in water. We'd neglected our bailing duties and were sinking.

"Think you can bail with your big feet?!" I asked.

That got us chuckling, which quickly became laughter, as we faced down old man death. Even if we failed, we had this moment, shoulder to shoulder, with each other.

We didn't go over the dam. Pumped full of adrenaline, we steadily pulled away, gaining the safety of an upstream shore. After beaching the boat, we leaned elbows on knees, panting. The sun laid a warm, comforting hand on our backs. I took a deep breath and let it out, releasing the tension.

We looked up at the drone of an airplane and saw a flash of light reflecting off the wings as it made a slow turn. An egret poised at the edge of a clump of cattails eyed us warily, while a carp leaped into the air and splashed back into the river. The world hadn't noticed two boys narrowly escaping destruction.

After catching our breaths, we set about bailing the river out of our waterlogged boat.

The sound of Grandma's silver police whistle told us it was time to come home. She'd used the same whistle decades before to call her wandering sons home. It could be heard for better than a mile upriver on a good day. It said lunch was ready and meant she wanted to make certain we were safe.

We slipped oars into oarlocks and began the journey back up the creek where the force of the water had already waned. We rowed silently side by side. The oars creaked and groaned as we dipped and pulled, dipped and pulled.

*

My family devoted little time expressing our love for each other. The fact is that sometimes we didn't feel terribly loving. Sometimes we just tolerated one another in a sort of coexistence. But on that long row back, I knew my brother loved me and I him. I could feel it in the oar as we shared the painful labor. Words would have ruined it or been embarrassing. Even now recalling the moment, words seem inadequate.

My brother's been dead for several years now and knowing that I can never share those memories with him hurts my heart.

I'm grateful for the clarity of the memory of that time as I once again see the sunlight filtering through the trees, smell the damp living river, hear the coo of mourning doves, and feel the smooth hardness of the oar in my blistered hands. I am forever thankful for that day on the river with my brother… my best friend.

OUR QUEEN VICTORIA

I wish you could have known my grandmother, Anna Victoria (Bonde) Christiansen. Well, since I'm wishing, I wish *I'd* taken the time to know her better.

Her birth in 1894 was near the end of Alexandrina Victoria's sixty-three-year reign as the Queen of England. Her time on the throne, known as The Victorian Age, marked the height of the UK's influence on the world. Her marriage to Prince Albert provided my grandfather with the name of his favorite cigarette tobacco. He rolled his own smokes for years out of a little red can with the dapper Albert's picture on the front. I certainly hope Albert contributed much more to the world than having his picture on a tobacco can.

Things were done properly back then. Women wore high collars and long dresses with long sleeves while the men wore hats, ties, and vests. The architecture of the time was elaborate and formal. People dressed for dinner or when going to town... well, at least folks aspired to... not everyone had the means.

Grandma's parents, Anna and Christian Bonde, emigrated from the Schleswig-Holstein area that's now Germany. The area had been claimed by Denmark off and on for centuries, but they considered themselves Danes and spoke Dane at home.

Chris, as he was called, eventually settled in Humboldt, Iowa, working in Callie's blacksmith shop. He was apparently able to earn a decent living, providing their only child, my grandmother, with nice clothes and surroundings.

Chris wanted his own shop, so they moved to the tiny Danish enclave of Rutland and set up a forge. It was a time when farmers relied upon draft horses to pull farming implements. The huge animals needed shoes and farmers needed repairs on their plows, hay rakes, harrows, wagons, etc. Welding was done with a hot fire, a heavy hammer, an anvil, and a strong arm. Great Grandpa Bonde had them all.

Again, the family did well.

Grandma Victoria, or "Vic" as her friends called her, married a fellow named Elmer Smith. I know very little about him as they divorced for unknown reasons, but not before fathering two sons: my uncles Virgil Bonde Smith and Elmer Wayne Smith.

Victoria moved back into the Bonde home with her sons and resumed life as a divorced woman in a small town. I can imagine it wasn't easy.

Along came a smiling, blue eyed, bandy-legged Dane, fresh off the boat from Denmark... my grandfather, Agner Christiansen. Uncle Emery was their firstborn, followed by my father Leo and then my aunt Joanne Marie.

They made a home in Rutland until a fire forced them back into the Bonde's Victorian household. Fires were common in the days before electricity, when homes needed kerosene lamps, candles, and wood or coal stoves. Everyone worked in one capacity or another, as the old blacksmith's declining health had forced his retirement. When the Great Depression struck, they lived off a huge garden from which Grandma canned, smoked, salted, and pickled the produce.

The boys did odd jobs while Grandpa Agner found work painting, digging drainage ditches, and butchering animals for farmers. There was little money, so many debts were paid through barter. Virgil left high school to work for the depression-era government program called the Civilian Conservation Corps, or CCC, to build bridges and roads all over the United States.

Grandma's second son Elmer Wayne tragically died at twenty-one due to an infection from a perforated appendix, well before the discovery of antibiotics.

Electric power and indoor plumbing were slow to arrive in little Rutland. Can you imagine the labor involved for women to keep a family going? There was water to pump, lamps to clean and fill with kerosene, mending, cooking, cleaning, and childcare.

Great Grandfather Chris and I never met, as he died from a stroke just a few weeks before I arrived in late 1948. His wife Anna had preceded him in death.

This is what I remember:

We lived a block from their house, and I delivered the mail to Grandma Vic on my tricycle every day. She rewarded me with sliced onion sandwiches on homemade bread covered with hand-churned butter.

The Bonde household was chock-full of dark Victorian furniture with its ornate carvings, claw-foot chairs, and horsehair-stuffed sofas. Grandma taught me to play Chopsticks on their upright piano in the parlor. Windows were decorated with thick drapes to keep out the winter drafts, and ornately framed photographs adorned the wallpapered walls. A tarnished brass lamp hung over a long table in the seldom-used dining room.

Grandma's kitchen was always warm, tidy, and busy. The new indoor water service and oil furnace must have made her life easier. It's hard to believe now, but all her children had their tonsils removed on the kitchen table, needed or not. Maybe there was a family discount?

After her three boys were back home safe and sound from military service in WWII, they all married and moved out, except for Joanne. The passing of Grandpa and Grandma Bonde didn't stop the family from gathering often at the old homestead.

My mother recalls how Grandma Victoria would come to our house for spring cleaning. She'd roll up her sleeves on her strong arms and announce, "Let's get it done." Getting it done involved washing the woodwork, walls, floors, curtains, and airing bed linens on the clothesline. As we lived on Rutland's then unpaved Main Street, which was only a short way from the surrounding fields, the dust and dirt blew unimpeded through the open windows during the hot dry weather.

I was four when the Bonde/Christiansen home caught fire. A friend of the family took my brother and me to Treloar's Drive-In in Fort Dodge for ice cream to remove us from the confusion. As we rode past the burning house on the way out of town, the smoke was still coming out of the windows, and volunteer firemen were carrying furniture out onto the lawn.

Grandma was given a sedative and bedded down at our house where she and Grandpa remained until they could find a suitable home.

Some days after the fire, I went with my father to the house to see the damage. It was shocking to see the familiar piano, furnishings, and rugs charred and waterlogged.

My grandparents found a small house in town next to a creek. It was a step backward, as they initially had to use an outhouse until a bathroom was added. There was only one bedroom, and the shower was in a damp, dark basement. Little of the Bonde furniture survived and the odor of smoke lingered for years on a favorite upholstered rocker.

Grandma set up housekeeping in their new home and put her remaining things in order the best she could. It must have been heartbreaking to lose so many of the nice things she'd known her entire life. Especially precious were the few mementos left of her deceased son, Wayne, my namesake.

My brother and I visited our grandparents for a week or two every summer. It was when we were introduced to Grandma Vic's many friends... and the game of Wahoo.

Her lady friends took turns hosting Wahoo parties. When it was Grandma's turn, she set out her fanciest dishes serving mints, nuts, and little thin sandwiches she called finger sandwiches. There were pitchers of lemonade and, of course, lots of coffee.

Her guests arrived in their vintage cars, dressed in light print dresses and sensible shoes with matching handbags. The scent of their perfume and powder filled the house.

They tittered and complimented each other on this and that and took their seats around the card tables Grandma had carefully arranged.

Competition was fierce and the winner of each game was required to loudly announce, "Wahoo!" The victor of each round advanced table to table until there was an overall winner. The lucky lady was awarded with a plant, a vase, or a fresh pie.

Wahoo time was the cue for Gary and me to grab fishing poles and head for the river.

After her last guest had gone and the house put back in order, Grandma explained the game. It was played on a wooden board with a pattern of holes just large enough to hold a marble. Players moved colored marbles about the board depending upon a roll of the dice. If you've ever played the game Parcheesi, you pretty much have the idea.

Grandma's friends could always be relied upon to staff church socials and funerals at the Lutheran church Grandpa Bonde had helped found. They were wonderful people, full of stories of growing up during the prairie days when Iowa was being settled. Most of them could recite poems and pieces of famous literature they'd memorized as children. They smiled often, exuded kindness, and loved my grandmother.

Victoria set a simple but bountiful table. There was fresh produce from their garden: radishes and green onions in colored glasses of ice water, cucumber slices in vinegar and onion bobbing in a covered glass dish, and jams and jellies sealed in jars with paraffin. A crock of milk with the cream floating, longhorn cheese, Roman Meal bread, and hand-churned butter were always present.

Grandpa made certain that we had the freshest and best cuts of meats from his butchering jobs. Each morning before he left for work, she made him fried eggs, bacon, black coffee, and wheat toast just the way he liked it.

When she went to a doctor to learn why she was easily bruising, she was diagnosed with myelofibrosis, a disorder of the bone marrow. Years later, the condition converted to chronic myelocytic leukemia, which eventually led to her passing. She must have suffered but bore it without complaint. "It can't be helped," she said, and just kept on keeping on.

Grandma never had a paying job and certainly had no time for one. She worked hard, loved to laugh, and loved us.

Whenever I made her laugh, she exclaimed, "Oh, Wayne-y, you are just the berries!" I'm certain it was a compliment because I never heard her say an unkind word about or to anyone... not ever... not once. If there is a heaven, she's there.

I'd like to forget some of my adolescent years. It's not for lack of trying, believe me, as some of those memories are still painful. Out of the blue, something will remind me of an embarrassment or humiliation and they're back... fresh and raw.

This is what I remember:

I don't know how it happened, but once I left the sixth grade, I found myself on the outside looking in.

I thought of most of my grade school classmates as friends. We were invited to birthday parties, played together, and came to know each other well.

My friends were a smorgasbord of athletes, eggheads, nerds, goof-offs, extroverts, and introverts. No, our class hadn't been utopia, but it was just fine to be whatever you were. There were exceptions, though, like Vera Freunde, who openly picked her nose and ate the harvest with such gusto.

But when I entered junior high, everything changed, and whoever was in charge neglected to send me the instructions.

School clothing was different now. Gone were our tennis shoes, blue jeans, and T-shirts, replaced by slacks, button-down shirts, and loafers. If your family had money, you had the advantage of dressing for success, but if your family was financially strapped like ours, it was tough going.

My seventh-grade class was a mix of kids from our rival school on the "rich side" of town, and an infusion from the local Catholic school. I was acquainted with most of the boys through summer little league baseball, so it wasn't like they were total strangers. Nonetheless, we didn't really *know* each other.

I'd already checked out the girls at the public swimming pool and movie theater, but they'd only been a curiosity, and I was far too shy to approach them.

Coming from the wrong side of the tracks, I'd gone to school with the rough and rowdy. In contrast, most of our crosstown classmates were from families with successful businesses or were professionals. The mixing was bound to cause confusion.

The Catholic kids seemed to have some aura about them. The boys who played sports were always blessing themselves and evoking saints (Christopher, Jude, Joseph, etc.). Somehow, they seemed to know something we didn't about convincing God to be on their team. It was most evident in the batter's box where they began crossing themselves in earnest. It didn't seem fair that they kept it to themselves and not let the rest of us in on the secret. I was perfectly willing to learn how to use a rosary if it would help my batting average.

When I asked a teammate to teach me how to "do the beads," he smiled in a far-off way, as if listening to a heavenly choir.

"Nope," he said shaking his head, "I can't teach you 'cause you ain't no Catholic."

A lame excuse, I thought, but I let it slide.

We postwar babyboomers were stressing school systems to their limits. Junior high was in the three-story, ivy-covered walls of the high school building. Grades seven through twelve and the students from a two-year community college were packed in there like words in a dictionary.

The congestion in the halls was such that we were allowed ten minutes between classes. We moved like swarms of South American driver ants, crushing and trampling everything in our path. It was awesome and frightening, not only for us, but for the teachers as well. You could see them standing near the open doors of their classrooms with panic-stricken faces. We had to have been in violation of multiple fire codes and state guidelines for teacher/pupil ratios. A new junior high building was being constructed, but a year away from completion so we were told to make do.

There was no orientation session introducing us bottom-of-the-barrel underclassmen to our new surroundings. Consequently, I knew the location of only one boy's bathroom until well into my second nightmare week. By the class period just before lunch and the last one in the afternoon, I was obsessed with my bursting bladder.

On the first day of school, we left homeroom to join the shuffling masses coursing through the corridors. I spotted a familiar face, Mike Ulrich, my best pal from grade school. His family owned a successful trucking company on the edge of town.

"Hi, Mike," I shouted above the noise, "how ya doin'?"

It seemed that he hadn't heard or seen me. He was talking with a kid from our crosstown rival school. They were laughing and joking like long-lost buddies.

"Ulrich!" I tried again.

He glanced at me briefly, nodded, and whispered something to his chum. They looked at me, laughed, and moved on without comment.

I was puzzled. Had I already committed some social gaff? A quick once-over revealed there was no "call me stupid" sign taped to my back, my fly was zipped up, and my socks matched, so what was wrong?

There was no time for reflection as I slammed headfirst into the hip of a large upper classman. When he flicked me aside like a horse brushing off a fly, my notebook spun from my arm and fell to the floor. My immediate impulse was to stop and retrieve it, but I got swept off by the swift current of humanity.

I fought my way back to the notebook and bent to pick it up while being jostled by the pushing and shoving. I had the odd perspective as if being underwater. All I could see were disembodied legs and feet. I heard: "Who's the dork?" Then, "Move it, shrimp!" and "Just step on him. I did."

I saw an opening and able to rescue my battered notebook from further destruction. It was scuffed and covered with dusty footprints but intact. I arrived at my first class disheveled, bruised, and late.

As the weeks ground on, I learned more about survival in junior high. I discovered how to wear an athletic supporter (a triumph in deductive reasoning), how to take a shower with thirty boys bent on snapping you with a towel, how to walk behind the bigger kids letting them "break trail," the location of the boy's restrooms, and… I learned my rung on the social ladder.

I discovered that I was in a sort of no-man's-land. I wasn't a Creep or a Cool, nothing that concrete. I just… wasn't.

The old friend who'd snubbed me had somehow taken up residence on the loftier ladder rungs with the Cool kids. The Cools dressed, talked, and acted alike. Those of us on the lower levels who attempted to copy their style were ridiculed.

The girls accepted as Cool by the same unseen jury were allowed to pursue and be pursued by boys from the same strata. We'd been judged and sentenced without so much as a trial. Kids I'd known most of my life, like Mike, no longer seemed comfortable speaking with me, or worse, ignored me. Those relegated to the Creep level skulked around the fringes of the school's mainstream, bewildered and dazed. I recognized their shocked and confused faces... they looked like me.

Everyone became obsessed with maintaining their status or finding the secret of moving up. Just when we began to figure it out, the rules changed. It was apparently the job of those at the top to periodically alter the rules to keep us off balance. Overwhelmed, I retreated into a protective shell that left me uninformed, oblivious, and lonely.

Take the afternoon I was late dressing after gym class. It was the next to the last period of the day and I'd forgotten my new gym locker's combination. Recall of the numbers was made more difficult by having to dodge snapping towels and unkind comments about my IQ.

I raced up the stairs with dripping wet hair to find the halls deserted and the building quiet as a tomb. I discounted this to being later than I'd thought. But I soon discovered that all the rooms were mysteriously empty. I sat for a moment at my desk wondering what to do.

The sounds of my footsteps echoed eerily as I walked the halls, peeking into classrooms, and was shocked to find all three floors empty. The thought, I admit, occurred to me that I might be the target of the original TV prank show, Candid Camera. I fancied that the entire school was in on it and we'd all have a good laugh.

The mystery was solved when I heard the faint sounds of cheering from the auditorium on the first floor. On tiptoe, I peeked through one of the unfrosted windowpanes of the door at the rear of the auditorium. There they were! The whole student body and faculty were watching cheerleaders jump around on the stage. It was a pep rally in preparation for the first football game of the season. There was even a band!

Before the days of announcements over an intercom, information was posted on bulletin boards above drinking fountains. Adrift in my own little world, I'd completely missed the notice about the assembly.

Embarrassed that someone might see me wandering the halls like a fool, I took refuge in a restroom. I selected a stall, closed the door, and settled on a commode for the duration. Twenty long minutes later, I joined the happy throng in the hall on the way home for the day. I was truly a lost ball in the tall grass.

In the middle of the first semester, a comely girl I knew from the other side of town caught my eye. She and I were in the same civics study group. I found her to be in possession of a keen sense of humor, easy to talk with, and ridiculously cute. She had a way of laughing that turned her eyes into little crescents and scrunched up her nose in the most fetching way. I tried to make her laugh just to watch her face do those tricks.

Her name was Karla. She was a cheerleader and most definitely a Cool. Inside a week I was in love and well on my way to disaster.

Karla's friend, Julia, had been a grade school classmate of mine. I walked partway home with her one afternoon and after some small talk and a pledge of confidence, I confessed that I "kinda liked" Karla.

She giggled, and after scrutinizing my face in that unnerving way girls have of checking for sincerity, agreed to tell Karla.

That was good by me. I'd followed protocol to the letter by having a go-between relay my interest; Julia would then report her response back to me. If the feelings were mutual, we could sit together at lunch and meet Saturdays at the movies. It was complicated, but that's the way it was done.

I walked home floating on air in the autumn afternoon sunshine. Tomorrow held a promise I hadn't felt in weeks. Things were looking up. Yes, I was late getting out of the starting gate, but once I was in the open... look out! Moving up the ladder a few rungs by dating a Cool like Karla would certainly be an added benefit.

The next morning, I could scarcely wait to get to school and see Karla. As I approached my locker, I saw a covey of Cool girls standing near the water fountain with their heads together in hushed conversation. As I passed, they stopped talking and I heard stifled giggles.

"Shh, he'll hear you," one said in a stage whisper that ended in a muffled guffaw.

Uh, oh, I thought, *trouble...*

Karla breezed by without so much as a nod and made a beeline for her locker, giving the girls and me a wide berth.

Yep, trouble for sure.

For the rest of the morning, I kept noticing awkward silences as I walked by classmates. Things came to a head when one of the jocks, the King Cool himself, approached me at my locker just before lunch.

"Hey, who do you think you are, anyway?" he sneered. "What makes you think a cool girl like Karla would have anything to do with a turd like you?"

So, that's it, I thought. My infatuation had been made public and the public had rendered its opinion.

"I, ah, I just kinda… like her, you know... as a friend," I said, with a shrug. I hoped that my body language communicated just how absurd I thought it was.

He poked his finger into my chest for emphasis and growled, "You keep to your own." Then he pushed past me and rejoined his friends watching nearby. They slapped him on the back and laughed. The King Cool had been the designated spokesperson for the Preservation of the Upper Rung.

My face burned and I heard my pulse in my ears, not with anger, mind you, but with profound embarrassment and humiliation. Until that moment I'd believed that somehow, I was not included among the Cools due to some oversight, but if given the chance, I'd soon be revealed as one of them.

At lunch I spotted Karla being consoled by her friends. She caught my eye from across the cafeteria and shot me a cold hateful look. She turned her head quickly and deliberately, leaving no doubt as to her feelings. Realizing that she'd, too, been embarrassed made me feel even worse. My heart sank into a dark pit landing with a wet *smack* in the cold muck at the bottom.

I'd been wrong about my ability to ascend the ladder. I'd been wrong, too, that I was in No Man's Land. Oh, no! I'd sunk to a special level… the Creep Level.

A verse from my nursery school days came back to me. It was the last verse in the *Farmer in the Dell*: *"The cheese stands alone. The cheese stands alone. Hi ho the Derry oh, the cheese stands alone."* How could I have dared to step out of place? My mistake had served as an example for other Creeps to keep their leper's distance.

I sat at a table amid the clatter of the cafeteria, absently pushing a piece of mystery meat from place to place on the tray with my fork. I knew those sharing my table were fully aware of what had transpired.

There was fat ole Terry Kerr begging for leftovers from his neighbor's tray; Earl Dinkel with a face ravaged by acne; and Bruce Wean, sitting across the table. Bruce's folks were poor farmers eking out a living on their miserable sixty-acre combination farm/junkyard. His eyeglasses were held together with a Band-Aid, and he wore patched hand-me-downs from his two older brothers.

I knew my fellow diners only slightly but well enough to recognize what we all had in common: faces, clothing, bodies, abilities, and personalities that were, well... different. We were the *also ran* kids who warranted little comment from teachers, coaches, or even each other.

Earl caught my eye, then nodded and smiled slightly. I didn't see any of the scorn on his face I'd witnessed all morning. I didn't see pity either, or "I could've told you so." But what I did see was that there'd be no faceless jury passing judgment, no ever-changing rules for admittance, and no dues to pay... just acceptance.

Of course, we yearned to be the star athletes, the brightest scholars, and homecoming royalty. We wanted to be invited to the school dances and rock all night with the person of our fondest desires. But instead, we settled for standing with our noses pressed against the windows, watching, and waiting...waiting to be respected and accepted, and waiting... to grow up.

*

As for me, I had to learn to forgive and keep that time from poisoning the rest of my life. I had to not just forgive those who'd cast me out but forgive *myself* for letting them define who and what I was.

Those lessons were painful, taking years to put into perspective. We didn't know it then, but we were the largest group within the school's social order, and had been all along. The power that was held sway over us was only that which we gave away.

Decades later while attending a class reunion, I wondered, *Why did I ever let these fat, bald, wrinkled old buzzards rule me?*

When I look at some of my government leaders, I have the same thought.

PEDDLING PAPERS

There's an old expression you don't hear much anymore. It was reserved for those who beg for "a moment of your time" to sell a product, service, or ask your support for some cause. That's when you'd say, "Oh, go peddle your papers!" Meaning, they should take their BS elsewhere. It was usually followed with a slammed door for added emphasis. My grandmother could slam a door that rattled windows.

The expression seems a bit gentler than some of the phrases used today, ones that tend to be crude, even if they are effective.

This is what I remember:

While growing up in Iowa, I literally did peddle papers from time to time.

My first employment in the news biz was delivering a weekly paper for the Eagle Grove Eagle. The paper was free, so I wasn't responsible for collecting money each week. That was a good thing, as I was only ten at the time, and admittedly not too swift with money management.

I'd heard through the grapevine (my father no doubt) that it was a lucrative after-school endeavor I only had to do once a week. On that day, I rode my bike a mile or so to the newspaper office to pick up my allotment of papers. I got there early to watch the typesetter preparing the next edition at a clattering machine that made letters and punctuation marks on lead slugs.

The newspapers were left for the delivery boys on a bench. I carried mine in a canvas bag embossed with the newspaper's name that I hung over the handlebars of my bike. It made me feel like I was a real paperboy.

Before leaving the office, I carefully folded each paper into a square so I could easily sail them onto the front steps. If it was raining, I put them into mail slots, between doors, or chucked them onto porches.

My route was a zone on the southeast side of town where homes built in the 1920s and 30s were still in good shape in the late 1950s. It was pretty much your average neighborhood for a Midwestern town of six thousand. Most of the houses were single family, two-story homes separated by a driveway or a well-kept lawn landscaped with shrubs and mature elms. The back of each house faced an alley where the trash burn barrels were kept. Everyone burned their trash and called the public works department to empty them when full of noncombustibles.

I began a week before resumption of classes in mid-August. The days were bright and sunny, and everything was hunky-dory for a couple months or so. But when the days grew shorter, and the weather colder, I was finishing my route around twilight and eventually in the dark. The falling autumn leaves swirled around me as I pedaled my bike up and down the sidewalks. With no one to talk to, I felt alone, isolated, dispirited, and yearning to be home to watch the Mickey Mouse Club with my brother and sisters before supper.

I began avoiding the creepier houses and those that never seemed to pick up the paper I'd left there the week before. Then I started skipping the more distant houses altogether. *Who cares?* I reasoned. *Who reads this stupid paper anyway?*

Dirt piles around street excavation sites were shielded with wooden barriers. Black cannonball-shaped oil pots, arranged near the holes to warn motorists, burned all night and were perfect for the disposal of my excess papers. I smiled with secret malice as I burned them one by one in the smokey flames.

Then one day, I turned in my paper bag and never looked back.

Five years later, my family relocated to a smaller town of about three hundred. Before the local farmers discovered us, my brother and I delivered the popular afternoon paper, the Fort Dodge Messenger. Gary had the east side of town and I had the west.

My best friend, Jack, delivered the Des Moines Register, including the thick Sunday paper, to the entire town every morning. I both admired and pitied him. In winter, he had to get up before school and trudge around in the cold and snow. As an athlete, the early route allowed him time for sports after classes.

Our town was divided in half by Main Street. Most of the inhabitants were retired farmers, widows, teachers, and small business owners. They were church-going, hardworking, honest folks who took pride in their homes and property. There were no mansions, as almost everyone was lower middle class and shunned ostentatious displays of wealth. Yes, there were some wealthy folks, but we only knew them from rumors. You really couldn't tell otherwise.

Newspapers were dropped off daily at my dad's barbershop.

By now my brother and I had trashed our bikes and were on foot. It wasn't a big problem, as the town was geographically small. The canvas bags slung over our shoulders became lighter with each delivery and when empty, we went to the only restaurant in town for a cold Pepsi.

As it was a daily paper, we were committed, regardless of weather. Our parents firmly believed that our job was just that...*our* job, and not theirs. It was assumed they would not be driving us around.

One Saturday in mid-January, I was preparing to leave on my route. I looked out the window at the thermometer that read minus 20 degrees, with the wind blowing snowflakes past the windows. I approached my mother, "Gee, Mom, it's sure cold out there." (It was a subtle but futile hint for a ride, as it turned out.) She was working at the sink and never even looked up. "Guess you'd better put on an extra sweater, then." So much for helicopter parenting.

Every Saturday when we went "collecting," our customers were expected to pay what they owed for their paper. Out of that money we had to pay our paper bill, which was the money we owed the newspaper. Anything left over was profit. What about tips, you say? Right... that rarely happened, and if it did, it was a dime or a Norwegian pastry fresh out of the oven (no complaint there). Most of my customers left the money in cups inside their backdoor or on the porch. I carried my customers' postage-stamp-sized receipts sandwiched between two metal plates held together with large rings. Each little receipt tab was torn off a page containing the name and address of the customer. It wasn't easy with numb fingers in subzero weather.

Junior enterpriser that I was, I always bought extra papers to sell in the town tavern, restaurant, and Dad's shop. It was easy money.

My paper route introduced us to the community. Soon, everyone knew Gary and me, and I mean everyone! There was no chance for misbehavior, as they knew my parents, and had no qualms about informing them of any infraction.

When there was a heavy snow, I knew exactly where to go to make extra money shoveling sidewalks and driveways. My friends and I formed shoveling crews to cover more area. We took pity on the old widows who reluctantly offered fifty cents for a half hour's work, and often settled for a cup of hot chocolate and yet more Norwegian pastries.

Gary became involved with sports, and I found employment with the local farmers, so we handed our routes off to someone else. Farm work paid better, and I didn't have to work in arctic cold.

*

I guess most people don't read newspapers much anymore and if they do, it's from an online subscription via computers or on their phones. Too bad, as I kind of liked peddling my papers.

This is what I remember:

My parents married shortly after my father's return from military service in the Pacific during WWII. They started their lives together in Rutland, a tiny Iowa town where he'd grown up and still had extended family and friends.

They rented a house that, like the others in town, had no indoor plumbing, requiring my mother carry water from a pump. It also meant we had to use an outhouse. Obviously, the community was a bit behind the times, but at least there was electricity. Mom was one game gal. She'd come from a larger nearby town that had had all those luxuries for years.

I clearly remember the horrors of the outhouse. It smelled like you'd imagine and drew flies, attracting spiders of every imaginable shape and size. Their dusty cobwebs were everywhere.

In a corner of my parents' bedroom was a small closet with a privacy curtain. Inside was a wooden "potty chair" over a chamber pot. It was used mostly during inclement weather or in the dark of night and fell to my parents to later empty into the outhouse…. usually my mother.

Thankfully, our house was the very first to get running water. I have the newspaper clipping of the event with my mother's happy face as she turns on the tap. This quickly led to the installation of a modern bathroom complete with sink, tub, and commode; the outhouse became a relic of the past.

Dad bought a fuel oil delivery truck and went into business. It took about three years for him to go broke, as many of his customers, all of whom he knew, couldn't or wouldn't pay their debts. He finally sold the business to a friend who had no qualms about demanding payment at delivery.

What to do now? It was off to barber college in Sioux City. He had to leave our family, which now included my brother, Gary. After classes, Pop worked for a funeral home, driving a hearse doubling as an ambulance. To save money he slept at the funeral home, sometimes in one of the coffins (He claimed that they were quite comfy.), but I strongly suspect this was a tall tale.

After graduation, he worked for a year as an apprentice in a barbershop in the neighboring town of Bode. As a newly-minted barber, he began the search for a shop and a home. We were now three children with the birth of my sister, Lee Ann.

He found a Main Street shop in the larger community of Eagle Grove and moved us into an apartment on the east side of town.

The shop was sandwiched between two larger buildings with a roof, storefront window, and a backdoor, making it long and narrow, reminiscent of a boxcar.

Unfortunately, the plumbing only supplied a single, white porcelain pedestal sink. There was no bathroom, so he had to adapt. When he needed to relieve himself, he had only to open the backdoor overlooking the alley. After the shop was closed for the day and the shades were pulled down, the sink served as a urinal. I'm sure the state health inspectors would have frowned upon it, but a man's gotta do what a man's gotta do. The friendly owner of Wimpy's, the diner next-door, provided a place for other bodily functions, and Dad returned the favor with free haircuts. He continued to use this bartering tool to pay for things throughout his career as a barber.

Pop really took to barbering, starting with a few secondhand tools and a knack for cutting hair into the popular hairstyle called a flattop. With a gift of gab and an obvious like of people, he quickly became known. His good-natured banter and ability to remember details about customers made him popular. He got involved in the community as a volunteer fireman, little league baseball coach, commander of the American Legion post, and Boy Scout leader.

He took pride in his work. I remember the day an out-of-towner dressed in a suit and driving a big expensive car stopped in for a trim. When he was leaving, he handed Dad a tip, and Pop told him that he was a professional and didn't want it. The arrogant fellow smirked, reached for his barber smock, and stuffed the money into his pocket. I watched Dad literally chase him onto the sidewalk to shove the money back into the man's sport coat. I'll never forget the look on that city slicker's face! Needless to say, no one tipped my father.

When old enough, I was put to work sweeping, mopping, and tidying the shop each night at closing around five. I arrived early to read the comic books reserved for waiting customers and listen to the arguments and banter. Dad had opinions on just about everything and loved to argue his point of view. I swear I heard him take different sides of the same issue. Men dropped in just to have a discussion.

My price for janitorial duties was a dime a night, but over time I was able to get it up to twenty-five cents. My strategy was to approach him for a raise whenever he raised his prices. Gary and I took turns with the cleaning chores and years later my sisters took over.

On Saturday mornings, I bicycled or walked the mile to the shop to get change for him at the bank. He didn't use a cash register and kept coins separated in cupcake baking pans inside a drawer.

Saturday in farming communities is the busiest day of the week. It's when farmers come to town to shop for groceries, catch up on gossip, and get haircuts for Sunday church. On those nights, Dad stayed open until the last customer was shorn, often until nine or ten o'clock. On Sundays, he'd sleep late then sit bleary-eyed at the kitchen table, trying to wake up with coffee and cigarettes. We wisely stayed clear until later in the day.

On those long Saturdays, he stood behind his barber chair, working with his hands in the air, chain-smoking cigarettes. Back then, almost all adult men smoked, making my eyes burn as I waited for him to finish. The smoke turned the cloth I used to clean the mirrors yellow. After he left to wet his whistle at the tavern, I opened the front door, regardless of weather, and fanned the smoke out with a piece of cardboard.

My least favorite task was when I had to burn hair clippings in the trash barrel in the alley. What a stink! But my favorite job was using the dollar he gave me to replenish the comic books. At ten cents apiece, it was a bonanza.

Eventually, he became so busy he had to turn away customers, so when asked if he'd apprentice a young barber named Emmit, he happily consented. When Emmit's year was up, Dad offered him a partnership. It was a friendly business relationship that lasted for many years. It helped that they were drinking buddies.

Two barbers meant extra work for my brother and me, but it also meant more money. After cleaning up, I joined them across the street at the tavern for a bottle of soda pop. I usually left them at the bar and wandered over to the pool tables to watch the old gents play. I remember the smell of the place: cigarette smoke, stale beer, and stale urine. Mom didn't like this nightly ritual that often made us late for supper. He truly did seem to prefer the company of his bar friends to that of his family. I didn't blame him, in a way. With the addition of another sister, Kim, our house could be a noisy and confusing place. Conversation was not as stimulating either, I suppose.

The two partners eventually found a more modern location that had once been an insurance office. Thankfully, it had a bathroom, but Dad made certain that there was no telephone. He didn't want to be interrupted with phone calls, asking if he was busy.

I was a sophomore in high school when he got an offer to buy out the owner of the barbershop where he'd apprenticed seven years before. It was a chance to start again after racking up considerable debt. The plan was to sell our house to some sucker and have a little money left over, but his debts had to be settled. A lien on the sale of the house left us with little.

We packed everything into the back of a farmer's truck and hit the road. It was exciting contemplating new schools, friends, and surroundings in a smaller town. We must have looked like the Joads out of the *Grapes of Wrath* riding into town, with Gary and me sitting guard on top of our worldly goods.

The barbershop was the only one in town and had a well-established clientele. For its size, the little town was bustling, and he was busy right from the start. As we lived in the spacious apartment above, he finally had access to indoor plumbing and regular meals.

My brother and I kept our jobs as janitors but were no longer paid, as we had plenty of farm work that Dad sent our way from his farmer customers.

I still enjoyed sitting in the shop listening to the discussions and arguments, but I could tell he'd lost enthusiasm for cutting hair. When longer hairstyles prevailed over flattops, thanks to the wildly popular Beatles, he bristled. High school boys were waiting longer between cuts, and when they asked for the new style, he mocked them. "Do you wanna look like a Beatle or do you wanna look like a human being?" he'd ask.

Obviously, this was not good for business, and it suffered. He was never very good at money management and with cash in his pocket at the end of each day, it was all too easy to spend it at the tavern.

Eventually, he lost the will to continue barbering and briefly took up welding. Later, he went for training to work for the Iowa State Department of Agriculture as a meat and poultry inspector. He took great pride in the job and did well until his retirement.

*

Pop's shop was where I first earned money, learned about the wide variety of people, and realized that I did not want to be a barber. The shop was a large part of my life for nearly twenty years and most certainly a major influence.

I miss my father and appreciate those many hours I spent so close to him.

TENDERFOOT

Early adolescence was a formative time of my life. The Boy Scouts of America engaged me on many levels, and I threw myself into it wholeheartedly. At the age of fifteen, I became an Eagle Scout. But first, I was a Tenderfoot, a beginner, the lowest rank in Scouting.

This is what I remember:

My initial outing with my scruffy, rough-and-ready troop was a Friday afternoon "cookout." It included a two-mile hike out of town to Swank's Woods where we built small cooking fires, made supper, and romped in the woods until dusk. Later, the scoutmaster and two or three assistants drove out after work. When it was time to leave, we rode back to town packed in their cars like smoked sardines.

I joined fifteen of my fellow Scouts at a pre-arranged location for the hike. Most of the boys were older and I found myself bringing up the rear of the column.

As we trudged down the road, I became painfully aware that my backpack was twice the size of everyone else's. By the time we'd hiked halfway in the afternoon sun, I was huffing and puffing like an over-worked mule. My shoulders ached and the straps dug into my arms, making my hands numb.

The Scoutmaster's son, Bucky Sherman, an older experienced camper, was keeping a wary eye on me... the new Tenderfoot. He paused to let the others slip by and waited for me.

With a knowing grin he asked, "Hey, need some help?"

I exhaled through flushed, puffed cheeks and nodded.

"Hold up guys!" he called. "Take five."

The troop wandered off into the ditch at the side of the road and removed their packs for a rest.

"Big pack for such a little guy, let's see whatcha got in that sack of yours," he said, reaching for my burden. He untied the canvas top and whistled low. "Wow, you got *some* stuff in here, dontcha, Tenderfoot?"

The Boy Scout motto is Be Prepared and I'd done my best. Having never been to woods of any size other than a farm grove or the trees along the river near my grandparent's house, I had no idea what to expect.

"Why do ya need an extra pair of underwear, Tenderfoot?" he queried. "Figure on messin' yours? And would ya look at this... not one but *two* pairs of socks!"

"Hey, Gerry," he called to his buddy, "come 'ere and look at this."

"This," of course was an open invitation for everyone to gather around my bulging knapsack as if it were Santa's gift bag. It was embarrassing.

As Bucky drew out each item and held it up for inspection, there was a collective gasp or guffaw.

Among the shameful contents were: a sweatshirt, matches, flashlight, a half-pound of hamburger, four slices of bread, a container of milk, a mess kit, knife, fork, spoon, spatula, a stick of butter, a deck of cards, my Boy Scout Handbook, salt, pepper, a raw potato, a package of pudding mix, an onion, ketchup, a pack of cherry Fizzies, two packs of Double Mint gum, a paper bag, an SOS pad, a metal mirror, a can of shoe-string potatoes, a can opener, and a length of twine.

"How long did ya figure on bein' gone?" Bucky smirked.

This produced another round of laughter.

I blushed deeply, shrugged my sore shoulders, and looked to my dusty sneakers for comfort.

"Isn't the Scout motto, 'Be Prepared?'" I asked.

"For what? World War Three?" one of the guys finished.

There was more amusement.

Bucky realized he was responsible for embarrassing me. "Okay, 'nuff of this. Let's get a move on."

"Don't worry, Tenderfoot," he said in a low voice, "I'll tote yer stuff for ya. Just remember, next time pack only what ya need, then bring half 'a that."

He smiled and began stuffing things from my pack into his. He winked at me and trotted back to the head of the troop. I was grateful when the backpack incident was not mentioned again. They'd all been a Tenderfoot once, too.

As we neared the woods, I could see the stand of maples, oaks, hickories, ashes, and ironwoods high above the surrounding fields. I had never seen so many tall trees in such density.

You must understand, we folk of the plains have a deep respect, bordering on awe, of the majesty of trees. Our pioneer ancestors discovered that trees were in short supply and were only found bordering rivers and lakes. The trees planted by our forefathers in and around settlements grew as America grew.

No one took them for granted. If one was blown down in a storm or felled for some reason, an appropriate period of mourning was required. An example of such an event sounded like this: "Aw geez, Lars, that big oak over to the neighbor's got blowed over in the storm last night!"

"Yah, I know it. That's a real shame, dontcha know. Gonna replant one next week though, I hear."

I found myself drawn to the towering giants as our troop neared.

The gravel road we were hiking dead-ended at the edge of the woods. Fields of corn and soybeans rolled away on both sides of the road, creating a striking contrast between their neat, long rows and the wild randomness.

As we entered the trees, it seemed as though they engulfed me and then silently closed a curtain from behind. A faint but inviting footpath meandered into the lush green.

The happy chatter of my fellow Scouts became eerily muffled and muted. From the upper branches the call of a blue jay, normally saucy and raucous, sounded forlorn. The heavy stillness produced a faint ringing in my ears and the dense canopy cast dark shadows in the silence. The ground was thickly carpeted with decomposing leaves, rotting wood, lush ferns, and multicolored fungi of every size and shape. Gooseberry and elderberry bushes grew in abundance, their green leaves splashed boldly against the brown and gray tree trunks.

The silence pressed gently upon me. The damp, pungent smell of the forest filled with life and decay permeated the air, inducing a momentary nausea. I was dumbstruck by the sense that I'd entered a church. It seemed like an immense, holy cathedral full of something divine and powerful.

The initial feelings of unease and strangeness were soon replaced by a sense of belonging and peace.

"Ya wanna camp with me?" a thin, blond-haired boy asked. "I'm Neil."

"Yeah, sure, okay." I whispered like I was at church services.

His blue eyes smiled but flickered with suspicion. The jury was still out on me.

"C'mon, let's pick a spot," he said, and led me off the path to a small clearing.

We set our packs down near a fallen tree and stretched sore muscles.

Neil eagerly rubbed his palms together and suggested, "Let's hunt up some firewood."

In no time we'd gathered an ample supply of dry, dead wood. I watched as he scraped a small area clear of leaves making a fire ring. Then, using small twigs he called "squaw wood," he struck a wooden kitchen match and started our fire. Soon, a yellow tongue of flame was licking the larger sticks. As Neil built up the fire, I began preparing supper.

The hamburger was easy as I only had to divide and compress it into patties. The potato was altogether a different story, as it had to be peeled with a pocketknife in my unskilled hands. The result was a greatly diminished potato resembling an asteroid. After I'd sliced it into my official Boy Scout aluminum frying pan, added onion, salt and pepper and a chunk of butter, I was ready to cook.

From here out, I had little better than a vague notion of what to do. Bucky had told us to cook on the hot coals, as the slow, even heat from a bed of coals would allow for better temperature regulation and remain hot longer.

But I'd seen enough western movies to know that the skillet was always directly over the flames, so I ignored his advice. I'd yet to learn that an unseasoned camper wisely listens to the experience of others.

I was soon rewarded with the sizzle and mouthwatering aroma of cooking hamburger and onion. Due to the open flames, I had to deal with an intensely hot, uneven fire. A heavy deposit of black soot quickly accumulated on the new, shiny surface of my pan. At one point, the flames leaped around the pan, setting fire to the grease, scorching my hand. *Note to self: bring oven glove.*

A good camper never fries raw potatoes; instead, the potatoes are pre-boiled, then simply heated and browned to taste. In a flash, my potatoes became charred on the outside, while the interior stubbornly remained raw. The hamburgers cooked much faster than the potatoes, so I removed them to allow the potatoes to catch up.

While extracting the hamburgers, they slipped off the spatula and plopped onto the ground. I began to sweat from the heat of the fire and a growing anxiety. Although Neil pretended not to see me floundering, I knew that he knew what a twit I was, and figured he must be regretting his choice of camping partner.

Faced with the likelihood of having no supper to slake a now ravenous appetite, I decided desperate times called for desperate measures. I rescued the fallen hamburgers, brushed off the biggest pieces of detritus, and rinsed them with water. Unfortunately, I'd made an earlier decision to drop two cherry flavored Fizzies into my canteen. I could only guess at the results.

I turned my attention to the obstinate potatoes. Over the next ten minutes, I watched them turn to charcoal briquettes; I gave up and fed them to the fire.

Once the burgers were done and placed between two slices of bread and doctored with ketchup, I judged them to be without a doubt, the best tasting hamburgers I'd ever eaten.

Vanilla pudding was on the dessert menu, my 'piece de resistance.' I mixed the package contents with milk in a small pot and set it on the same scorching fire. The pudding never completely thickened, and the clumps that successfully made the transition to pudding bobbed around in the goo. After scorching my hand yet again, I removed the pot to let it cool and sorta... well... drank it. It was tasty, but decidedly not the way Mom would have served it.

Neil, old hand that he was, had wrapped his entire meal in an aluminum foil pouch, dropped it into the coals at the edge of the fire, and disappeared to explore with the others. He returned later panting and sweating, retrieved the package from the fire and opened it with a fork. From his seat on a log out of reach of campfire smoke, he gobbled his dinner.

He eyed my blackened mess kit and observed that it truly was a "mess kit." "Man, you got an hour at the sink cleanin' that up when you get home," he told me.

I winced; I hadn't thought about cleanup. My mother was sure to rightfully insist the job was mine and mine alone.

The sun had slipped nearer the horizon, darkening the shadows. Heavy, lazy smoke from smoldering fires filled the cooling early evening air.

Heralded by whooping and shouting from the troop, our Scout leaders arrived. I could hear their deep reassuring voices.

The four men quickly assessed that we were all present and accounted for and managed to avoid significantly damaging ourselves.

I took notice of Bucky engaged in conversation with his father, the Scoutmaster. They were glancing and nodding in my direction. I pretended not to notice and concentrated on gathering my belongings. As I picked up my filthy mess kit, I felt a passing wave of queasiness.

Mess kits are designed to fit one into another in a self-contained unit and, after a few attempts, I recalled how to reassemble it. It wouldn't do to place the sooty pans against the other things in my pack, so I stuffed the kit into the paper bag I'd brought. *Hey,* I thought, *guess I was prepared after all.*

I discovered a yet uneaten can of shoestring potatoes. *Maybe they'll settle my stomach*, I thought.

I munched the chips then washed them down with the Fizzie water. I wished that I'd had time to explore like everyone else, instead of devoting all my energies to cooking.

"Let's go! Get a move on!" I heard Mr. Sherman shout.

"Aw, gee, already?" said a voice.

"Can't we stay a little longer?" whined another.

The Scoutmaster approached my campsite.

"Get that fire completely out, Wayne," he said.

"Yessir," I said weakly. My nausea was back.

I think he mistook my meekness for embarrassment over the backpack fiasco. He came to stand in front of me and placed a fatherly hand on my shoulder.

"Don't worry," he said reassuringly, "it all gets easier with practice. You'll see."

Suddenly I hunched forward and upchucked my weird supper onto his shoes.

"WHOA! WHOA!" he exclaimed, backing away like a scalded cat.

There was no stopping it. It happened without warning, the *coup de grace* to my initiation to woodland camping.

From a safe distance, he asked, "Are you alright?"

I wiped my mouth on my sleeve and mumbled, "Yeah, I think so. Gee, I'm sorry, Mr. Sherman. I couldn't help it."

"Forget it," he said. "Maybe your cooking didn't agree with you?" he suggested as he appraised his shoes.

"Yeah," I agreed. At that moment, I didn't want to even think about my fiasco supper.

I offered my canteen to clean his shoes, which he took obligingly. As he rinsed, he stopped, looked quizzically at the water, then tasted it with his finger. His face puckered sourly, and then shook his head with pity for the pathetic Tenderfoot before him.

*

It's a wonder I ever went camping again, but I did... again and again. In my dreams the woods called to me in the whispering of leaves, inviting me to learn, be comforted, and commune.

Then, one day, I found myself in Bucky's place at the head of the column, the blazer of trails, and caretaker of Tenderfeet.

Some of the happiest and most fulfilling hours of my teens were with the Boy Scouts of America. The BSA gave me focus, purpose, and an opportunity to excel when I was floundering.

This is what I remember:

A few miles west of my one-time hometown of Eagle Grove, Iowa, is a forested area called Swank's Woods. Most likely it was named for a local family, although I'm not certain. The woods spread outward from the Boone River and was bordered by farmland. For many midwestern kids like me, it was the only dense growth of trees I'd ever experienced.

It was like entering a cathedral when first I walked into those woods. I'd never been in a cathedral but imagined it was how it must feel. The dense tall trees and profound silence, save for the call of birds, created a sense of awe and reverence. The combined scents of decaying vegetation and new life can best be described as fecund. I felt at home and part of some ancient secret.

Those of the forestless plains of central Iowa enjoy and love our trees… provided they aren't in the way of farming. How that stand of trees escaped saws, axes, and plows I do not know, but I'm thankful for it.

My Scout troop had permission to use the woods and went there often for cookouts and overnight camps. I began going as a know-nothing Tenderfoot, and over time, became an experienced camper. It was expected that older, higher-ranking scouts would pass their knowledge and skills onto the younger ones.

Troop 54 was my troop, one of two in town. We were East Side kids from lower income families and a bit scruffy, but we made up for it by being very active, due to our terrific Scoutmasters. They were all WWII veterans and knew how to lead, when to follow, how to develop character, how to live in groups, and how to "rough it." They did not tolerate disobedience, disrespect, or misbehavior. We all knew instinctively that they wanted us to succeed and one day become good men.

My father was an assistant Scoutmaster and did what he could, but his time was limited by his barbershop, duties as Commander of the American Legion Post, and coach of our little league baseball team. Our cross-the-street neighbor was an assistant, too, who'd been an army cook in Europe during the war. His son and I were pals in the same Scout patrol that held monthly meetings in their basement. At these meetings we heard talks on how to safely handle tools, hiking and camping tips, identification of plants and animals, and how to live off the land. Together, we hiked, camped, and worked on projects for the troop.

Scout troops within a geographic area belong to a council. Ours was the Winnebago Council named after a tribe of Indians once living on the

117

great plains. Troops within the council took turns providing locations for winter and summer camping jamborees.

One summer, our town's two troops decided to jointly host a jamboree in Swank's Woods. There were troop competitions in fire starting, knot tying, woodlore, and the like. Each night we gathered around a large council fire to sing songs, present skits, and learn how to be good Scouts.

Each troop set up their camps in designated areas. We slept in tents owned by the troop or brought our own puptents; the Scoutmasters kept us awake with their loud snoring. Meals were communal, cooked on a central campfire where our army cook neighbor excelled. (I still use his recipe for chili con carne.) Metal mess kits were washed in hot water heated in two clean trash cans, one soapy for washing and the other for rinsing.

One sunny Saturday afternoon when the contests were finished, we were left to our own devices. Four of us went to gather firewood and discovered that much of the nearby down wood had already been gathered. Cutting live wood was forbidden, so we set off armed with a two-man crosscut saw and axes to find a standing dead tree. Channeling lumberjacks, we shouted, *"timmberrr!"* and sent up a loud cheer when it landed with a crashing thud. Other troops took this as a challenge and, not to be outdone, went about sawing down dead trees of their own. Soon, the woods were full of the calls of *"timber!"* and the crash of felled trees. By mid-afternoon, the Scoutmasters had had enough and put a stop to it, but not before we had firewood to spare. They directed us to drag our excess harvest to the council fire site for that night's gathering and the religious services the next morning.

The word was passed that my father and the town baker were bringing hot chocolate to us that evening. They were a bit late as Pop had to finish closing his barbershop and then ride herd on the baker who liked to drink. I think Dad got talked into having a few with him and the result was a vat of scorched hot chocolate. Boys will be boys, and it was readily consumed, nonetheless.

A belief in God is a tenant in the Boy Scouts, so we were expected to attend religious services that Sunday. They were held on a gentle, grassy slope that made a natural amphitheater.

It was my first time at a nondenominational service. Sitting on the logs that we'd cut, awash in the bright morning sun, we listened to inspiring words void of church doctrine. It was an eyeopener for me and I felt uplifted in a way I'd not experienced before. The Catholics were driven to services in town.

When I returned home after running around in the woods all weekend, I gave my smoky clothes to my mother for washing, aired out my sleeping bag on the clothesline, and took a long nap.

Later that same year, the council decided to hold a winter jamboree, and it was back to Swank's Woods.

Winter camping is very different from the summer and not for the faint of heart. There were fewer scouts in attendance and troop campsites were set closer together. We tamped down the snow and set up among the leafless trees. Straw spread beneath the tents helped to insulate them from the cold ground.

There were no night council fires; instead, each troop stayed to themselves for their own activities.

The first two days were sunny, and the snow was melting. There were places to explore and tracking games to play; we were all warned of the importance of not getting wet to avoid hypothermia. In the evenings, we talked around our campfires for a while and then went to bed much earlier than in summer. It didn't take long to figure out that it was warmer nestled deep within a sleeping bag versus sitting beside a smoky fire.

That night, the weather turned bitterly cold with a stiff north wind. When I awoke the next morning with a full bladder and intentions of finding the latrine, I quickly realized things had drastically changed. There was frost covering the opening of my sleeping bag from my frozen breath and wind was buffeting the tent. I could hear the muffled conversation of men, and noticed it was very cold. My three tentmates were awakening, too, rubbing sleep from their eyes and discovering that winter had found us.

Bucky, our head Scoutmaster, shouted, "Everybody up and at 'em!"

The decision had been made to end the weekend early. Nobody wanted to hang around in the cold anyway, so there was no grousing.

We packed up quickly but found that retrieving tent pegs from the now frozen snow was a challenge. Axes were needed to free them, and I have no doubt some are still there today.

*

Learning to work through adversity and discomfort is a good thing. Many events in life are adverse and must be overcome or just plain endured. I have so many fine people to thank for setting such a fine example for me to follow.

This is what I remember:

TAAA, TAADAA, TAAA, I tooted through the brass tubes. *TA, TA, TAAA...BLAT*. I winced at that last sour note and glared accusingly into the flared end of my cornet.

I sighed, rolled my eyes to heaven in an imitation of Louie Armstrong, and blew another blast of air and spit.

Spotty, our cocker spaniel, raised her head, formed a little O with her mouth, and matched the pitch from my tortured horn. *ARRROOOO!* Her eyes looked upward in her own imitation of Ol' Satchmo.

"Beat it, Spotty," I growled.

Spotty beat it.

Tapping time with my right foot, I lurched through a rendition of *Lightly Row*. I thought, *Hey, I don't sound half-bad*. I blew saliva from the spit valve and pulled off the mouthpiece. That was enough practice for the day. Fifteen minutes wasn't the half hour I was supposed to log, but I'd make up for it tomorrow. It was the same promise I'd made the day before.

But sunshine leaked through the slots in the venetian blinds, illuminating the dust motes, and the green grass called my name. So I put the instrument back into its scruffy black case and closed the lid. The hinges creaked like Count Dracula's coffin. Its edges were battered, and the surface badly scratched, and the shoelace handle cut into my hand.

The case and cornet were on permanent loan from a friend of my father's. We couldn't afford a new one and who knew, maybe I'd be a dud as a musician. It had been a chore cleaning the tarnished brass. The valves were stuck, and the bell end of the horn badly dented. With some elbow grease and the help of a handy neighbor, it became a reasonable facsimile of a musical instrument.

Music lessons were free through the community school system. Bandleaders were expected to bring along new talent from the lower grades, much the same as athletic coaches. The constant sifting and separating the wheat from the chaff must have been endless. The stream of uninspired, unmotivated no-talents flowing through their doors couldn't have been much fun. I suppose it was all made worthwhile when a gem turned up to be polished to brilliance, or when the school band stirred the hearts of proud parents.

In the beginning, I had grand illusions of blowing a cool horn in some smoky Chicago nightclub. As colored lights glinted off the brass, I'd steal the show during my solos and girls would swoon with my name on their lips.

Then things changed… I hadn't counted on needing to spend hours and hours practicing. No one told me there was actual work involved, and that my lip would swell up as if stung by a wasp. I did, however, enjoy the challenge of learning something new. The language of music came easily for me, and I accelerated quickly past that stage. It was in the actual application where I lagged.

I showed up weekly for my lessons, having practiced for the first and only time ten minutes before leaving the house. The teacher sighed and asked, "Did you practice this week?"

"Yes, sir," I answered truthfully.

"How much?"

"Not enough, I guess," I replied. I should have brought a recording of the conversation; it would have saved us both time. But little by little via osmosis, I progressed.

On the rare occasions when I practiced, my parents had the opportunity to listen to my growing repertoire and came to recognize the tunes I was butchering. They smiled at each other and nodded their heads knowingly. "Sounds good, Son," they said. Neither of them could read a note of music, making their credibility as music critics suspect. However, they encouraged me, and I could see that they were proud of my accomplishments, paltry though they were.

When an unfortunate and unsuspecting relative or family friend came for a visit, the conversation eventually got around to us kids, what we were doing, which grade we were in, etc., and I knew what was coming...

"Oh, Wayne's our little musician now," said my mother.

"And he ain't bad, either," Dad added. "Say, why don't we get him to play us a little something?"

I cringed. "Aw, naw, Dad," I whined. "Please don't make me."

"Baloney! Why the hell do I pay for those lessons if I can't hear you play occasionally?"

As far as I could tell, he didn't have any more than four bucks invested. My music book had been a dollar and a half, and a bottle of valve oil was two dollars tops. Who did he think he was fooling?

Eventually I gave in. "Okay, I'll get my music."

I arranged myself in the center of the living room with my back to the TV. On these occasions, the TV's sound was turned down and the glow from the picture tube served as backlighting.

After a sigh of resignation, I pumped the three valves with my fingers, raised the mouthpiece to my puckered lips, and plunged headlong into *Jingle Bells* or some such piece. As I played, I watched the faces watching me. There were my parents, brimming with pride, my two sisters absently twiddling their hair, and my brother, jealous of the attention, shooting me cross-eyed looks with his tongue stuck out. Then there were the guests with fake smiles frozen onto their faces, trying to look enthralled with the boy prodigy.

Okay, okay, maybe I did like the attention, I'll admit. But all things considered, I'd rather have been doing most anything else. After a polite patter of applause, I made my exit. No one ever asked for an encore.

Slowly, I began to lose the dream. That smoky nightclub in Chicago gave way to the more realistic goal of playing in the junior high band.

One Friday evening, our band was to present a concert in the high school gymnasium. Members of an orchestra are arranged by chair within each section: brass, woodwinds, strings, etc., according to their skill levels. I had the distinction of being last chair.

My parents, glowing with pride and dressed in their Sunday clothes, sat front and center. I avoided making eye contact and nervously rearranged my music for the tenth time.

The collar of my white shirt and tie choked me in an unfamiliar embrace as I fought the urge to squirm, waiting for the appearance of the bandleader. When he approached the podium, the audience gave him a small, polite applause. This was my first performance in front of anyone other than the poor saps in our living room and I was momentarily confused and started to stand.

The kid next to me hissed, "Sit down, you idiot!"

I sat.

The bandleader looked like a man with his neck in a noose. He had wide damp circles of perspiration under his arms, and his face was shiny with sweat in the bright lights reflecting off the waxed gym floor. He wore an expression both pleading and hopeful as he raised his stained armpits, baton in hand, and we were off.

We played that night with abandon. I couldn't believe my ears! The music flowed from our instruments in a steady stream of pleasant sounds that delighted and surprised us. It was one of those moments when everything seemed to coalesce into perfection with an effortless, clean, seamless performance.

My fingers flew, pumping the pistons of my ugly cornet. The notes seemed to leap from my horn to join the others. I was a MUSICIAN! *Look out, Chicago, here I come!* The dream was back.

The director, flushed with pride, beamed joy, confidence, and love. He loved us and we loved him. We loved each other. We loved the world.

When it was over, the audience went berserk, and we were applauded into an encore. I thought my father was going to embarrass me when it looked like he was getting up for a one-man standing ovation. *Don't get carried away, Pop*, I thought. He caught my mother's sober eye and settled.

Backstage, we were in ecstasy. It was our first time out of the blocks, and we'd blown them away. We'd walked among the clouds in the dizzy heights of the exalted and found it wonderful.

After the concert my folks took me for ice cream. It was just the three of us, as they'd wisely left my brother and sisters home with a babysitter. It hadn't been this way for as long as I could remember, and the specialness was not lost on me.

"Whatever my son THE MUSICIAN wants," Pop told the waitress.

I ordered a hot-fudge sundae and a Coke. The cold felt good on my swollen lip... the lip of a MUSICIAN.

The following week my music teacher called a conference with my parents and me. I figured that because of my sterling performance at the concert, I was to be given some sort of recognition. Unfortunately, this was not the case; instead, I was dealt a devastating blow.

He tactfully explained that I didn't have the ability to consistently hit the high C note required in more advanced music. He'd noted this for some time and was waiting for my "lip to mature" but my lip had stubbornly remained a juvenile delinquent. It was called "embouchure" or some such thing.

He recommended I drop the cornet, "just for now," and take up the drum. Then, with my sense of rhythm developed, I could take another crack at it.

So, for the next six months I beat on a brown, rubber practice pad with drumsticks, tapped my foot in time, and... lost all interest. I finally mustered enough courage to tell my teacher I was through. He seemed disappointed. Gee, I was disappointed, too, but my heart just wasn't in it. I'd lost the dream, you see.

My parents were displeased with me and Dad told me he was worried I might be embarking on a career as a quitter. This made absolutely no sense. If a guy had to repeatedly and painfully stick his finger into an electric light socket, shouldn't he be allowed to stop?

*

I still love music and have flirted with several different instruments, including the blues harp, piano, concertina, and kazoo. I even played guitar in a rock and roll band for a short time in my late teens. But even now, I can still see that smoky nightclub with a spotlight that waits for me.

Imprisoned in my pipsqueak body lies the heart of an athlete. It wasn't easy in small-town Iowa for twerps like me to find an outlet for athleticism. Strapped school budgets often lacked funding, except for the meat-and- potato sports like football and basketball.

Until my sophomore year I lived in a town large enough to offer a sport Iowa has claimed as its own for decades… wrestling. Frank Gotch, from the nearby town of Humboldt, Iowa, was a famous world champion heavyweight, catch-as-catch-can wrestler.

This is what I remember:

I got hooked in the fifth grade when on Saturday mornings during wrestling season, I trekked off through the snow to the high school for "wrestling clinic." There, the town's very successful wrestling coach sacrificed his time to find and nurture new talent.

My pint-sized friends and I met in the workout rooms clad in our black high-top PF flyers *("the shoes that winners choose")*, T-shirts, shorts, and long underwear.

The long underwear was not only armor against the Iowa winter but also protected us from friction abrasions or "mat burns," as we grapplers called them. My bony knees and elbows were constantly challenged to grow new skin.

At these clinics we learned the various moves and holds which allowed you to score points on your opponent or pin his shoulders to the mat long enough to declare yourself the immediate victor.

The sport seemed to fit me. Each wrestler was equally matched based upon weight, thereby negating the "shrimp factor." It was a lonely kind of sport, as there was no team on the mat with you and no one else to blame nor anyone to help you out of a tight spot. The thrill of victory and the agony of defeat were yours and yours alone.

When I entered junior high, practices and meets were conducted after school from mid-November through February. Practice sessions were grueling and intense. Any workout room worth its salt was a small space carpeted wall-to-wall with mats and required to smell like a forgotten sweat sock in an old sneaker.

You had to be tough to face that odor every day, but it was nothing compared to the stench after two hours of sweating with the heater turned to the Blast from Hell setting. Add twenty grunting adolescent boys in various stages of personal hygiene awareness and you really had something.

In the front of the room, dressed in his gray sweatsuit, a silver whistle clamped in his teeth, was the coach.

"Tweet. Tweet!" he blew. "Again! Do it!"

"Ugh," we moaned.

We'd been practicing the same move for an hour, trying desperately to satisfy whatever it was he was looking for. I reached to grab my partner, Gerald Halsrud, in the prescribed embrace for wrestlers: in the standing position bent forward, head-to-head, right ear to right ear, grasping each other's neck and left arm. It was this position that prompted my father to dub us "armpit smellers." That's exactly what we looked like: two guys trying to stick their noses into each other's armpits.

"*Tweet!*" the whistle chirped, signaling us to commence *The Move*.

Gerald wobbled in exhaustion as he leaned against me for support. Our faces were locked next to each other; he panted the toxic miasma of his breath. I was thankful to be breathing through my mouth and thus bypassing my nose.

"Man, I can't stand much more of this," he puffed.

"Me neither," I said and ducked under his left arm, pulling his head down to the mat in a maneuver called a take down.

We lay on the mat panting, tangled in each other's limbs, stalling for time to catch our breaths.

"*Tweet!* Do it again! On your feet! Move!"

We struggled to stand and assumed the position.

"Ya know," Gerald gasped, "your sweatshirt is really gettin' rank, man. Did yah ever think o' warshin' it?"

I always took my workout clothes home for a well-deserved washing over Christmas vacation, still two weeks away. "Look who's talkin'," I said, "I gotta hold my breath every time I get near you!"

"*Tweet!*"

It was my turn to be taken down to the mat.

"Get up! Again!" the coach commanded.

The world had become a fuzzy blur. Long ago, I'd entered the trance-like state well-known to wrestlers: *I'll do this until I drop and then you'll have some explaining to do, mister!* We were rag dolls flopping on top of each other in damp stinking heaps. No one spoke as we waited for it to be over.

Then, it *was*.

"*Tweeeet... tweet!* All right, fellas, hit the showers."

We resisted the urge to lie on the mat in blots of sweat to wheeze life back into our bodies but knew it wouldn't look good in front of the coach. Instead, we remained standing, leaning with hands on knees, red-faced, gasping like landed fish.

"Good work-out, guys!" Coach smiled. He beamed with happiness at the pitiful pulps he'd produced in just sixty minutes.

We staggered off the mats, beckoned by the soothing massage of running water and purification.

Some of the brown-noser types hung back, stretching and exercising so Coach could see just how dedicated they were.

"Look at those jerks!" Gerald said.

"Yeah," I said, "Jerks!"

"You ever see me doin' that, you can pull that sweatshirt of yours over my head," he grinned.

"Do me a favor, Gerry," I returned, "brush your teeth tonight."

The steam was rising from the showers as I peeled off my soggy clothes. Entering the dense mist I saw my fellow masochists, weak with fatigue, clinging to shower heads to remain standing. Contact with the floor was avoided at all costs, as it was littered with a disgusting compost of Band-Aids, wads of tape, clots of bloody cotton, slivers of used soap, and unclaimed athletic supporters. It was bad enough to walk barefoot on that floor, let alone allow some part of your body touch it.

The hot water streamed over me in a wondrous caress that sucked the remaining strength from my muscles and swept it down the drain. I wasn't sure if I was going to make it out of the showers, let alone home.

I felt better after I'd dressed and stood out in the December evening. As the cool air flowed into my lungs, strength returned to the rubber bands that were my legs. The sudden exhilaration made me giddy.

The walk home was much the same as wrestling: a lonely, personal event, filled with pain and punctuated by rare moments of pleasure.

Few of us wore caps in those days, preferring the hood of a parka or sweatshirt. My ears burned and my damp hair turned stiff in the cold. I switched my schoolbooks to the other arm to relieve the cramps in my shoulder and blew on my fingers to warm them.

I crossed the railroad tracks dividing the town into West and East Sides. We lived on the East Side, the "wrong" side of town.

In the light of a streetlamp, I saw the glint of the rock salt used to keep railroad crossings free of ice. I bent to pick one up and popped it into my mouth. The salt tasted good and helped to satisfy my craving after two hours of heavy sweating.

Darkness came early that time of year, and stars had already dotted the sky-roof over our town. Moments like this were a time of reflection during the twenty-minute walk. It was the only time of the day when I was alone with my thoughts.

Not for the first time, I contemplated why I'd agreed to this torture. The practices were bad enough, but the constant maintenance of my weight was worse.

Luckily, I'd always been one who could eat as much of whatever I wanted, whenever I wanted, and not gain weight. There were restrictions requiring a wrestler not to exceed the limits of his weight class. If he could not maintain at or below this weight, he had to wrestle at the weight class above. This often meant being paired with a stronger and more experienced kid who also wanted the position. As there was room for only one at each weight class, there was constant vying for position. The rules were that anyone could challenge and win a place on the starting team.

It was vital for me to stay at ninety-five pounds so I might continue to be a starter for the eleven-man junior varsity team. Not to do so meant I would only be a sparring partner, as Gerald was for me. The kid wrestling at my weight on the varsity team was stronger, more agile, aggressive, and most importantly, more motivated than I. It was all right with me; I knew where I belonged.

As I moved through adolescence, it became harder and harder to keep my wrestling weight. Whenever I gained a pound or two, I skipped meals and restricted sweets. For me, it was more difficult than the worst workout.

On the day of a wrestling meet I wouldn't eat all day until after classes, when we were officially weighed-in at the gym. It was hard to concentrate on my schoolwork on those days, especially if I was overweight and refusing even a sip of water. After the official weigh-in I would run to the nearest drinking fountain and vending machine for some quick energy and hydration. Healthy, huh?

If my parents had known, they would have had a fit. It was a little secret between us and our coaches. We kept our mouths shut about how we stayed at weight and the coaches pretended they didn't know what was going on.

Some used drastic measures to lose those last pounds by chewing gum and spitting the saliva, taking laxatives, inducing vomiting, or starving themselves. Despite the rules limiting how much weight you could cut in a season, it continued. A method of desperation on weigh-in days was to roll up in a plastic mat cover and lie next to a hot radiator to sweat off water weight. This way everyone got what they wanted. The coach didn't have to forfeit a wrestler disqualified for being overweight and we got to do our stuff in front of our fans.

In fairness, the coaches weren't happy if we had to resort to this strategy, as ultimately it produced a weakened wrestler. They discouraged unrealistic weight cutting, but winning was the goal.

My father and his two brothers had been basketball and baseball jocks. They didn't understand wrestling but thought they did. Most of their information about the sport came from watching the likes of Gorgeous George, Vern Gonya, and Haystack Calhoun on Saturday night television. The TV show was just that... show. It was a rehearsed, choreographed performance by muscular men and women for their audiences. The holds and throws they used on each other were not allowed in the real sport, but my family didn't understand that.

Mom was aghast to think that her son would be "in the ring" being beaten, thrown, gouged, bitten, and kicked. After carefully explaining the differences between the two forms of wrestling, she reluctantly agreed to let me participate but refused to attend a meet.

Dad, on the other hand, wanted to see me in action and secretly hoped, I suspect, that he'd watch me tear an arm off my opponent and beat him over the head with it. Pop was a real competitor.

One of my uncles, Emery, was a huge television-wrestling fan. At family gatherings, he pumped me for stories about my fledgling career "in the ring."

"There's good money in it if you play your cards right, big boy," he said. He was always saying things like that.

"No. No. You got it wrong," I said. "You can't intentionally hurt someone in sport wrestling. You…"

"Yeah, yeah," he cut in, "that's just for now, until you learn the business. Then you'll be a poundin' and a gougin' just like the rest of 'em."

"Why don't you come and watch a meet sometime and find out what I'm talking about?" I suggested.

"Someday I will," he winked, "if you play your cards right, big boy."

Uncle was one of those characters I suppose every family has. He'd been a strong powerful man in his youth but was slowly turning into a big fat guy. He had no neck; instead, his large head rolled around on top of a barrel-shaped torso, and he wore his greying hair in a short flattop. No slave to fashion, he wore coveralls and a yellow baseball cap that said CAT.

His most striking feature was his mouth. He talked loudly and incessantly in a wonderfully comic way that was a mixture of Iowan twang and affected Southern drawl. He frequently spoke before thinking. "Hey, you can just take me the way I am or git the hell outta my way," was his standard response to criticism.

Dad was certain I'd selected wrestling for spite. He didn't care much for the sport but as it seemed important to me, he gamely tried to learn. It was difficult for him to take time away from his barbershop to catch a wrestling meet. Nonetheless he made as many home meets as he could. When the team ran out onto the edge of the mat at the start of the meet, I would scan the crowd to see him standing in the back in his old gray coat.

One January evening we were to wrestle in a meet in Fort Dodge, a town twice the size of ours with a rough reputation.

I was two pounds overweight and had spent an hour rolled in a plastic mat cover. After a quick shower I ran to the waiting team bus.

The coach was irritated. "Where's your uniform?" he barked.

"Oh," I said, "I thought they were already loaded."

I turned and sprinted back to the locker room and found the nearly empty rack holding our red and white uniforms. Spotting the number 1 on the sleeve reserved for the 95-pound wrestler, I grabbed it and dashed back to the bus and my scowling coach.

"Now that we're all here," he said sarcastically, "sound off for roll call."

When we'd answered "yeoh" to our names, he spoke, "Okay, you guys, this is a tough one. These kids are always a challenge for us. We'll try to make certain none of them carry switchblades to the mat," he joked.

Nobody laughed.

"Maybe you've noticed," he continued, "that we didn't suit up our heavyweight today. Yoddle's got the flu so we must forfeit his match, which puts us five points down right from the get-go. We can't afford to lose a single match."

A team received three points for a match decision, one for a draw and five points for a pin, also called a "fall." To pin a wrestler, both his shoulders had to be held to the mat for three consecutive seconds. A forfeit counted as a fall.

I sat alone on the bus, lost in thoughts of how and what I was going to do in my match, as butterflies fluttered in my stomach. My anxiety was worse than usual, as my Uncle Emery had agreed to join my father to attend the out-of-town meet.

By now I'd turned into a fair wrestler. I was no great shakes, but I'd never been pinned and had a winning record. Just the same, I lacked confidence.

I rode in silence over the bleak, wintry countryside, staring out of the steamy window and wishing, not for the first time, I'd taken up some other activity, like chess.

When we arrived, we were directed to the girl's locker room, as was customary for the visiting team. Immediately the one hundred-twenty pounder, Shultzy, located a Kotex dispenser and performed his routine. He loved to entertain us by punching eyeholes into a pad, taping it to his head, and then strutting around the room in his jock strap. Shultzy boasted that after he finished school, he would wrestle as a professional under the name of the Kotex Kid. It had become a sort of good luck ritual for us.

Today, however, I wasn't laughing. I was dismayed to discover I'd picked up the wrong uniform. Instead of my number 1, I'd taken number 11! The other numeral had been hidden behind the sleeve's crease. Number 11 was the number of the heavyweight, Big John Yoddle.

I brought my predicament to the coach. He'd know what to do...

"Oh, just great!" Coach rolled his eyes and shook his head in disbelief. "Well, you're just going to have to wear it!" he said and turned away, washing his hands of me.

There was nothing left to do but suit up.

I milked the baggy tights up my legs and rolled it down from my chest to my hips. The singlet that buttoned at the crotch sagged to my thighs. Next, I hitched up the over shorts and secured them with the drawstring. There was lots of extra string, and I stuffed it all into my athletic supporter, hoping that the now-crowded contents wouldn't result in something unpleasant.

The stuffed shorts ballooned, causing Shultzy to guffaw loudly from beneath his mask. "Hey, you look like you got a load in your pants!"

A quick check in the mirror reflected a ninety-five-pound clown, freakishly swaddled in a red and white costume. *Maybe they'll think I'm the team mascot*, I mused.

The call came for us to run out onto the mat to warm up. As the lightest weight, I wrestled first and led the team out from the locker room. Our cheerleaders leaped and twirled, and those loyal to us stood to cheer. The cheerleaders held up a drawing of the school's mascot: a snarling, mean-looking eagle dressed in a wrestling uniform. The paper was spread over a door-sized wooden frame.

My job was to crash through the paper doorway and onto the mat. It was supposed to be an inspiring moment. I lowered my head and leaped through the paper, got my bearings and trotted to the edge of the mat in front of our team's bench. Maybe it was my imagination, but I could have sworn the noise dimmed and the cheerleaders' smiles faded as I made my entrance in the billowing clown suit.

Head down, I avoided eye contact and begged God to not let my pants fall down.

Thirty seconds later, the home team took the opposite side of the mat facing us, ushered in by a deafening roar of welcome from their fans and the school's pep band. We sized each other up. At thirteen, I wasn't old enough to shave, but the fellow I was to wrestle had a five o'clock shadow if I ever saw one. He looked strong, mean, and, well… old.

The coach helped me out of my oversized warm-up jacket, which slid easily from my skinny arms. "This kid's flunked two grades, Wayne," he said, "and is undefeated in two years. For heaven's sake, don't get pinned! Okay? Just don't get pinned." After that ringing endorsement of confidence, he rubbed my shoulders and patted my butt in the way athletes and coaches seem compelled to do.

I stepped out onto ground zero in the center of the mat to shake hands with the tough guy. He gripped my hand briefly, then flung it aside in a move meant to intimidate me. He snickered as he surveyed me in my oversized uniform. I felt my face flush with embarrassment.

We squared off and in moments he'd taken me down, gaining a two-point lead. I fought him off through the rest of the first period. It wasn't easy, as I kept getting tangled in the folds of my uniform.

We started in the down position for the second period. I knelt at his left side, my left hand above his left elbow and my right hand wrapped around his waist. He had to crouch on his hands and knees as we waited for the referee's whistle.

In short order, he'd completed a reversal by getting himself behind and on top of me for another two points. Things were looking grim.

I stole a glance at the coach as I struggled to free myself. He was shouting and waving his arms frantically. I read his lips, "Don't get pinned!"

My teammates shouted encouragement while the cheerleaders chanted, "Turn him over, show him the lights, come on, Wayne, fight, fight, fight!"

Then I saw them... my father and Uncle Emery, sitting two rows back. I caught the look of concern in Pop's eyes. "C'mon, Son!" he shouted.

Uncle sat next to him like a big mountain with his hat pulled low. He opened that famous mouth and bellowed like a Hereford bull, "Grab his hair! Grab his hair!" Followed by, "Punch him a good one!" He punched the air demonstrating how it was done.

Please, I thought, *let this be over soon.*

Mercifully, the third and last period arrived, without me getting farther behind. This time we changed places with me on the bottom.

I looked up into the bleachers and saw my uncle make a slow movement with his finger across his throat, pantomiming that now was the time to cut my opponent's throat.

From the bench, the Kotex Kid shouted, "Wayne, he's riding you too high! Fake a switch and roll him!"

I was near the fatigue that accompanies the last period of a match, and I decided that since I didn't really have a plan of my own, I might as well try the Kid's.

When the referee blew his whistle, I feigned a move to pull myself around behind my opponent. When he countered as anticipated by pushing hard against me, I hooked his elbow with mine and rolled him.

In a flash I'd scored two points and the crowd, as they say, went wild.

The maneuver had put him on his back, and I quickly applied a pinning hold, pressing him to the mat. In three seconds, the ref slapped the mat and blew his whistle, indicating I'd pinned the tough guy.

My teammates carried me off the mat on their shoulders. I was exalted! I grinned and whooped, basking in the glory of a moment I was to remember the rest of my life.

Dad and Uncle Emery, amid an ocean of angry, disappointed Fort Dodge fans, were clapping and cheering for all they were worth. They pounded each other on the back and hooted, ignoring the disdainful looks around them.

In one move I'd turned Bozo into Hero and tied the score.

Inspired, the rest of the team wrestled like wild animals, and we won the meet.

The trip home was jubilant and noisy. Coach sat in the front seat behind the driver, smiling and smiling. As we left the bus after arriving home, he stopped me.

"Good job, Chris!" he said and patted me on the shoulder.

"Maybe I should wear Yoddle's uniform all the time, Coach?" I said and we shared a laugh.

On the walk home, bathed in a warm glow, I felt like I was floating. This was why I was a wrestler, I decided. It was for a chance to feel like this.

*

After my freshman year, we moved to a town too small to support a wrestling program, and my career as a small-time jock came to an end. In retrospect, it was for the best. I was never dedicated enough nor had the talent to be a champion armpit smeller and knew it. Instead, I turned my attentions to my classes and making money by working on farms after school. Just the same, it was wonderful to have had that little moment of glory.

Our two daughters were at the dining room table, carefully writing on the cards they'd put into their classmates Valentine's boxes at school the next day. Shoeboxes wrapped in white paper and decorated with little red hearts had slots cut into their tops to receive Valentines from others.

"Make sure you sign your names on your cards," I butted in.

They looked at me as if I had two heads, puzzled that I'd remind them of something so obvious.

"Dad, do you think we're stupid or something?" the oldest asked.

"No," I said, "I guess not." Duly chastised, I returned to my paper.

This is what I remember:

In second grade, like my girls, I'd performed the same ritual the night before Valentine's Day, wrapping a box with a cut-to-size brown paper bag. I had enough foresight to make certain the outside of the bag was facing inward so that the words *"Paul's Pay'n Take It"* weren't visible. Next, I slashed a slot into the lid with blunt-nosed scissors. They were the only ones my wise mother would let me use.

I drew lopsided, misshaped hearts on the sides with red crayon, piercing each with a small arrow from Cupid's quiver.

When I finished, I paused to admire my work. There was enough cellophane tape to wrap a twenty-pound turkey and pieces of frayed cardboard stuck out of the slot in a hairy fringe. I proudly wrote my name on the top but had misjudged the space needed, so the last two letters bent around the corner.

I punched out my cards from the perforations in a book of Valentine's cards from the Five & Dime and put them into envelopes. Then I glued them shut without smearing an inordinate amount of Elmer's glue and wrote the first name of each classmate on them. Choosing the card was important and I was careful to match them with their personalities and how I felt about them.

The Valentine marked "For My Special Valentine" I kept for the blond-haired, blue-eyed angel who sat in the row next to me... Arlis. I drew an extra off-kilter heart next to her name on the envelope to let her know just how special she was.

The next day at afternoon recess, we distributed our Valentines before going out to play. As I happily dropped them into the boxes set around the room, I took the opportunity to compare the craftwork of my fellow students. After I'd made my way around the room, I no longer felt that proud of my little box. It paled in comparison with most of the girls' and a few of the boys', except for Al Knutson's, who'd covered one of his mother's Kotex boxes with transparent white tissue paper.

I went outside for recess, haunted by a nagging, sinking feeling. While on the jungle gym, I suddenly knew what was bothering me... I'd forgotten to sign my name on the cards!

I sprinted back into the schoolhouse in an adrenaline-fueled frenzy. Panic- stricken, I began opening boxes, fumbling through the thirty-odd cards in each box, looking for mine. I tore open the envelopes I'd so carefully sealed the night before and with a trembling hand, scribbled my name. I was on the sixth or seventh box when the bell rang, ending recess. My heart sank. There were twenty-five more to go.

I continued to stall for time until the teacher became irritated and told me to take my seat.

"But..." I started to explain, then shrugged and went to my desk next to Arlis. I hadn't gotten to her Valentine box in time.

The last half hour of the day, we opened our boxes and read our cards. The teacher gave each of us a heart-shaped cookie sprinkled with red sugar. I sat chewing the cookie, reading my Valentines while keeping an eagle eye on my classmates. When I saw a puzzled look, I called to them, "Oh, that's from me. I forgot to sign it. Would you like me to sign it now?" Most declined.

When Arlis opened her anonymous card, she cocked her head in puzzlement. Embarrassed, I pretended to not see her and continued munching my cookie. *She'll know it was from me*, I thought. But when I saw her shrug her shoulders and then carelessly toss My Special Valentine onto the pile on her desk... with it, she tossed my heart.

That evening my father brought home a red heart-shaped box of chocolates for my mother. She hid it for a time on the topmost shelf of a cupboard, but my brother and I sniffed it out just the same. Standing on tiptoes, I could reach inside the box and send my fingers shopping. From their shapes I could tell which were the cream or caramel-filled and which were the dreaded nut or fruit-filled.

Mom thought the box was pretty and decided to keep it in the hall closet near the stairway where it remained, forgotten, for the next six years.

Having reached the ripe old age of thirteen, many of my waking hours were involved with unraveling the mysteries of s-e-x. My friends and I had developed a curiosity about the females of our species. The "B" movies at the theater featuring heaving bosoms became a Saturday afternoon staple.

One of my pals came into possession of a magazine with lewd pictures of women in various stages of undress. The cheap, dog-eared pages were entrusted to me for safekeeping for some reason.

I smuggled it home after a frenzied hour of pawing through the pages in the neighbor's garage. I snuck it past my mother under my shirt and slipped upstairs to the hall closet. I looked around for a likely place with easy access to hide the forbidden fruit.

Mom's Valentine heart under a stack of boxes fit the bill nicely. I opened it, noting the lingering aroma of chocolate, slipped in the magazine, and returned it to its original position. I smiled at my cleverness.

I heard someone say that you leave childhood when you start keeping secrets from your parents. My secret remained hidden for many months.

One rainy Saturday afternoon my brother, two sisters, and I were inside with nothing to do, and were in the process of driving our mother crazy by teasing and tormenting each other.

She'd had enough and announced, "All right, since you all have so much energy, you can help me clean house."

It seemed like a good idea, and we pitched in. We dusted, picked up our toys, vacuumed, and polished the silver. During all the activity, I lost sight of my mother and found her, cleaning rag in hand, in the upstairs hall closet. Immediately my antennae were up. *Egad!* I thought.

I rushed to her side anxiously watching, contemplating my next move should she notice the red box.

I still had no ideas when with a wistful smile, she reached for the box. It was in her hands one moment and open the next.

In the movie *Psycho*, whenever a shocking scene is revealed to the audience, several violins repeatedly strike a single, strident high-pitched note in unison. The effect chillingly magnifies the intensity of the events on the screen.

I heard those violins as I watched my mother lift the lid and remove the tattered magazine. I made a desperate attempt to snatch the book from her hands.

"Aw, that's nothin', Mom," I said, reaching for the box.

She pushed my hands away. "This is yours?" she said in disbelief.

"Well, sorta…" I felt faint.

She began thumbing through the pages. I looked over her shoulder at the familiar faces leering from the photos. They seemed silly and stupid, not at all like the steamy sexpots they once were.

"Oh! Oh, my goodness!" she said, with each turn of a page.

Finally, she took the magazine in one hand, held it over my head, and said, "Just wait till I tell your father!"

Dad ran the criminal court in our house as judge, jury, and executioner. He seemed to have an aptitude for it. When it came to thinking up new and unusual punishments, his creativity knew no bounds. Most cases of a serious disciplinary nature were left until he arrived home at the end of the day. His usual beer or three prior to coming home did little to improve his mood, and he waited at the supper table like a hungry wolf for transgressors to be presented to court.

I was filled with dread as I contemplated my fate. Slowly, inevitably, the day wore on. When the aromas of supper filled the house, I knew he'd be home soon.

Late as usual, we started supper without him. I had no appetite and picked at my food until it was cold while my mother and I avoided each other's eyes.

One by one, everyone finished eating and left the table. I alone remained poking randomly at my food, as the Sword of Damocles hung overhead on a frayed thread.

At last, my father arrived for his supper. He saw me at the table and asked, "Well, what's your problem?"

He left the room to hang up his jacket, and I heard him talking with my mother. Although I couldn't make out the words, I had a good idea as to what she was saying. Court had convened. I hung my head and waited for the sword.

He came into the kitchen and stood by the table, magazine in hand, flipping the pages. He snorted once, walked to the trashcan, and dropped it in.

I glanced up for a quick peek.

"Well, well, looks like my little boy is growin' up," he said quietly, and took his place at the table, ate his supper, and never said another word.

That was it? From the man who'd practically invented the concept of grounding? Was this the man who once condemned me to a week of washing the supper dishes for breaking one lousy window? Hadn't he broken three wooden laths, one after the other, over my brother's behind for telling a lie? There had to be a catch. There had to be.

But there wasn't. No one ever mentioned it again, apparently slipping from the minds of my parents as an obscure blip in our family history, chalked up to adolescent curiosity.

*

I hope that if the time comes for such a moment with my children, I act with as much wisdom and generosity.

This is what I remember:

The heavy thud at the bottom of my bag told me it was an apple. The tiny eyeholes of my mask hadn't allowed me to see what the old woman was handing out, but I knew what it was immediately. It made sense now why most kids were avoiding this house. As a novice, I'd missed this very important clue. I was disappointed but mumbled a thank-you and moved back down the walk.

The cold October wind blew easily through the thin fabric of my cheap skeleton costume, but there was no time for retreat. My bag felt too light for that. I was spurred on by the many houses on our street with their lighted porches announcing, "Get your free treats here."

As an eight-year-old, it was my first solo foray into begging. I believed it was required to keep my mask on as I stumbled along the brick sidewalks in the dark. Moisture from my breath made it wet and soggy, adding to the discomfort. I'd scorned my mother's advice to wear a jacket, fearing it would cover my costume and deprive people the privilege of seeing it.

I spied a group of kids and decided to join them. There was comfort in numbers, as well as the advantage of shared knowledge to avoid mistakes like the apple lady.

As per Halloween protocol, our group boldly walked onto a porch and rang the doorbell. When a woman opened the door, we greeted her with a chorus of "trick-or-treat!" After the perfunctory exclamations of appreciation for our costumes, we took turns opening our bags to receive the treats.

My fellow beggars and I continued house to house, repeating the ritual. After I'd tripped, fallen, and skinned my knees on the sidewalk, I heard a boy's disdainful advice. "Why dontcha take your mask off between houses, dummy?" And so, I did. It made a world of difference. Another lesson learned in the art of Halloweening.

When we reached the hinterlands near the end of the street where the porch lights were dark, we turned to walk back up the other side. I could see groups of kids in the distance flitting about. I felt like I was truly part of something... something old, passed on through the generations.

My parents told us that during the Great Depression they were happy to receive a cookie, an apple, or an orange. My father remembered Halloween night mischief called "tricks," when the outhouses of the local curmudgeons were moved back from their foul pits. There were funny stories of people needing rescue from the filth after falling in during a midnight visit to the privy. It was common then for children to make a racket with noisemakers while making their rounds. The windows of unwelcoming houses were smeared with soap and their trash cans overturned. Ahh... those were the days.

When my bag felt sufficiently heavy, I returned home and dumped the loot into one of my mother's mixing bowls. There were reports of hidden dangers in the treats, prompting a careful inspection.

I gazed with satisfaction upon my treasures. Some of my favorites were there, as well as the unfamiliar. This was the only night of the year we were allowed to eat candy without restraint. I made a mental note to bring the less desirable items to school to be traded at recess. I was hoping to fob off treats containing nuts like Squirrels or Peanut M&Ms onto some sucker. It was an introduction to free market capitalism.

As I grew older and wiser, I learned to make Halloween plans to trick-or-treat with friends. It was when I learned of the secret bonanza at "the big green house."

My pal, Roger, did not have the adult supervision I enjoyed. Free to wander where and when he liked, he'd discovered the house the year before and agreed to take me. Apparently, it was a closely guarded secret and when asked for details, he cryptically said, "You'll see."

When we crossed the railroad tracks separating the east side from the west side of town, I became apprehensive. I'd always stuck to a familiar geographic area near home, and this was unexplored territory.

"How much farther, Roger?" I whined.

"You'll see," he repeated.

Just as I was about to turn back, he pointed to an old Victorian house on the corner. "Here it is!" he exclaimed. From a dim streetlight, I could see that it was in fact, pale green. All the windows were brightly lit and inviting, so I decided it was probably safe; after all, Roger had been there and lived to tell the tale.

We joined others gathering on the porch and rang the bell. A stooped, elderly woman holding a cane greeted us with a toothless smile. "Oh! Do come in, children." Immediate thoughts of the Hansel and Gretel story came to mind. *Maybe I should have dropped breadcrumbs or candy wrappers*, I thought.

"Just go on up the stairs," she said pointing with her cane to an ornately carved, well-worn stairway.

We creaked single file to the top of the stairs and entered a double doorway into a long, brightly lit room. On one side, sitting on rocking chairs and couches decorated with crocheted doilies, were several elderly ladies in old-fashioned dresses, smiling happily. A long wooden table in the center of the room immediately caught everyone's attention. On it was a smorgasbord of every kind of candy imaginable from overflowing bowls.

One of ladies directed us to walk around the table and take whatever we wished. The only requirement was that we had to walk past them so they could admire our costumes. They were an appreciative audience, pointing and clapping their hands with excitement. "Oh my! Look at that one!" said one. Another exclaimed, "Aren't you all just wonderful!"

It did feel a bit weird, but I was easily and cheaply bribed. They seemed to enjoy our Halloween parade and who were we to deprive some old ladies of happiness?

On the way back across the tracks, Roger said proudly, "See? I told ya."

The Halloween just before I turned thirteen, I decided I was too old for trick-or-treating. Inspired by my parents' stories of amusing Halloween mischief, two friends and I decided to pull pranks of our own that we could one day tell our own children.

We gave our parents vague plans of a Halloween party at a friend's house where we'd be bobbing for apples and what not. Under a streetlight, dressed in dark clothing, we conspired. The days of outhouses were long gone, so we settled upon soaping the windows of a few stores. The idea had infused us with a forbidden excitement previously unknown. We were bad boys of the mean streets.

Our first victim was a tool and die business where we went right to work rubbing soap on the reachable windows. Suddenly, a bright spotlight from a passing police car illuminated the area. "Run!" someone shouted, and run we did, down the narrow space between buildings to an alley where we hoped to lose them.

The police, anticipating our destination, sped to head us off.

I ran into a backyard. Instinctively, I knew I couldn't outrun the searchlight and lay flat in the shadows on the cool, dewy grass. It took all my willpower to lie still as the cruiser's powerful spotlight swept back and forth, hunting me. I thought of old war movies where GIs with blackened faces hid to avoid the enemy.

My two fellow mischief-makers were quickly spotted and apprehended. I watched as they were put into the back of the police cruiser and hauled away to an unknown fate.

That took the wind out of my sails for good, and I slunk off for the safety of home. So much for amusing stories of daring do... yet another Halloween lesson learned.

At school the next day, my fellow bad boys told me that the police had driven them home and escorted them to their doors. Their parents were not pleased in the least. In the language I believed boys of the streets used, I thanked them for not being "rats" and "squealin'" on me.

When my age disqualified me from further Halloween begging or mischief, I stayed home, safe and warm, to watch TV and hand out candy. The baton had been passed to a new generation.

*

Trick or treating taught me several useful things: 1) How to observe others and discern where the "apples" are in life; 2) How it was wiser to wear a warm jacket over a costume; 3) How to ration and barter perishable goods; 4) How some rewards are worth the extra effort; and 5) I wasn't cut out to be a bad boy.

A HONKY-TONK XMAS

This is what I remember:

"OK, pull the shades, Son," my father said, announcing the end of his workday. I was slouched in one of the waiting chairs of his barbershop, reading a Batman comic book. I stood, put the comic on the chair, and walked to the big storefront window facing the street. My brother and I alternated weeks cleaning the shop and this was my week.

On tiptoe, I tried but failed to reach the drawstring and climbed onto the radiator. As I pulled the shade over the steamy window, I looked out on the town's twinkling Christmas decorations. Each lamppost was trimmed with sparkling garlands and hung with giant candy canes, angels, or snowmen. The decorations suspended on wires over the streets danced and swung in the gusty winter wind. Plows had piled snow five feet high along the edges of the sidewalks, burying the parking meters up to their tiny windows. Fine snowflakes revealed themselves as they passed through the headlights of the few cars rushing down Main Street. I could faintly hear Christmas music from the strategically placed loudspeakers.

The sun had just set, draining the world of color; it was a small-town Christmas postcard in black, white, and sepia. The sudden rush of excitement from the impending Christmas welled in my chest and I smiled.

"What're you grinnin' about, Sunshine?" My father had noticed.

"Oh, nothing," I said, "just daydreaming, I guess."

"What's the weather gettin' to look like out there?" he asked.

I peeked around the shade. "The snow's comin' down even harder now," I reported. "Will we be able to go to Grandma's tonight for Christmas Eve?"

"Guess we'll have to see when I finish here and that's gonna be some time yet, it looks like," he said, gesturing to the waiting men.

I looked around the room and knew what he meant. Besides the customer in the barber chair, there were another half dozen. Most were farmers who'd put off getting haircuts until the last moment. They sat talking among themselves about crops, the weather, the prospects of the high school basketball team, and plans for the holidays. Some just sat in their striped overalls reading the newspaper or a magazine while little puddles of snow melted from their buckle overshoes. I sighed, seeing the extra cleaning I had to do when everyone was gone.

Thick cigarette smoke in the shop stung my eyes. It was always like this. After cleaning the mirrors, the cloth would be stale yellow from the smoke.

I resumed my seat only to rise again to answer a knock at the locked door. I opened it slightly and a young man shouted through the crack,

"Hey, Leo, it's me, Kenny Worth. Let me get a haircut, will ya? I gotta usher at Mass tomorrow morning and I look like a Shetland pony."

Dad nodded, but I could tell he wasn't pleased.

"Thanks, Leo, you're a real pal!" Ken said, stomping the snow from his boots. I took note of yet another dirty puddle on the mat in front of the door.

"Yeah, the more the merrier," Dad said flatly, as he took another drag from his cigarette and resumed working.

The man took *my* seat, crossed his legs, and picked up the evening paper.

The clippers whined in Dad's hand and the hair rolled down the barber cloth onto the floor. The shaving lather machine buzzed as he prepared to shave the neck of the customer sitting in the porcelain chair. He honed his razor on a leather strop, making a *whick, whick* sound.

The assembly line of customers moved inexorably as the clock slowly ticked deeper into Christmas Eve. Outside, the snow drifted higher as the hair piled deeper beneath the barber chair.

Dad chain-smoked cigarettes while he conversed simultaneously with everyone in the shop. Sometimes there was good-natured banter and joking; other times, there were heated arguments about an endless number of topics. Often the center of conversation was gossip about the latest scandal or who was seeing whom.

Eventually everyone was drawn into one debate or another. *Didn't they realize it was Christmas Eve?*

The newly installed pay phone in the corner rang. I answered it, "Barbershop." It was my mother. "When are you going to be finished there?" The impatience in her voice was clear.

"Just three more to go, Mom," I said, trying to sound upbeat.

Dad glared and said, "Tell her to hold her horses. We'll be there when we get there."

I relayed the message which she didn't take well. It was with her family we traditionally spent Christmas Eve.

"Next victim," Pop called as another customer donned his coat to leave. "Merry Christmas, Leo," he said and stepped out into the snowy night.

"Same to you, Les," Dad called after him. He slapped clumps of hair off the chair with a towel, preparing for the next head to shear.

I decided to get a jump on the cleanup and began the ritual of straightening the magazines, emptying the ashtrays, and sweeping the floor. I caught Dad's eye in the mirror over the back bar and saw him chuckle and shake his head at my haste. He lit another cigarette, inhaled deeply, and fired up his clipper. The smoke curled around him as the hair fell.

The man in the chair winced as the hurried clipper pulled his hair. "Dammit, Leo, watch it, will ya?" he complained.

"Tell you what," Dad growled, "next year, go find another barbershop on Christmas Eve." The man wisely shut his mouth.

When the last customer had left, he removed his smock, hung it on the back of the barber chair, and reached for his coat. "See you next door, Son," he said, glancing at his wristwatch. "I got time for a quick one."

A quick one meant a beer at the tavern across the street. It was never quick and never one.

I hurried along emptying the wastebaskets, scrubbing the sink, and mopping the floor. After a last look around, I turned off the lights and pulled the door shut behind me.

The night air was refreshingly cool and filled with snowflakes. *Three inches already*, I thought, *a white Christmas, for sure.*

The fresh snow crunched under my boots. The street was empty except for the cars parked in front of the tavern where neon beer signs assured it was still open for business.

I pushed the door open, entered the dimly lit interior, and heard the familiar clack of billiard balls and jukebox music. The bar smelled as always: stale beer, cigarettes, and the faint odor of urine.

The men seated at the bar looked up briefly as I walked in, except for Earl, the town drunk, who was passed out face down on the bar. Seeing it was only me they returned to their glasses and conversations. Earl didn't stir.

Dad motioned me over to his barstool. He was speaking with the bartender, gesturing as he spoke.

A middle-aged couple danced a two-step on the tiny dance floor near the Wurlitzer, their cowboy boots clomping time to a country western tune.

Suspended above the bar was a revolving beer advertisement, fashioned to resemble a giant pocket watch. One side pictured the Anheuser Busch Clydesdales, and the other an electric clock with roman numerals. I noted the time… six thirty.

I could see Dad was comfortably settled in, having had his first quick one and working on the second. He broke off his conversation long enough to order me a Pepsi and my favorite candy bar.

The cloying odor of cooking hamburgers from the small grill hung in the air. My stomach growled, but I kept my hunger to myself. I wasn't going to provide another excuse to delay getting home to Christmas.

Someone punched in Bobby Helms' *Jingle Bell Rock* on the Wurlitzer. I hated it. *What kind of Christmas song is that?* I thought. The tune fit this honky-tonk, Midwestern bar with its unpleasant smells and loud voices. *Don't these people have some place else to be?*

Boredom set in and I slid from the barstool and walked to the bowling machine. After sprinkling the alleyway with sawdust from a can, I dropped a quarter into the slot. The lights flashed and the bells clanged as the score reset to zero, but I didn't care what the score was. I just kept slamming the little metal disk against the back of the machine until it was over. How could I express my anger and disappointment with my father? I knew trying to hurry him would only make him dig in his heels. This was "his time" to relax after a long day and he'd made it very clear that no one was to infringe upon it.

Back at the bar, the talk had turned to the weather and speculation about the prospects for travel. Through the steamy front windows, I could see the snow blowing past the streetlights.

My heart sank, my mouth went dry, and I could feel the burn of tears… just for a moment. I bit the inside of my lip, and the feeling passed, leaving in its place a smoldering anger.

How could my father prefer the company of these people to his family? How could he choose to remain in this dim, stupid place when he might be at this moment… home? *Sure*, I fumed, *he deserves time to unwind from a long day of standing in one place with his arms in the air. But come on, enough is enough! This is Christmas, isn't it?*

I recalled Christmas Eves at Grandma's house full of aunts, uncles, and cousins, where the noise and confusion grew year by year.

The uncles sat on the living room couch joking and kidding each other. To relieve boredom, they'd find a likely nephew or niece with whom to amuse themselves. I'd learned to steer clear, as they often teased me until I blushed.

The fortress of brightly wrapped gifts beneath the Christmas tree was the focal point for us kids. After what seemed forever, the signal was given to pass out presents, and the noise level climbed to the decibel level of a rock concert.

Paper flew, flashbulbs popped, and cousins squealed as that year's treasures were revealed. The aunts frantically tried to keep track of who gave what to whom for the thankyou notes later. Everyone immediately opened their gifts… everyone that is, but Grandma.

She sat on her rocker like royalty as each package was laid at her feet or on her lap. The aunties, all seven of them, focused their attentions on her like drones around the queen bee.

When the din faded, she'd peek and wave over the stack of gifts while her daughters rushed forward to take pictures of her in the same pose, every year.

Then it was time to load the car for the perilous twenty-mile trip home. Iowa weather is not particularly pleasant during that time of year... if it ever is. Often the trip was made through storms, snow, or ice-glazed roads, our hearts pounding as my father cursed and muttered into the night. What a relief it was to arrive home at last and fall into bed to await the arrival of Santa Claus!

I was startled from my reverie by my father's hand on my shoulder.

"Ready to go, Son?" he asked.

My God! Did he have to ask?

Waving goodnight and wishing all a Merry Christmas, we zipped up our coats and buckled our boots to face the weather. Earl, weaving his way back from the men's room, waved his good wishes in our hazy and uncertain direction.

My mood was dark and somber. The smell of the tavern lingered on my clothing and hair while I sulked five steps behind as we walked to the car.

Silently, we brushed the snow from the car and scraped ice from the windows. Dad pumped the accelerator and turned the key. When the engine fired, he patted the dashboard. "Good ol' Ford. Good girl."

We backed out into the street and began making our way through the snow. The car fishtailed now and again, but he kept control. On we went, skidding and sliding around corners, over the railroad tracks, and on to Christmas.

I slunk lower in the seat with hunched shoulders, my hands stuffed deep into the pockets of my coat.

He saw the scowl on my face in the glow of the dashboard lights.

"What's eatin' you, then?"

"Nuthin'," I said briskly, "nuthin' at all." I looked out the side window at the blurred snowflakes.

"Guess you're pretty sore at me for not rushin' right home and takin' on those extra customers, huh?"

"Yeah," I blurted, as the dam burst. "Why, Dad? Why of all nights did you have to do this?" I didn't usually speak to my father in this manner, but I figured… what the hell, he'd asked for it.

He stiffened slightly and turned the wheel sharply to avoid a pothole.

"Well, I'll tell ya," he started. "First off, we need the money to pay for Christmas and the extra customers helps. Last, just how damned bad did you want to drive to your grandma's and back tonight?"

My silence was enough of an answer.

"Well, me either!" he said emphatically.

"If we'd a gone home right at quittin' time, your mother would a put her little foot down, and that's where we'd be right now. The thought of gettin' snowed in and spendin' Christmas Eve sleepin' on the floor of your grandma's house with my in-laws is not my idea of a good time. Puttin' my family at risk drivin' into a storm isn't something I care to do either."

I pushed myself up in the seat and turned to look at him in a new light.

"It's all in the timin', kid. It's all in the timin'." He winked at me as we turned safely into the driveway of our home.

*

We never made the trip to Grandma's. Mom was very displeased, and she let him know it. I think that she surely knew that driving in such weather was ill advised. If we'd come home two hours earlier there would have been indecision and strife. The pull of the heart to join family on a special occasion and the opposing tug of the realities of the situation would have been trouble. The real issue was my father's method of dealing with the conflict, and that was never truly resolved.

I remember the evening passing peacefully in serenity as we opened our gifts and enjoyed a quiet Christmas Eve in the bosom of our family. My parents sat on the couch in each other's arms watching us play with our new toys, while the wind swirled snow around the eaves.

Later, snuggled in our beds awaiting the arrival of St. Nick, I wondered: *Was my father a sly old dog who'd manipulated a situation to his advantage, a cowardly bully who'd ducked a confrontation, or something else altogether?*

I still don't know.

"Tell me why the stars do shine,
Tell me why the ivy twines,
Tell me why the sky's so blue,
And I will tell you why I love you."

I first heard this beautiful old love song around a summer campfire, sung in two-part harmony with my Aunt Jan's soprano and Aunt Jeanne's alto. Their voices seemed to thirteen-year-old me to rise with the smoke and join the Minnesota night stars. I'd never heard my aunts sing, but that night they sang as if their duet had been practiced till perfect. And it was… perfect.

This is what I remember:

At the end of a long day, we gathered at our campsite fire. Uncles Virgil and Emery nodded sleepily in their folding chairs, arising now and again to tend the fire. My brother and I sat nearby at a picnic table playing cards in the brilliant white light of a hissing Coleman gas lantern.

Later we'd be going to our tents to snuggle into our sleeping bags, but for now we listened to the low murmuring of the grown-ups and the singing. It was a song I would always remember for its simple beauty and lovely harmony.

The drive to Alexandria, Minnesota, from Iowa had taken several hours. Gary and I rode in the back of Jan and Virgil's station wagon on top of a pile of carefully packed camping gear and supplies. From the rear window, we could see Uncle's powerboat following along on its trailer. It was also loaded with necessities and covered with a brown canvas tarp.

Traveling close behind were Aunt Jean, Uncle Emery, and their sixteen-year-old daughter, Barbara.

The radio was tuned to a station out of Minneapolis carrying the Twins' baseball game. When the game was over, we listened to "Whoopie" John Wilfahrt's band endlessly playing the polkas for which it was famous. I dozed in the sun and dreamed of the fish I'd catch.

Our home for the week was a large State Park on the shores of Lake Carlos. Because we'd arrived on a weekend, our reserved campsite would not be available for two days. In the meantime, we had to set up in a less desirable location uncomfortably surrounded by other campers. No one was happy, but knew it was temporary. Still, there were too many people for much privacy. Making matters worse, it was peak mayfly mating season.

We learned from park rangers that for about two days each year, the flying insects emerged to mate, lay eggs, and die. Although harmless, they swarmed around lights and clung to every surface. They were a bit pesky,

147

requiring everyone to be mindful of open containers lest you get "bug flavoring."

Gary and I were frustrated, waiting to be "gone fishin'." There appeared to be no urgency to do so with the endless tasks that seemed to require the adults' attentions. Uncle Virgil left to secure a nearby place to beach and unload his boat while Uncle Emery busied himself rigging fishing poles, pitching tents, and getting firewood. The aunts, sensing our boredom, took us into Alexandria for groceries and a trip to the famous Runestone Museum.

I was fascinated by the little museum built to display a large hunk of rock found in a field by a Swedish immigrant farmer named Olaf Ohman. The stone was supposedly carved with ancient runes from Viking explorers in 1362. In addition, there were other artifacts like anchor stones, indicating visits centuries before Columbus.

The Vikings must have left directions for the thousands of Scandinavian farmers that later settled in much of Minnesota.

Near dusk, we were treated to an outdoor movie the rangers projected onto a large screen. We sat on the ground on blankets and watched the mayflies chase one another through the projector's beam. It was a warm, clear summer night with nothing to do but enjoy this simple pleasure with our fellow campers.

At the end of the weekend the crowds and most of the mayflies were gone. We moved to our new campsite under large oaks that was more secluded and nearer the lakeshore. A screened-in fish cleaning station that we hoped to be frequenting was a short trip up the hill.

After settling in, it was time to get down to business... fishing business.

The uncles got us up early to load gear into the boat. We cast off and made way for the edge of a reed bed scouted on a previous trip. Once Emery explained the technique and rules of trolling, we wet our lines. Uncle Virgil kept a cigar clamped in his teeth, a fishing pole in one hand, and the steering wheel in the other.

"Well, Gib Dean, are you happy now?" Uncle Emery asked, using my brother's nickname.

Gary nodded and grinned, making the uncles chuckle. Neither of them had sons and we were perfect substitutes.

By the time the sun was full up, I'd become more alert and felt the need for something livelier than the drone of the motor. I'm a fan of jokes and amusing anecdotes and possess a good memory for them, so I launched into my repertoire unasked. The uncles laughed and shook their heads, which of course only encouraged me.

"Well, looks like somebody's finally awake," Virgil observed.

"Hey, Uncle Virg, how can you tell the sex of a squirrel?" I asked.

"I don't know, but I'll bet anything you're gonna tell me." He sighed.

"You chase it up a tree and shake it. If it's a male, you'll hear his nuts rattle."

The groans told me that the joke hadn't landed.

"Why don't you tell that one to your Aunt Jan?" he suggested with a wry grin.

"I don't think so," I answered. My aunt didn't like that sort of thing.

"I didn't think so," he said.

It wasn't long before the fish started hitting and we were catching one northern pike after another. "Fish on!" we called when our lures were struck. Virg put the boat into neutral and everyone did their best to keep fishing lines out of the lucky fisherman's way.

Our stringer was quickly full of the slender fierce fish, and we put into shore. At the cleaning station, jealous fisherman came by to admire our catch and asked: "Where'd you go? What were you using?" Of course, being good sportsmen, we told them.

"Take a look at this!" Uncle Emery exclaimed, indicating a fish with his fillet knife.

After performing an autopsy on a large pike, he'd discovered the fish's stomach was full of mayflies. "Lucky for us, pikes never seem to know when to quit eating," he observed.

After lunch, the sun was hot and the cool lake inviting. Time to play...

It had already been decided that we were to learn how to water ski.

We motored out not far from shore and rigged the tow rope harness to the stern. Gary was first up to don his lifejacket and jump into the water. He put on his skis as Aunt Jan floated them to him one by one.

Uncle Virgil circled to bring him the tow rope and then on Gary's signal, he gave the boat full throttle, pulling him to the surface. I could see his proud happy grin at having gotten up on the very first attempt. As his confidence improved, he took his hand off the tow handle to wave and began showing off by jumping the boat's wake.

When he signaled that he was ready to quit, Virg slowed the boat, allowing him to sink back into the water.

It was my turn, and I felt the pressure of getting up on the first try.

I tried to relax as I bobbed in the water and let the rope slip through my hands until I had the handle. When I gave the go signal, I popped up like a cork, relieved not to have my kid brother show me up.

Virg swung the boat into a wide circle, letting me build speed from the centrifugal force. I could feel little jolts on my skis as they skimmed the choppy water. While maneuvering back into the smooth zone behind the boat, I lost my balance and pitched forward.

The world was a gushing geyser of lake water, rendering me unable to breathe or see. I faintly heard my aunt's voice above the sound of the rushing water: "LET GO OF THE ROPE!"

Oh... yeah. I'd forgotten to let go and turned myself into trolling bait. I coughed and spat out water and bits of lake weed, waiting to be picked up.

Gary was laughing. "Boy, are you stupid, or what?"

What could I say? Lesson learned... know when to let go.

Later that day, Barbara, Gary and I walked to a little swimming area on the beach and swam out to a diving raft. After a few dives off the rough-planked diving board, we lay on the raft in the warm sunshine to doze.

As evening set in we prepared for supper. We pushed picnic tables together and set out the utensils while Aunt Jeanne fried fresh fish in a black iron skillet. I was sure it was the best fish I'd ever eaten.

At dark, I heard a strange eerie sound coming from the nearby wetland... a constant high-pitched hum or whine like nothing I'd ever heard before.

"What the heck is that sound?" I asked.

"It's the sound of the mosquitoes," Emery explained. "They're the state bird of Minnesota, ya know." (Iowans love jokes about Minnesota and vice versa.)

It was stunning! *How many mosquitoes must it take to make a noise that loud*? I wondered. *Thousands? Millions? Trillions?* My next thought was how miserable you'd be if you were out there, unprotected. It made me shudder.

The day had exceeded my wildest dreams. I was exhausted and it was time for bed. There'd be fish to catch tomorrow and the tomorrow after that. I smiled to myself as I nestled into my sleeping bag, listening to my aunts' strong, sweet voices.

"By the light of the silvery moon,
I want to spoon, to my honey I'll croon love's tune,
Honeymoon keep a shining in June,
Your silvery beams, will bring love dreams,
We'll be cuddling soon,
By the silvery moon."

A REAL McCoy

My grandpa Agner Christiansen was a character. Note the omission of adjectives like exasperating, sensible, funny, inspirational, etc., because he was all those things and more. I prefer the word... character. It's not as limiting; descriptions that confine my grandfather would be a shame.

Like many at the turn of the last century, he was one of the "huddled masses" emigrating to the promised land of the United States of America, making his way via ship from Denmark to Ellis Island, NY. At twenty-one, he arrived with eighteen dollars US in his pocket and a few clothes in an old leather suitcase. After denouncing all Kings, Princes, and Potentates, he worked off his passage as a gardener for the wealthy owner of a wire factory in Palmer, Massachusetts. Lured by letters from Danish friends in Iowa, he made his way by train into our family's history.

Physical labor was the only way for a man with an eighth-grade education to make a living. It was backbreaking, bent over, sweat labor that seems so foreign and repugnant to many now.

Much of the Grade-A soil in the United States lies within Iowa. There weren't many rocks to move and few trees to fell, but there were plenty of marshes and sloughs that needed draining before meeting the plow. He found himself on the working end of a shovel, digging trenches for the tile that emptied into meandering dredge ditches.

After enlisting in the US Army in 1919, he was granted US citizenship. Fortunately, WWI ended, and he was discharged before being sent back to Europe to fight.

"Back in the old country," he told me, "I wanted to be a doctor, but it took money we didn't have. Better to work with your brains," he said tapping his forehead, "than your back."

He soon singled out my handsome grandmother who needed help raising two strapping sons from a previous marriage.

Denmark is a small country so Grandma's parents, both Danish immigrants, readily welcomed one from their homeland into the family. They were married and promptly had three children... one of them my father, Leo.

Grandpa had learned the butchering trade in his youth and called upon it to make ends meet during the Great Depression, traveling in a Model-T Ford to butcher animals for farmers. Money was scarce and he was often paid in barter with part of the beast. They joked how they ate everything from the "rooter to the tooter."

When there were no butchering jobs, he found work mixing mortar for masons, painting buildings, and any task that paid. My father and his brothers were kept busy cutting wood for the great black stove, doing odd jobs, or hunting small game.

Despite hard times, Gramps managed to educate his children through high school, fulfilling a pledge to "give my kids better than I had."

After the end of WWII and his sons returned safe and sound from Europe and the Pacific, I entered the picture. Gramps was very proud and excited with his firstborn grandchild.

My earliest memories of him are of a short, wiry man with a wide toothless grin (He seldom wore his "store-bought" teeth.) and two of the bluest eyes I've ever seen. Picking me up in his arms he'd say, "How's my Number One?" I also remember how he smelled: a mixture of perspiration, Old Spice aftershave, tobacco, and beer.

The old gent was very fond of his beer, finding every opportunity to run as much of it as possible through his kidneys, earning him a reputation as a live wire, and often making him present at closing time at the tavern.

A very outgoing person, he easily started conversations with strangers. Somehow, he was able to remember everybody's name, including what they did for a living, to whom they were married, and their children's names. He could not go anywhere without bumping into someone he knew, offering him the advantage of never having to drink alone.

Naturally, his carousing took a toll on the family, especially my grandmother, who was a teetotaler. She could deliver one of the most severe tongue-lashings allowable for a Christian woman. The scolding was kept for the next morning when it would be most effective. Inebriated, a scolding was a waste of time, but when delivered while nursing a rip-roaring hangover in the cold, sober light of day, it could bring any man to his knees begging forgiveness.

But my grandpa was not just any man, and he did not beg forgiveness. Instead, he sat at the table, propping his aching head with one hand, and stirring black coffee with the other. With drooped shoulders and a pained look on his swarthy face, he patiently bore his wife's Danish temper. Those were times when my brother and I made ourselves scarce.

Later, he'd retreat to the haven of his junkyard of a garage to paw through an amazing disarray of rusting tools strewn about on benches, in cardboard boxes, or hanging from nails. Here, at last in silence, he could take up some odd job that needed tending, having been put off for such occasions.

Early one spring well before WWII, he was working for the local electric company. Iowa in those days had much of its electricity supplied by a multitude of small hydroelectric dams. Our little town of Rutland had its own dam on the East Fork of the Des Moines River.

Along the top of the dam were wooden barriers allowing additional water to be stored above the dam as potential energy. During the spring thaw with the river at flood, the boards were pulled out to allow ice and debris to flow down the river.

A cable car suspended above the dam provided a moving work platform. Grandpa and another man were working in the late afternoon removing the waterlogged planked barriers. With a rope lifeline around his waist, the stubborn Dane wrestled an equally stubborn barrier. Suddenly, while heaving and pulling against the force of the bobbing ice and surging water, it came free, and the force of the water pulled him into the river. The ice severed his lifeline in an instant.

I can only imagine the numbing cold of a Northern Iowa river when the ice is just breaking up and the melting snow is pouring into the stream, creating a very swift current. He certainly didn't have time to think of the cold, as in a flash he was swept over the dam along with tons of ice, tree trunks, branches, fence posts, and whatnot, awash in the flood.

At the bottom of the dam, the water boils and whirls, throwing brown foam into the air. The loud roar of the water drowned out the other worker's shouts, leaving Grandpa's frantic coworker to pull himself along the steel cables back to the planthouse for help.

The alarm was sounded and soon the able-bodied men of town were afoot, lanterns in hand, searching the dark, swollen river for Grandpa. In the nearby town of Humboldt, the main feature in the movie theater was interrupted to ask for volunteers.

Back home, Grandma paced, rocked, and prayed. She wrung her hands and cried on the shoulders of neighbors gathered to await news. Secretly, they must have believed no one could survive that fall with pieces of ice the size of boxcars. They knew, too, the short time it took to die from exposure (hypothermia). So, the old widows rolled their eyes, sipped strong coffee, and knowingly shook their heads. The Lutheran minister arrived to lead them in prayers and the consumption of more coffee.

One of the men searching that night was stumbling and cursing his way along the muddy riverbank, wishing he were home with his family eating supper instead of looking for a dead man. "*Just another hour,*" he thought, "*and I'll call it quits. Someone has probably found his body by now anyway.*"

Then he heard a faint call. It was coming from the river; he was sure of it!

"Halloo," the rescuer called. "Is that you?"

"Yah, it's me, all right," answered my grandfather as he clung to a flooded island in the middle of the river.

In due time, they had him wrapped in blankets and delivered to his doorstep.

My grandmother was joyous! She cried tears of happiness and hugged her blue-lipped, shivering husband, returned from the dead. The old widows, a trifle disappointed perhaps, smiled bravely. There was always the chance of pneumonia....

My father and uncles stripped him and piled on quilts and blankets. Grandma fed him her hearty oxtail soup from a steaming white mug. But best of all, according to Grandpa's later accounts, was the stiff drink of good brandy, compliments of the town's mayor.

He reported to work the next day with only a few bruises to show for his ordeal.

This is what I remember:

During summer vacations, my brother and I often spent a couple of weeks with our grandparents.

There was milk fresh from the cow stored in an old crock, covered with a plate to keep off the flies. We were fascinated by the butterfat collecting on the surface. After it had separated enough, Grandma let us skim it off and turn it into butter with a small hand churn.

At breakfast she fed us thickly sliced bacon, fresh eggs, wheat toast dripping with honey, and tall glasses of that sweet, cool milk. With a wink, Grandma allowed us to pour a small amount of coffee into our milk to pretend we were grown-ups dawdling over breakfast before going to work.

Most days were spent running wild along the banks of the creek bordering their property. The fishing was good and there were wild grape vines to swing on, a raft to build, or a snapping turtle to tease.

I loved to accompany Grandpa on one of his steadier jobs. At that time, he was employed by a locker-plant in a nearby town. After securing permission from the owner, he allowed my brother and me to tag along and "go a butcherin'."

These days, folks go to the supermarket to buy their meat from a refrigerated counter with the various cuts neatly packaged in little trays and covered with clear plastic. Or they buy it from companies specializing in meats that are flash-frozen, to then be stored in the family freezer.

As most families back then couldn't afford freezers, a small, locked box was rented at a locker-plant to keep the meat frozen until needed.

Meat could be purchased from the plant, or customers could buy parts or an entire hog or steer from a farmer, then have the animal processed by the locker-plant. The owner charged a fee for processing, wrapping it in white paper, and keeping it frozen.

The slaughter area was behind the building with a large double door facing an alley. It was where farmers unloaded their doomed cargo into a chute leading to a small pen. The floors were concrete and the thick walls white. Hanging near the killing pen was an electric hoist with its scary, jangling chains and hooks.

On one such trip, we arrived around 8 a.m. with a full schedule. Grandpa laid out his bone saw and knives with their gleaming blades and worn, wooden handles. They were the only tools he kept spotless and rust free.

He propped his .22 rifle against a post, hung up his jacket, and walked to the pen to size up the day's work. He grunted displeasure at seeing a steer and two hogs standing in the holding pen, representing more work than he'd anticipated.

"Okay. Let's go," he said to Mr. Cook, the owner.

The steer was first. We chased it into the narrow killing pen and closed the door behind it. He picked up his rifle, chambered a round, and walked to face the animal. Cooing in a low soothing voice in Danish, he slowly raised the rifle.

I held my breath, anticipating the shot with my fingers stuck tightly in my ears. The loud, sharp *CRACK!* always took me by surprise, and I jumped every time. The steer immediately fell, and the side rails swung open allowing it to fall out onto the floor.

Whistling a little tune, Grandpa deftly slit the unconscious beast's throat at the carotid artery. The trick was to do this quickly before the heart stopped beating so every possible drop of blood was pumped out of the body.

I watched its dark, liquid-brown eyes glaze and fog as its life flowed into the floor drain. The old man saw my shocked face and smiled his toothless grin, "Don't worry, boy. He don't feel nuthin'. Your grandpa, he make sure of that," he said with a wink.

It's no exaggeration to say that people would come to watch the old man hide an animal. His knives became extensions of himself as he skillfully sliced off the thick skin. Care had to be taken to ensure the hide was not perforated nor the meat damaged. It seemed to me that the animal's hide was merely pulled away in his hands, leaving only the fat-encased carcass. I heard low murmurs of approval from those who'd come to watch a master.

The rest of the procedure was even more terrifyingly wonderful as Grandpa conducted an autopsy/magic show for us. "Look'a here, boys, this here's the heart." Then he sliced open the organ. "These are the four rooms of the heart... here, here, here, and here." He indicated each with the tip of his knife.

He took us on a tour of each animal's body, indicating pathology such as a piece of swallowed barbed wire ulcerating the stomach, or a parasite in the critter's gut.

Steam arose from the carcass as he stripped to his shirtsleeves, warming to the job.

One by one the animals fell before him.

In a small backroom, we paused to eat lunch that was packed by Grandma into his black tin lunchbox. I didn't think I could eat at first, but quickly changed my mind as we devoured thick, yellow-cheese sandwiches, beet pickles, and homemade bread smeared with apple butter.

"Most people, they don't want to know 'bout this part of makin' food," Grandpa said, taking a sip of coffee from his steel thermos. "The farmer, he raises them cows and hogs, feedin' and a waterin' 'em. The storeowner, he don't want to see nuthin' with its hide still on and the smaller the pieces the better. The wives? Why, they just want to feed their families. Shoot, they don't want to even think 'bout how that nice piece a meat got in their grocery carts.

"Now I figure, somebody's gotta do this dirty job, and I'm just glad there's somethin' in this ol' world that I'm real good at. Even the dirtiest job's gotta have somethin' to take pride in."

"You boys'll grow up to be educated men someday, and somebody like me will be doin' yer butcherin' for ya. But I want ya to remember that somethin' dies to feed ya, to put shoes on yer feet, and make a livin' for folks."

He leaned against the side of the double doors in the early afternoon sunlight for a smoke. I can still see his bowed, bandy legs arranged in that odd way he had with one leg cocked off at an angle and the other out straight to hold his weight. He puffed on a Pall Mall, holding it the European way between his thumb and index finger. The gray hair cropped close in the classic flattop of the 50s revealed ears too large for his head, and what a nose! No one in the family had one that size. It put Jimmy Durante's proboscis to shame.

He finished his smoke and crushed it out on his worn work shoe. "Time to pay the rent," he said, and laughed the laugh I wish I could hear just once more.

*

Agner Christiansen was not only a character, but he was a man *of* character. I love and miss him dearly.

TO CATCH A FISH

I'm not crazy about fishing. By that I mean, if there's a good chance that I'll catch fish and it's not too inconvenient, you may count me in. Then there's with whom you go fishing, the frequency of a catch, size of the fish, species, etc. I don't want to get too picky here, but these are all factors in the equation.

I have a friend, John, who fits the "with whom" factor nicely. He has a jon boat we... well...*I*, dubbed *John's Boat*. At the time of said dubbing, he grunted disparagingly and even though he was sitting behind me in the boat, I sensed an eye roll.

John's a good listener, I think, but there are times when I suspect he's only lost in private thoughts, waiting for me to finish rambling. His conversational contributions are usually short and to the point but much appreciated, as I become easily bored by listening to myself.

Generally, not having an outboard motor is a negative factor in the 'go fishing' or 'no go fishing' decision. The fact that John prefers to row, however, is a big plus. He believes rowing is good exercise, and I encourage this. With him on the oars, I have time for trolling. For those unfamiliar with trolling: it's dragging a fishing lure behind a moving boat in hopes of enticing a fish. It's probably one of the laziest ways to fish.

A bit of a wise guy, I thought it amusing when I pounded the side of the aluminum boat in a fast rhythm and shouted, "Ramming speed!" My attempt at humor was met with silence and a deadpan face. I preferred to believe that he hadn't seen the movie *Ben Hur,* when Charlton Heston's character is chained to an oar on a Roman war ship, rather than believe it wasn't funny. I could be wrong here.

One morning we were drifting along in John's boat, catching enough fish to keep my short attention span content, when I got the feeling that I was being watched. Looking around, I saw a field mouse near my feet, huddled next to a tacklebox. It was intently watching me with little beady eyes conveying extreme apprehension.

When not in use, the boat was kept upside down on shore resting on two-by-fours. It probably had seemed like an ideal mousey hangout, but little did it know that a cruise was in its future.

I was perfectly happy to share the space, but the little fellow thought better of the idea and began scrambling about looking for an exit. Supercharged with adrenaline, it jumped up onto the gunnel, briefly looked at the water, and abandoned ship.

I don't believe that mice are particularly known for their diving ability, but it managed a graceful belly flop. I gave it a 7 out of 10, losing points for form but gaining for commitment.

We watched as it paddled for the distant shore, leaving a tiny wake. We can't be sure if it made it, but in my opinion, he should have stayed onboard and maybe learned something new about the world.

This is what I remember:

I grew up fishing the rivers, creeks, and lakes of Iowa and Minnesota with my father and two uncles. They taught my brother and me the rudiments of fishing and then left it for us to figure out the finer points on our own. There was a long period of trial and error involving events that varied between life-threatening and pure stupidity. If our parents had known the risks we took to find ideal fishing spots, they'd never have allowed us to bait another hook.

One hot summer day comes to mind. My brother, a friend and I had commandeered an abandoned waterlogged raft. We'd found it upstream near the remains of a concrete wall, once part of a small hydroelectric dam in Rutland, Iowa. Some three feet wide, fifty feet long, and ten feet above the water, the wall ran parallel to the current and looked to us like an ideal fishing spot.

With some old boards, we managed to get the raft through the swift current out to the wall and tied up to a piece of rebar. Once on the wall and assuming a somewhat precarious perch on the downstream end, we commenced fishing.

It was lucky we never caught anything too large, as cranking a fish up ten feet allows ample time for failure. Around noon, the cement became too hot to stay, and we decided to return to shore.

By now the raft was completely awash and barely afloat, but having no choice, we climbed aboard with tackle boxes, fishing poles, and a stringer of catfish. As we cast off, we knew full well that the current was going to have its say. The boards we laughingly referred to as paddles turned out to be shockingly inefficient, and we were quickly swept down the tree-lined bank farther than calculated. Eventually we came to rest on a sandbar, allowing us to wade ashore.

It was a long, hot walk in the tall weeds, brush, and poplars. Did I mention the mosquitoes? Fortunately, we made it back in time to hear my grandmother blow her police whistle, calling us for lunch and proof of life. She was delighted with the not-so-fresh fish. We wisely omitted to say how they were caught, and she wisely never asked.

One spring my younger brother Gary and I decided to make some money selling nightcrawlers; we caught them by the dozens in the yard after a hard rain. Rumor had it they stayed healthy longer in refrigeration. So we put them into Folgers coffee cans with some dirt and moistened shredded newspaper, then stashed them in the back of the refrigerator.

After staking a hand-painted sign in the front yard that read: "Nite Crawlers for Sale 25c/doz," the Christiansen boys were in the bait business.

Things went well until a few worms escaped from a too hastily replaced lid. Alternate plans had to be made when Mom found them crawling around near the leftover meatloaf. We heard her scream as she pointed at the worms dangling from the shelves. "I want them out of my refrigerator, and I mean now!" It was clear that she did not care to entertain any promise of "we'll do better."

Once we'd found a large tank, lugged it into the root cellar, and filled it with bedding and worms, we were back in business. Everything was fine until the midsummer fishing lag when it's too hot for good fishing. Business fell off, as did our interest and attention, and we became daily regulars at the town's swimming pool.

Periodically, one of us remembered to add water to the tank to replenish moisture; however, there's a fine line between moist and wet. The worms finally gave up and drowned, resulting in a foul, fetid soup that emitted a horrific stench. When the odor reached the interior of the house, we were told something had to be done... NOW! Dad made it clear that he wouldn't be assisting in any way, except for supervision. The nasty chore was ours and ours alone.

When the outside cellar door was opened, the smell hit us like a ballpeen hammer, causing me to start gagging. Dad grinned, puffed his cigarette, and moved farther upwind.

We held our breaths and plunged down the wooden steps. Little by little, Gary and I pushed and tugged the tank of decaying worms across the floor and up the wooden steps. Between breaks to catch our breath and renew our courage, we eventually got the tank out of the worm tomb. As we hungrily gulped the fresh, early evening air, Dad flipped his cigarette butt into the garden and said, "Guess the bait shop's closed, huh, boys?" and left for supper.

*

When I think about it, it's nothing short of a miracle that I survived my childhood. Many, but not all, occasions when I could have been badly injured or worse seem to involve fishing. Now, older and wiser, I fish with a compatible companion from a small, dry boat wearing a life jacket and splashed with 30spf sunscreen.

If you live long enough, you're bound to learn a thing or two, such as when, where, and how to venture out with fishing pole in hand. After many decades of experiencing the highs and lows of angling, I can take it or leave it. It all depends on the equation.

A GOOD MOVE

This is what I remember:

I'm a small-town guy. I lived my first seven years in tiny Rutland, Iowa, a place where everybody knows everybody and not much happens. Keeping track of each other's business was a kind of entertainment in the days before television. The telephone party lines back then allowed for several households to access the same phone conversation, making it easy to snoop.

Until midway through second grade, I attended classes in the same sturdy, red-bricked schoolhouse used to educate my father, his brothers, and sister. Situated on the edge of town, there was plenty of open space for a playground, ball field, and to just run amok. In a town the size of Rutland, most everything was on the edge of town, or nearly so.

My great grandfather, the village blacksmith, had designed and constructed the school's merry-go-round out of metal rods and old thrashing machine parts. Generations of kids spun themselves to nausea on that clanking monstrosity.

Reminiscent of old country schools, our classrooms contained more than one grade, with each row or two of desks representing a grade. In my room there was kindergarten, first, and second grades. The teacher only had to move to the head of each row to address lessons for each grade level.

Above the blackboard, sandwiched between the pictures of Abraham Lincoln and George Washington, hung the US flag (48 stars then). Every morning, we stood with our hands over our hearts and pledged allegiance to the flag and to the republic for which it stands.

Things really changed after moving to Eagle Grove, a town large enough for two grade schools. The town was divided into East and West sides by sets of railroad tracks. We lived on the scruffy, blue-collar East side.

It was very different from my previous situation, as my new second-grade homeroom had thirty babyboomers crammed in there. Floundering in bewilderment and confusion, I quickly became a timid lost soul. For the next seven years, I eked out lackluster grades, excelling only in shyness and clumsy social skills. I came to accept the opinion of others that I was a failure and a loser. Despite this, a tiny stubborn spark inside of me said it wasn't true.

Change came again when we moved back to a smaller town for a fresh start. Dad bought the town's barbershop, and we took up residence in the spacious apartment above. The community of about three hundred was only a few miles from Rutland, where we'd originally begun. I, for one, couldn't leave fast enough for our new life. I'm not sure that my sister Lee

Ann and brother Gary felt the same about being uprooted, but the youngest, Kim, was able to start fresh in kindergarten in the Twin Rivers school system.

The schools were the result of the merger of three small communities: Bode, Livermore, and Ottosen. Centrally located Bode was selected for the high school while the other towns continued to educate kindergarten through eighth grades.

The town's business zone, all two blocks, was situated on both sides of a north-south main street with no need for a traffic light. Within the town limits were a high school, Lutheran Church, two taverns, two grocery stores, a laundromat, two gas stations, a pharmacy with a soda fountain, and Norwegians aplenty. A hardware store, jammed aisle upon aisle and ceiling to floor with every imaginable item, stood on the corner across the street from Dad's shop.

Next to the indispensable CO-OP grain elevator was a sprawling lumberyard. A locker plant, a creepy old hotel, a photography-developing studio, and a small movie theater rounded out the businesses.

Townspeople were proud of their little musty library operated by the local piano teacher who smiled benevolently from behind an oak desk. It was a place in which you could spend hours and accomplish absolutely nothing. That suited me fine. It was where I mined for lurid stories and forbidden words.

On Saturday nights things got busy when farmers and their families came to town. It was when they bought groceries, got haircuts, went to the movies, or lingered over coffee in the café catching up on gossip. On those nights, the sidewalks bustled with people going here and there or sitting on benches chatting with neighbors. To keep folks in town as long as possible, businesses chipped in for a weekly cash drawing.

Friday nights could be busy, too, when there was a football or basketball home game. Afterwards, everyone gathered at the café for a snack or in the tavern for a "beer and a bump." Whenever the team lost, the coaches underwent an unforgiving postmortem by high school alumni ex-jocks. Coaches wisely avoided downtown… win or lose.

The only church in town was the Evangelical Lutheran Church. One group of churchgoers not attending services on Sundays there were the Catholics who'd been turned away by the town fathers decades ago. The narrow-mindedness cost the community dearly, as they took their families and prosperity a few miles north and set up the little community of St. Joe around their church.

Gary and I delivered the evening newspaper, the Fort Dodge Messenger. He had half the town, and I had the other. It was a chance to get to know people and make a little pocket money. Most of the old widows tipped me with homemade cookies and Norwegian pastries instead of cash. Yes, I truly appreciated the goodies and the kindness, but really would have preferred the money. An added benefit was the fresh air and exercise as I walked my route each afternoon rain, snow, or shine.

I picked up odd jobs for farmers and local businesses. The CO-OP hired me to shovel grain in the storage bins at harvest and the lumberyard had me unload lumber from freight trains. There was always something to do, as Dad was only too happy to find work for us from the men getting haircuts.

In the summer I worked in the fields with my pals, sweating in the hot sun by day and cooling off in the gravel pit outside of town. There was camping with the Boy Scout troop and pheasant hunting with friends.

The high school offered glee clubs, marching band, football, basketball (girls and boys), track, baseball, and a full curriculum. Most of the students were farm kids who'd grown up together.

On my first day of classes as a sophomore, I learned that previous testing and grade point had divided our class in half. I was assigned to what was dubbed the "the stupid half." We were the kids thought unlikely to attend college, with a curriculum of shop class, home economics, typing, bookkeeping, and business math, while those on the college track took algebra, geometry, English literature, chemistry, and physics.

I was pleased to discover that most of my classmates were friendly and welcoming. The girls were curious about me and not as conceited and cliqued as I'd experienced. The boys with athletic prowess tended to pal around together, but I wasn't ostracized by any means.

The old building's cafeteria, locker rooms, and shop were in the basement level of the two-story school building. There was ample classroom space for all of us babyboomers.

What a difference! I quickly felt comfortable in the old building with my classmates and with the town itself.

I choked on a mouthful of water the day I looked up and saw my name on the first semester's honor roll posted above the water fountain.

My favorite class was biology. The teacher, also the football coach, was an even-tempered no-nonsense man. I liked him right away and guess he saw something in me when my fellow dimwits and I set about dissecting earthworms.

Previously, my only experience with them had been for fishing. These, however, had been preserved in formaldehyde, making them stiff and rubbery. After placing them into dissection trays, we went to work. Tissues were held out of the way with pins stuck into the tray's wax bottom. Using a dissection guide, I carefully made the skin incision to reveal the wonders beneath and was amazed to discover the complex structures in such a lowly creature. My interest piqued; I had no difficulty memorizing the names and functions of each structure.

Next was the microscope, where I experienced the same sense of wonder and discovery in the algae and spirogyra (not to be confused with the band by that name). I quickly learned microscope skills and it wasn't long before I was helping classmates. All this was quietly observed by the teacher.

I was in Dad's barbershop one afternoon when he came in for a haircut. It always made me nervous whenever my teachers were in the shop, but I stuck around to listen to their conversation. They talked about the football team's pros and cons, eventually getting around to me. I was sitting in a chair only a few feet away, pretending to read a magazine.

"How's my son doin', Coach?" Dad casually asked.

"I think he's doing very well. No problems that I can see," he said. He shifted slightly to cross his legs under the barber cloth. "I think they made a mistake, though."

Dad's eyebrows went up and he paused, clippers in midair. "How's that?"

"He's in the wrong group. He's too smart to be where he is now."

"First time I ever heard that one," Dad said with a smirk. "Now what?"

The coach shrugged, "I'll see about getting him reassigned. He's going to have to get caught up, though. He's a year behind in some subjects."

Now what, indeed? I thought.

Getting caught up meant taking Algebra with the freshmen class instead of business math, making me eligible for geometry and advanced Algebra. Later, I'd have to take chemistry, physics, and English literature. I soon realized that there was no more coasting for me, and it felt good.

I fought off my shyness and found how much I enjoyed talking to other kids. It was easy, as everyone seemed non-judgmental. I felt most at ease with the shy, not-so-popular kids because I recognized myself in them. They didn't know that I was a loser. It was a fresh start, and I could be whoever I wanted, so I decided to be a friendly, cheerful person. Within a year or two, everyone knew me and I them. Some of the younger kids sought me out for advice as I was a good listener, and I liked that.

That little spark had caught fire.

Three years after our arrival, I began the first day of my senior year when we met to elect class officers. This year was important, as the seniors always took a class trip somewhere, usually Chicago. We would have to decide where to go, how to get there, and raise money for the trip.

I was stunned when nominated for class president and even more so when elected. The surprises continued. As class president, I had a seat on the student council and at the first meeting, elected president. When the mixed glee club elected me president, I thought, *what the hell is going on?* I didn't like the spotlight.

The week before the homecoming football game that autumn, a schoolwide election selected three senior girls and three boys to be on the homecoming court. The top vote getters were inaugurated homecoming king and queen at a rally in the gym that evening, attended by the student body and community.

That afternoon, a kindly teacher took me aside. "I want you to be prepared for tonight's homecoming events."

"What are you talking about?" I asked her.

"I think you're on the court," she said in a whisper.

Oh, crap, I thought. *I don't want any of this.*

It was a good thing she'd given me the heads up, as later that day, I was notified that I should wear a suit and tie to the rally. I was on the court! Anxiety set it. *This can't be happening to me*, the loser whispered in my ear.

I sat on the gym stage that night in my church clothes with the other members of the homecoming court. The other two guys were varsity football players, one of them the team's captain and best all-around athlete of the school. He was the most likely to be the homecoming king and knew it. The three girls were attractive, intelligent, and popular. Then there was me... Who the hell was I? I knew who... I was an imposter. This had to be an embarrassing mistake, maybe even a joke.

Then came the moment... the homecoming king was me!

I became lightheaded, and my legs trembled. In a daze, I took my place center stage for pictures with the queen. She got a bouquet of roses, and I plastered on a stupid smile. It was just the beginning...

At the end of the week, the queen and I appeared seated in the back of a white Pontiac convertible in the homecoming parade on Main Street. I waved to the crowd lining the street like an idiot. I was sure that she was embarrassed to be with me and not the football hero. She was polite enough, but I didn't know what to say so we sat in embarrassing silence.

Later that night at halftime, we rode in the white convertible onto the football field and were introduced to the crowd. There was applause from the bleachers, so I figured it was my cue to give the queen an obligatory kiss. I guess I moved in on her too fast, taking her by surprise, and delivered a peck on her quickly turned cheek. I felt awkward and ridiculous. In retrospect, it all seems like much ado about nothing, but it certainly didn't feel that way then.

The rest of the year was a blur. We had our senior prom, senior breakfast, and held fundraisers to pay for the trip to St. Louis, Missouri. The trip turned out to be a blast and the last time we were all together just for fun. Then it was graduation, and we were set loose on an unsuspecting world.

*

You'll be surprised to learn where I attended my first two years of college... it was back to my old hometown of Eagle Grove. Yup. But things had changed... *I'd* changed, thanks to a good move.

Bode, the small town of three hundred people, some in desperate need of shearing, was eager to welcome my father as their barber. The retiring barber, with an already well-established business, had offered Dad the opportunity to buy him out. He'd done his apprenticeship there years before and knew the area well. We were eager for a much-needed fresh start.

This is what I remember:

At that time, Bode was a bustling hub of activity, drawing farmers and their families into town to shop and socialize. Downtown was especially busy on summer Saturday nights. The center of activity was the restaurant where a sizzling, juicy T-bone steak with mounds of French fries, a salad, green beans, and fresh bread washed down with endless cups of coffee could be had for five bucks. Your choice of homemade pie was extra, though.

Customers sipped their coffee as they caught up on the latest news. And how those Norwegian farmers loved their gossip! Being a rather taciturn lot and isolated on their farms with hours of endless toil, they were hungry for diversion.

Anyone looking for a discussion or an argument along with his haircut could find it at Dad's shop. There was no extra charge, and he was happy to oblige.

This was before every mother's son and daughter sixteen years or older had a car. There was no place else to go if you lived in the country, except *to* town or *downtown,* if you lived *in* town. The phonelines on Fridays hummed with the making and remaking of plans for the coming weekend.

Our new home was a three-bedroom apartment above the barbershop. I could watch the comings and goings from the windows overlooking Main Street. I knew when a family came to town, vital knowledge if they happened to have a comely daughter my age.

Armed with this information I arranged chance encounters with them, employing a nonchalance practiced in the bathroom mirror. "Oh, hi! Nice to see you. What brings you to town?" I used a surprised expression combined with what I hoped was a winning smile.

It wasn't all that effective, as my follow-up was never very good. I probably came off like a car salesman lurking around a showroom. Once I'd judged the Saturday night crowd to be at critical mass, I cut through Dad's shop and hit the street.

The movie theater was the center of attention for us kids. No matter what the plans were, they eventually included the movies. It was of no concern what the feature was; the important thing was to see and be seen.

The theater, located diagonally from us, was very different from any I'd experienced. It was built some thirty years before by a man apparently inspired by railroad boxcars. A vee-shaped marquee lined with light bulbs (half of which were burned out) jutted precariously out over the sidewalk.

The movie manager claimed that some of the marquee's letters were either broken or missing, forcing him to improvise. I was never certain if he was very clever or a bad speller. The results were often amusing. For example: JAMEZ BOND IN "DOKTER NO" or VIKTOR MANURE IN "SAMSON AND DELILA." How could I ever forget, "HUSH UP SWEET CHARLET"?

Letters long devoid of paint spelled out the theater's name, BODE. It wasn't long after we'd moved in that the marquee was accused, convicted, and sentenced to removal due to loss of structural integrity… a red-letter day for all.

The ticket booth in the lobby was roughly the size of a phone booth, where tickets were dispensed from a spool suspended on a nail. After buying a ticket, you walked four steps to the ticket taker who ripped your ticket in half and dropped the stub into a tall wooden box that held half of every ticket ever sold. They were layered in there like sediment at the bottom of an ancient seabed.

The candy counter was entirely hit or miss. You just never knew. Sometimes it was open and sometimes not. Popcorn available for ten cents a bag was popped in an antique, glass-cased machine with the stainless-steel popper burnished to a deep brown by the cooking oil. No one seemed to care, as it was eagerly eaten with no reported ill effects. The place reeked of stale popcorn, spilled soft drinks, and musty old wood. It wasn't a terribly unpleasant odor and after a while, hardly noticed.

From the curtain-draped theater doorway, it was about five paces up a slight incline to the seating area. From there the floor abruptly pitched in the other direction to the seats. The decline was so steep that small children and old folks had to lower themselves down the aisle by clutching the backs of seats to slow their descent. The climb to leave the theater required those with cardiac or respiratory problems to pause periodically and catch their breath or pop a nitroglycerin tablet.

A box of jawbreakers was routinely released from the back row and rolled in a miniature avalanche to the stage area in front of the patched movie screen. The ritual was passed from generation to generation of youngsters and no movie presentation was considered complete without it.

Some of the cracked, red-leather seat cushions had protruding springs and the seasoned moviegoer had to use caution with seat selection. The back of the theater was a kind of movie seat graveyard, where stacks of them awaited repairs that never came.

Unfortunately, the Bode Theater's projectionist, Clement, also doubled as the town's very own drunk. Learning the operations of the two projectors had been child's play for him; he was reputed at one time to have been in possession of a very nimble mind. But due to his brain's regular and prolonged soakings in alcohol, his capabilities often left him unexpectedly.

It was around this time when I developed a keen interest in the restaurant owner's fourteen-year-old daughter. Her twinkling blue-green eyes and sweet smile had attracted me soon after my arrival in town. I used any excuse to visit the restaurant to see her while she worked with her family. Her name reflected her personality... Joy.

The ease of our conversations removed much of the shyness I felt with most girls, and we quickly became friends.

The ticket seller job had recently fallen to her. This was good news to me, as most Saturday nights she worked waiting on tables and was too busy to talk. Selling tickets required forty minutes or so, then she stayed for the movie before returning to work. Theatergoers usually made a beeline to the restaurant after the show where she'd be needed.

One Saturday evening, from my perch above the street, I watched for her on her walk to the theater. When I saw her skipping along the sidewalk waving to friends, my heart skipped, too.

I was down the stairs in three jumps and out the door, plotting a course designed to intercept her half a block from the theater.

"Hi, Joy!" I said in faux surprise, applying my best country-boy smile.

She turned and gave me a smile of her own, throwing another log on the fire in my heart. "Hi! Didn't see you today. Where were you?"

"I had to finish collectin' money from my paper route this morning and by the time I finished, it was noon," I explained. "Are you workin' the ticket booth tonight?" I asked (as if I didn't know).

"Yeah! Are you going to the movie?" She brightened.

"Thought I might," I said, trying to appear careless.

"Maybe we could sit together after everyone's inside?" she asked and twinkled another smile.

I got lightheaded. "Sure! You bet! I'll save you a seat, okay?"

I tried to calm down by telling myself I was merely saving a seat for a friend, and that was all. But my brain wasn't listening. *Just a friend, ha! Who was I kidding?*

"See you later, then," she said.

I floated home and up the stairs for supper.

"What are you ginning at?" My mother noticed my sunny disposition, a sharp contrast to my usual adolescent brooding.

"He's got a date," teased my brother.

"I do not!" I protested too loudly and shot him a poisonous look.

"A date!" said my mother. "Who with?"

"C'mon," I said, "It's not a date. For the last time, I'm just saving a seat for Joy at the movie."

Mom suppressed a smile. "Hmmm... meeting a girl at the movie and agreeing to sit with her sounds kind of like a date to me."

"Waayne's gotta date! Waayne's gotta date!" sister Lee Ann teased. She was enjoying this.

I rolled my eyes and gave up, clearly outnumbered.

After supper, I spent fifteen minutes worrying over the new blemishes that seemed to have appeared on my face in the last hour. There were limited options available for boys to deal with this problem. Curiously, I hadn't cared that much how I looked until the past few weeks. *Oh, well*, I thought, *it's dark in the theater.*

Later, I crossed the street to the theater and approached Joy at the ticket counter. We smiled at each other, and as she slid the ticket to me our fingers touched briefly. I was electrified!

By arriving early, I was able to carefully select our seats and prepare to defend them against poachers. The choice seats were in the far back corner, and it was there I staked my claim, draping myself over two seats.

One of my buddies stopped to visit. "Hey, man, what's happening?" he asked.

"Oh, not much. How 'bout you?"

"Same old, same old," he answered. "Got anybody to sit with?" he asked nodding to the empty seat.

"Ah, well, a... yeah," I stammered, "sort a..."

"Anybody I know?"

"Well, ah... sort' a, it's sort' a... Joy."

"Joy? Hey, all right! Since when did you two become an item?"

This was exactly what I feared... the pressure of being an "item" at school. In this town, a single Saturday night together at a movie was enough to label us as a couple. I wasn't sure if I was ready for the commitment, and I wasn't sure if Joy felt the same way about me. What would she think?

The lights saved me when they dimmed for the movie, and everyone rushed to find their seats.

A very blurry image appeared on the screen. Garbled cartoon music stuttered and faded, then the screen went dark.

"C'mon, Clem, fix it!" shouted several kids.

"Focus!" others hollered.

A small window from the projectionist booth above us flew open. Clem stuck his grizzled head out and spit, "Shut up, you stupid brats!"

"Oh, great, Clem's pie-eyed for sure," I muttered.

There were sounds of empty cans and bottles being kicked across the floor, accompanied by muffled cursing and muttering.

In short order, a better-focused cartoon appeared. I was reasonably certain Clem rarely saw much in focus, and projecting movies must have represented a fair amount of guesswork.

By the time introduction music for the main feature had begun, I was nervous as a cat in a room full of rocking chairs.

Should I hold her hand? I wondered. *Should I put my arm around her and how would I get it there? What do I say? Should I buy her popcorn? Why was I so nervous?* I'd had plenty of conversations with her before this.

My hands were sweaty, and my heart thudded. What was worse, I had to pee and kept crossing my legs, first one way and then the other. What would happen if she came looking for me and I was off relieving myself?

Then I saw her enter the theater. When the entrance curtain parted, she was briefly backlit by the lobby lights as she tried to accustom her eyes to the darkness.

"Over here!" I hissed.

Joy turned with outstretched arms in a sleepwalker's pose and groped her way to my voice.

"Here she comes, Wayne. Here comes your sweetie pie." I heard my friend's stage whisper from the dark.

Heads turned and I heard snickering. Thankfully the darkness hid my blushing.

I stood and guided her to her seat.

"Hi," I whispered.

"Hi," she sighed as she settled in.

For a few moments we sat in the dark pretending to watch the movie, then she made the first move.

Reaching for my hand she closed mine in hers, entwining our fingers. I looked at her from the corner of my eye and swallowed. She smiled and gave my damp hand a gentle squeeze.

We remained like that for half an hour or more, enjoying the closeness as I tried to ignore my complaining bladder.

When Clem switched projectors at the change of a new reel it was rarely a smooth transition; this time, it was seamless. His rare triumph was marred by the fact that he'd mixed up the sequence, and we were being treated prematurely to the last reel. It was quickly discovered by the audience who immediately turned hostile.

"Hey, Clem, why dontcha have another beer?" and similar insults were slung his way. This was mild in comparison to the night when, unable to take the abuse any longer, he'd simply stormed out of the projection booth and took up residence in the tavern, where no amount of coaxing could persuade him to return.

After Clem corrected his error, we resumed handholding and squeezing. I'd managed a popcorn and bathroom run during the break and felt more on top of my game... whatever that was.

Handholding was entirely new to me, and I was thrilled with my progress. But it left me wondering what was next.

Once again, it was Joy to the rescue. Turning to me she pulled me close and whispered, "You're the sweetest boy I've ever met."

Well, that was a first, too.

She tipped her head back, closed her eyes, and parted her lips ever so slightly, ever so sweetly. I recognized the pose from the movies. She wanted me to kiss her!

Whoa! Moving a little fast here, aren't we? I thought. *Nah*, was the answer.

I leaned and planted the firm, dry kiss of a complete amateur on her waiting mouth. I noticed how her hair smelled like the French fries from the restaurant. It was only a little kiss and all I could muster on short notice. *Was she disappointed*? I wondered.

We sighed, resting our clasped hands on her soft thigh until the credits rolled into infinity at the top of the screen.

*

I suppose no one forgets their first case of puppy love. It springs up like fresh rye grass, full and strong, but fades as quickly. Not meant to last, it prepares the ground for longer-lasting growth. We eventually parted as we'd met... friends. She went her way, and I mine.

The Bode Theater is long gone, just another weedy empty lot among the wrack and ruin of my decaying adopted hometown. Almost all the businesses are closed now, as people have followed the jobs offered in the larger towns and cities... following opportunity. They've even closed the high school, the final nail in the coffin lid of a town quickly fading away.

Preserved in my memory, though, are all those places and people that still live on just as they were, like pressed flowers in a book. I think that I'll always remember that special time, and how I felt that night after the movie, waiting for sleep with thoughts full of Joy.

At unexpected times the smell of French fries still takes me back to the Bode Theater and my first kiss.

I had a very close relationship with work as a teenager. I knew how to find it, do it, and even enjoy it. Work was how I made money for the things I wanted and a way to socialize.

This is what I remember:

The group of pals I worked with most often somehow found a way to make time pass as pleasantly as possible. We sang songs, told jokes and stories, and teased each other. This is one of the songs we sang to the tune, *If You're Happy and You Know it:*

"My name is Johnny Small, f#*k'em all.
My name is Johnny Small, f#*k'em all.
My name is Johnny Small, and they say I only have one ball,
F#*k'em all, f#*k'em all, f#*k'em all.

They say I shot a man, f#*k'em all.
They say I shot a man, f#*k'em all.
They say I shot a man and now I'm gonna swing,
F#*k'em all, f#*k'em all, f#*k'em all.

Oh, yeah, I'm gonna swing, f#*k'em all.
Oh, yeah, I'm gonna swing, f#*k'em all.
Oh, yeah, I'm gonna swing from a f#*kin' piece of string,
F#*k'em all, f#*k'em all, f#*k'em all."

We sang this dirty little tune with gusto, safe in the middle of a soybean field. It was adopted immediately as our theme from the moment we'd first heard it; an easy tune with simple, forbidden lyrics none of us would ever dare to sing within earshot of an adult.

Our song told us we were a crew with whom to be reckoned. We thought of ourselves as rough guys, doing rough work that called for rough language. Having reached our mid-teens, we'd begun catching glimpses of approaching manhood and were trying out how we thought men spoke and acted.

Our bean crew was me, Gary, and three friends Jack, Smitty and Rick. We'd worked and hung around together on and off for years, even though we were in different grades at school. We worked in the fields from 7:00 a.m. to 5:00 p.m., six days a week for $1.25 an hour during the summer.

Jack, although not a scholar, was an excellent all-around athlete. His good looks and muscular physic made him very popular with the girls.

Smitty was everybody's friend, with a wonderful self-deprecating humor and a big goofy grin; he was an intellectual more than an athlete.

At odd times Smitty began stammering and the more he tried to stop, the worse it got. Mostly we ignored it, but sometimes just couldn't resist teasing him.

Rick knew what work was, but it didn't often make his acquaintance. It would be a mistake to call him plump... especially to his face. Despite a layer of fat, he was as strong as a bull and, fortunately, slow to anger.

In Iowa, corn is king, but a close second is the soybean. Growing the same crop year after year depletes the soil, so these two agricultural staples are rotated; beans one year then corn the next. The field we were working had been in corn last season, and corn spilled during the harvest had sprouted this year among the beans. Left to grow, the stalks would interfere with combines during harvest, and so they needed to be removed. Stout, tall weeds were also cut down for the same reason.

The summer sun turned our skin brown and the hoes we carried calloused our hands. To relieve boredom as we trudged up and down the long rows, we listened to the radio strapped to Jack's belt or sang our Johnny Small song.

"Are we done singin' that stupid song yet?" Jack our resident smartass asked. It was he who'd taught us the song.

Without waiting for an answer, he switched on his radio tuned to our favorite top 40 AM station. We worked steadily in time to the music, occasionally stepping in to help each other when someone's row was "dirty" with weeds and rogue corn.

The Four Seasons' hit song, *Working My Way Back to You Babe*, got us singing again. When it was over Gary asked, "Smitty, who ever told you that you could sing?"

Smitty stopped and leaned on his hoe, waiting for everyone to catch up. "Everybody's a critic." He shielded his eyes with his hand and said, "Hey, is... is...isn't that Marie John...John...Johnson's girls crew workin' across the road?" he asked. The stammer bug had bitten.

Rick squinted his eyes in the shimmering heat. His exceptional eyesight made him an excellent marksman and girl spotter.

"It's them, all right. Her crew has some of the best-lookin' girls in the county."

He needn't have reminded us. We were aware of who worked on Marie's crew. When Marie came home from college each summer, she organized an all-girl crew to earn money for tuition. Her crews were widely sought for their excellent work reputations.

Rick took off his hat and wiped his forehead on his arm. "It sure would be nice to see what they're wearin' or not wearin' on a hot day, wouldn't it?"

We stared into the late morning haze, contemplating the potential for a break in the boredom. It was nearly lunchtime, so why not?

Smitty smiled, "Wha... what are we waitin' for, guys? They'll just cover up as they get close to... tooo... to the road."

We stashed our hoes and ran to the dredge ditch that meandered through the fields. The ditch passed under a small bridge, and then cut into the field the girls were working. The steep banks were fifteen feet high, but the water only four feet deep this time of year. After skidding down the grassy slopes, we paused at the water's edge, and then followed the stream to the promised land. In the shade under a rattling metal bridge, we stopped to catch our breath. A few yards farther, Jack scrambled to the top of the ditch to get our bearings.

We could hear female voices drifting on the hot wind.

"Oh, shit, they're almost here!" Jack whispered. "You guys get your asses up here before it's too late!"

We crawled up the bank, lying on our bellies in the tall grass. The voices were clearer now.

"That Randy Moser," one said, "all he wants is to get in your pants!" There was laughter. "The last date we had, I let him touch my boob, you know, just to keep him interested. Well, that was a big mistake. I had to fight him off the rest of the night. I came home worn to a frazzle. I finally had to sock him in the balls just to let him know "no" meant *NO*!" More laughter...

"That's not what I heard, Sandy. I heard you let him go all the way," said another.

"Where'd you hear that from?" Sandy demanded.

"Peggy Miller told me at the A&W last week."

"Come on. Everyone knows Peggy's a bigmouthed liar."

The girls were passing directly in front of us, and we held our breaths disbelieving our luck. The girls had rolled their shorts high on their brown legs and slipped off blouses to skimpy bikini tops. A good tan was one of the benefits of an otherwise hot, dirty job. More bare skin could be seen at the swimming pool, but forbidden fruit is always sweeter. I glanced at Jack whose eyes seemed to bulge out of his head. He caught my eye and mouthed the words, "Holy shit!"

Once the girls had passed, we returned to our field the way we'd come, retrieved our hoes, and innocently walked the fence line to greet the girls emerging from their field. We met on the gravel road and stood near Rick's car. I noted that blouses had been donned and shorts rolled down, just as we'd anticipated.

Rick snickered and Smitty elbowed him sharply, "Don't be such an asshole!" he scolded in a harsh whisper.

"Hi, ya, girls," Smitty called, "wa... waaa... wanna have lunch with us?"

Marie looked at her crew and seeing several "why not" shrugs said, "Okay with us. We're goin' to the Jenson's place. It's their field we're working today."

The girls got into the back of Marie's pickup while we climbed into Rick's car and drove down the road, kicking up clouds of white dust.

Farmers' yards were cool, shady places for crews working in their fields. The Jenson's farm was no exception. A grove of pines lining the north and west sides of the buildings helped cut the winter wind and blowing snow.

We ate and talked, mostly about where we were going to cool off after work. The choices were: the local swimming pool or the nearby gravel pit with its cold spring water.

We refilled our thermoses at the water pump and chased each other around the farmyard in a rowdy water fight. The girls didn't participate, wisely choosing to remain spectators, but we were happy to play the clowns for their attention.

Jack suggested a game of touch football in the haymow, and I was surprised when some of the girls agreed. Four of the nine climbed the ladder with us to the hayloft.

In a short time, the game degenerated into a pig-pile on whoever was unfortunate enough to have the ball. I could see things were getting ugly and getting late, so I suggested we get back to work... a decision Jack did not support.

"Aw, c'mon, ya big party pooper," he said. But the girls quickly announced they were done, and we climbed back down.

As we prepared to leave, one of the girls, Becky, shyly stepped forward and asked sweetly, "Would you boys like something a little stronger than water? We got some beer left, but it's kinda warm." She smiled and flashed her hazel eyes.

"No problemo," Jack grinned confidently. "We like it that way." None of us had any more than a sip of our fathers' beer and had no idea of how we "liked our beer."

Becky handed him a clear bottle half full of a slightly foamy, amber liquid, then climbed into the back of the pickup.

Jack unscrewed the cap and tipped his head back for a swig. He pulled a face tinged with surprise. "What do you guys think? Is it Pabst or Bud?" he asked as he passed the bottle along. We each in turn took a sip. "It tastes like… like pi…piss!" Smitty exclaimed and spit it into the dirt.

The girls burst into laughter from the safety of their pickup as they rolled away. "You're right, boys!" Becky shouted. "That's exactly what it is! It's what you deserve for lying like snakes in the grass, spying on us. We saw you!"

Jack snatched the bottle and threw it in disgust at the departing truck, then we ran for the water pump to rinse our mouths. It wouldn't take long for news of this humiliation to be all over town. The girls would be sure of it. There'd be no rinsing the taste of that away.

"Suppose we had that coming," Gary mused.

"Bull f*#@ing shit!" Jack shouted. "That was way over the top. We're never gonna live this down!"

*

But we did live it down. Most things are forgotten eventually, and what happened years ago in a barnyard in Iowa doesn't amount to, well… a hill of beans.

During our lives, we must try to face our shortcomings and find the paths meant for us. Those summer afternoons laboring in the hot Iowa sun helped shape us into the men we'd become. We learned the value of hard work, friendship, and the wisdom of never, ever, sampling an un-identified liquid.

This is what I remember:

Yawning and stretching, I opened one eye to see if my brother Gary was stirring. Bright sunlight was already calling from the window, but he'd yet to hear it. Ready to roll over for another snooze, I remembered it was Saturday.

The realization that I had the whole day to spend as I wished pushed me to full awake. I threw back the covers, pulled on my Levi jeans, socks, (now on their third day of service) and a fresh T-shirt. My Flash Gordon wristwatch registered 7:52 a.m. and gave me the time on Mars, Jupiter, and several other locations of equal importance to a nine-year-old.

"Still got time," I whispered and bolted down the stairs, headed for a Saturday morning ritual.

The cabinet Motorola sat in a corner of the living room, its screen blank. The tiny crescent wrench, jerry-rigged and clamped to the broken channel selector, stuck out like a silver tooth.

A clatter of dishes in the sink told me my mother was about. "Mornin', Mom," I called.

"Good morning yourself," she answered. "You're up bright and early."

The TV blinked on, and the test pattern greeted me like an old friend. I didn't have long to look at the maze of lines as the program I'd been awaiting began... Superman!

I loved those magic words, committed to memory and recited like a prayer: *"Faster than a speeding bullet, more powerful than a locomotive, able to leap tall buildings in a single bound."* Each statement was accompanied by the appropriate sound effects and visual images. *"Look! Up in the sky! It's a bird. It's a plane. It's Superman! Yes, it's Superman who came to Earth with powers and abilities far beyond those of mortal men. Superman! Who can change the course of mighty rivers, bend steel in his bare hands. Superman! Who, disguised as Clark Kent, mild mannered reporter for a great metropolitan newspaper, fights a never-ending battle for Truth, Justice, and the American Way!"*

At this point Superman stood in the clouds with the Stars and Stripes billowing behind him. Dark cape flowing, fists on hips, he stared reassuringly into my eyes. For me, this was the best part of all. And how I believed!

The plots and acting, even to my unsophisticated taste, left something to be desired, but the intro was the dessert before the meal.

At the first commercial break, I noticed Gary had pulled up a pillow next to me on the floor, three feet from the TV screen. Our threadbare carpet needed pillows to be comfortable.

After *Superman* was *My Friend Flicka*, then *Fury* and *Sky King*. What a way to start the day! We ate our breakfasts bathed in the light of the cathode tube.

The morning breezed past. If only mornings at school went as quickly.

Mom announced it was time for dinner (Midwestern for lunch). I took my seat at the table and caught the aroma of baking cookies, the promise of a late afternoon snack. As I poured myself a glass of milk, I recognized the glass as one I'd won tossing nickels at the Wright County Fair. Mom had a weird collection of mismatched glassware, thanks to our efforts.

After a bowl of tomato soup and a peanut butter sandwich, we were out the screened door for the day's adventures.

With the high-pitched shriek that was the neighborhood call, I summonsed our buddies, the Torgerson boys, from across the street. Larry, the oldest, answered with his own whoop. He and his kid brother, Craig, were ready to go.

During the late 1950s, the country was in full gear after the upheaval of World War II. Most of our fathers and uncles had been in the war to one degree or other. We loved to listen to war stories told by these men who'd whipped Hitler and Tojo. We knew it had been a special time for our parents by the reverent way they talked about it, and the faraway look they got when telling stories of home front rationing or lonely vigils in foreign lands.

Movies on TV as well as those at our town's theater were often based upon some aspect of the war. I worshipped John Wayne. *"The Sands of Iwo Jima"* was my favorite.

My Dad had been a Navy Corpsman with the First Marine Division during the Battle of Okinawa. "War," my father said solemnly, "is hell, but if I ever have to go back, it's gotta be with the Marine Corps."

It was around this time that the country was stirred up over a world takeover by Soviet Union communists. My fifth-grade teacher told us there were actual "card-carrying members" of the communist party living in our town. The looming threat of a nuclear attack arriving without warning or pity to wipe out the Heartland of America was a frequent topic. It made sense that to destroy a nation, you must attack its ability to make war. And after all, who can have a war without food? We all believed that Iowa was high on the target list. Why waste a missile on New York City when they'd just starve?

My brother and I tried without success to convince Dad of the need to build a fallout shelter. He said that the thought of living for months in the root cellar had no appeal, and he'd rather take his chances in the living room or, better yet, the kitchen.

Nevertheless, I'd hidden some cans of soup, beans, and a few jars of water behind the gas meter... just in case.

Larry bounded into our yard. "Hi, guys," he said, "what're we gonna do today?"

He wore his dark brown hair swept back into a DA or "duck's ass" secured with enough Brylcream to lubricate a Sherman tank. Our friend's lopsided grin said it all: *"It's Saturday and I'm ready for anything."*

"Whaddya feel like doin', Larry?" I asked.

Larry kicked at the grass with his PF Flyers. "Aw, I don't care. You guys decide."

He rarely had an idea and usually left decisions to Gary and me. We knew this, having already made plans on the back porch. It was a ritual we observed to avoid hurt feelings.

"Let's go over to the Alamo and then take in a movie downtown," I suggested.

The two brothers nodded agreement, and we were off, cutting through neighbors' yards.

The "Alamo" was a concrete partition next to the railroad tracks, just a block from our house. The wall was adjacent to a grain storage bin. There were several vertical slots running part way down from the top, making it a perfect fort. The famous Texas battle had been re-enacted there many times, with each of us taking turns as Davy Crocket.

Today, the Alamo became the shelled-out ruins of a French farmhouse, sheltering us from German soldiers bent on the death of we brave and outnumbered American GIs.

We gathered dirt clods from the nearby field for hand grenades and found pieces of discarded lumber for rifles.

Each of us had our own characteristic gun-sound when "spraying the enemy with deadly accurate fire." Gary's and mine sounded, *"Tussh, tussh"* for the M1 rifle, and a rapid trilling of the tip of the tongue for a machine gun. Larry's was, *"Pow, pow, pow"* and Craig used the traditional but uninspired *"bang, bang."*

We hunkered down behind the wall as the battle raged around us. "Take that, you Nazi cowards," Gary screamed as he heaved a dirt clod over the wall. The "grenade" went off in an explosion clearly heard by all.

"There's too many of 'em, men!" I yelled above the noise of battle. "Let's take a few of 'em with us to hell!" (I was a big movie fan.)

Taking the cue, Larry threw himself onto the ground clutching his left shoulder and said, "I'm hit, boys!" Craig was living the drama. Reality blended with imagination for us, but for Craig, it was very real. He began to cry as he looked at his older brother lying on the ground, grimacing in feigned pain.

"Ah, fer Pete's sakes, Craig," Larry chided, "Quit bawlin'! You're gonna ruin everything."

"I wanna… go… home," Craig sniffed. It was vintage Craig.

"See? I'm not really hurt," Larry said as he stood and swung his arm. He looked hopeful.

Craig rubbed his eyes. "Don't (sniff) care (sniff)!"

France dissolved into a vacant lot on the edge of a small Iowa town. We felt it go. Still sobbing, Craig shuffled off for home with an embarrassed Larry following closely behind, doing big brother duty.

"Pick you up for the movie," I shouted. Larry turned and waved his okay.

I joined the Boy Scouts of America at twelve, becoming an Eagle Scout at sixteen. Each summer, our Scout Master, Arly, took our troop on a weeklong campout in the woods along a river north of town. A decorated veteran of the Korean War, we never tired of hearing stories about his experiences.

On one trip, we built a monkey bridge across the river out of rope and a thirty-foot signal tower constructed of small trees and baling twine. He encouraged us to have a good time but didn't tolerate misbehavior.

I was sharing a tent with three others roughly my age. We were amusing ourselves late in the night and had gotten a bit rowdy. Arly shouted for us to pipe down. We quieted for all of five minutes and then stupidly resumed. Suddenly, Arly appeared at the tent flap, flashlight in hand. "Out. Now!"

We surmised he was very unhappy and indeed, he was.

He selected a heavy log and had us run up and down the riverbank with it on our shoulders, then had us raise it overhead and shift it back and forth to each shoulder. We were grunting and puffing when he ordered us to do sit-ups holding the log against our chests.

"Had enough?" he asked as he lit his pipe.

"Yes, Arly," we said.

"Well, I don't think so," he said. "You still look noisy to me. Let's go!"

When he was finally satisfied, we stumbled off to bed. Lesson learned: don't piss-off Arly.

We played two games on camp outs that we loved.

On warm summer evenings shortly after dark, we stripped to our bathing suits and hid in the brush lining the river. Arly positioned himself a distance away armed with a powerful flashlight. On his command we crept silently down the slippery, muddy bank and slipped into the water. The goal was to swim as quietly as possible downstream and then creep back into the woods undetected. When he heard a sound, he'd switch on his flashlight and if the beam hit you, you were "dead" and eliminated.

In cooler weather, the game was moved to a sand pit at the edge of the woods where he climbed a tall dune to smoke his pipe while we stalked him. Again, if he heard a sound, the flashlight beam "killed" the stalker, and he left the game.

I learned to wait for clouds to obscure the moon, to lie in the shadows enduring the insects, and to move slowly and silently.

We loved the challenge, and Arly seemed to enjoy it, too. He was a good man, and his games taught useful lessons.

*

Five years later, I was stalking and being stalked in the rice paddies and jungles of Vietnam, but there we played for keeps. I was better prepared than most, thanks to Arly.

THE MUSIC IN ME

This is what I remember:

With hands trembling in anticipation, I tore open the cardboard box. Nestled inside was the object of my heart's desire, a Western style, flattop, acoustic guitar.

Visions of my meteoric rise to fame flashed through my overheated brain: the bright lights, the stage, the rabid fans, and, well... the girls. The possibilities were limitless, and I held the very instrument to make it all happen in my sweaty, sixteen-year-old hands. For a mere twenty-five dollars plus shipping, Montgomery Ward had delivered a new world. Included was a booklet of guitar chord diagrams with small dots indicating finger placement. It looked simple enough, but first I had to tune it.

Any guitarist will tell you that before electronic tuners, tuning was an endless and frustrating pursuit of an elusive perfection. I set about the task described in the booklet.

An hour later, I was ready to smash my heart's desire against the chest of drawers in the bedroom I shared with Gary. Perseverance paid off and I finally succeeded.

Next came the chords. I started with C, then F, and on to G.

The strings, made of various gauges of wire, had to be pressed against the thin metal ridges along the neck of the guitar called frets. Enough pressure had to be exerted to produce a clear sound. It took practice, but motivated by visions of the stage, I pressed on.

My fingers hurt from the abuse, becoming so tender I could barely button my shirt; I had to pause periodically to soak them in cold water. Eventually, I developed callouses and discovered just the right amount of pressure required.

The next challenge was to switch smoothly from chord to chord without looking. The endless repetition to create muscle memory never seemed to bore me.

Learning to use my right hand for strumming was less of a problem. At first, I used a plastic pick, but with time and advice from a friend, I learned how to produce various rhythms by picking with my thumb and fingers.

I bought a paperback book with music, chord diagrams, and words to old songs. The old familiar standards were easy enough; I was already familiar with their tempos and tunes. I sang along with my guitar and slowly began... to drive... my family... nuts.

Gary: "Oh, my God! How many times do I have to listen to *On Top of Old Smoky*?

Me: "Go somewhere else, then. I gotta practice."

Gary: "YOU go somewhere else. I live here, too, you fathead!"

Me: "Philistine!"

I didn't know what a Philistine was, but I'd heard it used once and thought it sounded badass. It worked, as he abruptly got up, showed me one of his fingers (the middle one, as I recall), and stomped out of the bedroom.

My mother got into the act, too.

Mom: "Since you got that guitar, you're hardly ever around. Maybe you should come out of your room to eat or say hello once and awhile?"

Me: "Mom, music *is* my food now. It feeds my soul."

Mom with eye roll: "Well, when your *soul* gets hungry, I expect you to be at supper with us. Your guitar isn't going anywhere."

Me singing: "On top of Old Smoookey. all covered with snow." *Strum. Strum. Strum.*

Dad took to calling me "Chet Atkins" as in, "Well, there goes ole Chet Atkins again." *Whoever that was?* He asked me to play solo for him. "So low I can't hear you." *Yuk. Yuk. Har. Har. Stick to barbering, Pop.*

My two younger sisters never said anything one way or the other, but I got the message when I heard the bedroom door slam.

In time my skills improved, and I branched out into folk music. The folk genre was quite popular in the mid 1960s, and I closely followed TV shows featuring folk singers to learn their styles. I watched with envy as the girls in the audience fawned over them.

My first gig was leading our local Lutheran church youth group in a singalong. The pastor had latched on to me, seeing a way to connect with kids my age. That first appearance in the church basement was my last, as I quickly blew through my entire repertoire. Not wishing to fatigue my audience with repetition, I stepped aside.

My Uncle Dave, who was only a few years older than me, played guitar. Whenever the family gathered, he'd bring it along to teach me a new lick or two. We spent half the time endlessly fiddling with the knobs tuning our guitars together. When playing solo, a guitar only needs to be in tune with itself, but it's an entirely different matter when playing with others.

Uncle Dave: "I think your G string's flat, there, nephew."

Me: "Nope. I think yours is sharp, Uncle."

And so on and so on…

I discovered others who were learning to play and eager to share. To save us the tedium of tuning, we demonstrated techniques and riffs on each other's guitars. In addition to guitar knowledge, I learned the chords and lyrics to some very naughty songs.

Inevitably, I moved on to rock and roll and bought music books with popular songs. The Beatles were at the top of the list, but I found their chord progressions challenging. The Monkees were much easier on my fingers.

I didn't have the money to buy records or albums, so I listened carefully to songs on the radio. The local Top 40 stations obliged me by playing the same songs over and over.

The idea of moving to an electric guitar occurred to me. Folk music was fading in popularity, and guys with a couple of guitars and a drum kit were forming groups and rocking out. Watching girls screaming their lungs out on TV for the Beatles continued to be a big inspiration.

That Christmas, I got a hollow body, dual pickup, electric guitar. My parents made the down payment, and I paid the balance. *Gee... thanks.*

In a few weeks I'd saved enough to buy a small amplifier, and I was cookin'! I was able to turn the amp up loud, having been banished to my father's barbershop after closing for the day. I liked the acoustics in the big room.

An electric guitar was a breeze compared to my acoustic, and there were many ways to vary the sound. Due to lack of motivation in my earlier years, I'd tried and failed miserably to play the cornet; I was determined to see this through.

One Sunday afternoon, I was in the barbershop plunking away on *The House of The Rising Sun* with the amp cranked up.

My brother and two friends heard me from the sidewalk and came in. Soon we were singing along to popular songs that I accompanied on guitar. We'd all sung together in high school glee clubs and were harmonizing nicely.

"Hey," I said, "we sound pretty good."

They all acknowledged that we indeed sounded "pretty good," and resolved to get together again soon.

At our next meeting, we learned that one of Gary's pals, Shultzy, had been playing drums for a couple of years, and I knew Tommy, a classmate, who played bass guitar. Craig had a great voice and had been in the All-State Choir. We found another classmate, Dale, who played keyboards, and my brother resolved to learn some guitar chords ASAP. Tommy and Craig had amplifiers, and after I bought two used microphones, we had the makings of a band.

On weekends we practiced in each other's garages that drew small gatherings of young kids curious to see what the racket was all about. An audience was an audience, even if the average age was only nine.

Midsummer, our town held a street festival. A stage was constructed on a side street, and word was that there'd be a cash prize for the winner of an amateur talent show. Naturally, we eagerly entered the contest.

We practiced three songs until we were confident enough to play them in public. It was to be our debut.

Disaster was narrowly avoided the day before the contest, when Shultzy came down with mononucleosis and couldn't play. My cousin,

Mike, was a professional drummer with a band that had done some recording; as he was between gigs, he consented to play with us.

It rained off and on the day of the event, ending just a few hours before the contest. The MC asked us to play something to attract a crowd. We obliged and were pleased to see it did the trick, as people quickly gathered. The song we played was one of the three we were to perform, which meant we'd already used up a full third of our play list. Naturally, we decided to repeat it for the contest.

When it was our turn to perform that evening, the MC channeled Ed Sullivan and announced, "Next up is the rock group, the Steppingstones... take it away, boys!" The group's name had been decided the day before by unanimous decision.

We had to be careful on the wet, slippery stage as we walked on with our instruments. It had turned cool, changing the tensions of the guitar strings, so there was a brief but frantic period of re-tuning.

I introduced the group one by one and announced our first song, *I'm Not Your Steppingstone* by the Monkees. My cousin counted out the tempo with his drumsticks and we were off and rocking.

We were thrilled to see the crowd bopping and clapping to the music... our music. I looked around for the adoring girls and saw a group standing in front of the stage. Unfortunately, they didn't look very adoring yet, but we still had time with two more songs to go.

Before the next number, Craig caught my eye, raised his eyebrows, and showed me that whenever he touched the microphone stand, the hair on his arms stood up. I gave him a wide-eyed look and mouthed the word, *WOW!* He shrugged and wisely sang with his hands shoved into his pockets to avoid electrocution.

When we finished, the crowd applauded wildly. We weren't sure if we should bow or what, so we just grinned like idiots. We were, by God, a band!

There was no doubt we'd have won the contest, but had to disqualify ourselves having used a professional, my cousin. It didn't matter, as we'd accomplished everything we wanted, and more.

The next goal was to learn more songs and become more polished.

Gary quickly learned rhythm guitar chords and I did what I could on lead. Craig banged on a tambourine doing his best Mick Jagger, while Tommy thumped away on the bass. Dale, our best musician by far, wowed us on the organ. We got better.

Our first paid gig was for a dance at the high school. We set up at the end of the gym and went to it. The time passed quickly… too quickly, and we realized that we'd run out of tunes well before the dance was over.

The problem was solved by surreptitiously having a couple of friends make requests to repeat songs, and we were able to stretch out the rest of the evening without complaint.

Next was a weird gig at a youth center in a nearby town. It went well enough, and we were paid in hot dogs and soft drinks. It really didn't matter, as it was just so much fun.

The time neared when school was to resume, and I had to start college. There would be no way for the Steppingstones to continue. When push came to shove, none of us could envision a career in rock and roll. Sure, we fantasized about it, but in the long run we were practical, Midwestern, small-town kids. It just wasn't in the cards.

For our final performance, we rented the American Legion Hall and charged admission. The audience paid at the door, and we sold soda pop to make extra money. We knew almost everyone anyway, and they were happy to help us out.

We played like real rock and rollers that night. Everything seemed effortless. The harmonies were crisp and tight, Dale's fingers flew across the keyboard, and Craig sang his heart out. Tommy filled the music with a solid base line and Shultzy was on fire, keeping us together, driving the beat for the dancers. It was strange feeling simultaneously sad and exalted.

Then it was over. We paid the Legion Club, split the money, packed up, and said goodbye. I never saw most of them again.

I brought my acoustic guitar with me to college and played during study breaks and after classes. Without other guitarists it was difficult to progress, but I kept at it, playing the old songs.

Mr. Boe, the music professor, recruited me to sing and play in a college folk music group performing for church groups, college singalongs, and nursing homes.

While in the Navy, I bought a nice flat top guitar in a Navy PX in Norfolk, Virginia. I kept it in my locker and took it with me on planes, buses, and trains. With my guitar, I always had a companion, especially when arriving alone for the first time at a new duty station. It was a great conversation starter, as invariably someone in the barracks played.

While serving as a Hospital Corpsman in Vietnam, my sergeant and I were passing by the open door of a bamboo hooch and were surprised to hear an electric guitar. When we peeked inside, there was a Vietnamese teenager strumming away on an old Fender guitar. There was no electricity, so he'd rigged up military field-radio batteries to power an amp.

I indicated that I'd like to play. He smiled, shrugged, and handed me his precious "ax." Soon, we were trading licks and communicating through the universal language of music. I thanked him profusely, he bowed politely, and we went on our ways.

After marriage, I continued to pick out chords and tunes from our favorite albums, but over time, the duties of work and family left my old guitar gathering dust and rust. Eventually, the neck warped and that was that.

*

I don't consider myself a musician any more than a kazoo player, but I still enjoy listening. Having some knowledge as to how music is made only adds to my appreciation.

Music was and always will be an important part of my life. Many of my best memories are associated with the music of the time. I can often identify the year an old tune was popular by remembering where and when I'd heard it for the first time. Go ahead... just ask me, because I got the music in me.

Newly married and fresh out of the Navy, my wife and I were visiting my parents in my hometown during a break in college classes. A trifle bored, I decided to take a stroll around town. The stroll didn't take long in a town of around three hundred people. My brother and I once had paper routes, he with half the town and I the other.

On my walk I discovered a weed-covered baseball diamond now home to an assortment of old farm machinery waiting for someone to decide what to do with it.

I found an old friend rusting away among the nettles, milkweeds, and cockleburs. It was the corn sheller once owned and operated by Big Mel Bratland. It had sustained him financially for over three decades and was dear enough to his heart for him to name it. The chipped and faded name was barely readable... Shelly.

It was a massive, hulking machine that clanked and whirred loudly as it separated the kernels from the cobs of countless ears of field corn. A gasoline engine belching black smoke from the back of a beat-up truck powered the monstrosity. Arranged on each side were racks carrying sections of the drag.

A drag is a metal chute assembled to the length required for the task. At the bottom of each trough-like section was a series of horizontal blades that conveyed corn to Shelly's hungry maw. Our job was to keep the drag filled to keep her fed.

Corncribs and shellers have been made obsolete by the invention of the picker-sheller. As the name implies, the implement simultaneously picks and shells the corn saving the extra step and expense of shelling later. At harvest, the kernels are augured into a wagon and stored in bins.

It's important for the corn to stay dry to prevent rot. Every load of corn brought to market at the local CO-OP has its moisture content measured. The drier the corn, the higher the price and vice versa.

Corncribs before modern pickers were designed to store and protect the ears of corn from weather until the market price was right. There were many variations and I've been on the end of a shovel in many.

The round-type were enclosed in heavy gauge wire and covered with a metal roof. The drag slid into a slot in the concrete floor covered with boards that were removed one by one as the corn above was cleared.

A cheaper, more common type was a long, narrow structure made of two-by-fours and wire. A roof kept out the weather while the wire walls provided ventilation. Hinged panels along the bottom of one side allowed the corn to be shoveled into the drag. The sheller was parked at one end, and we as we worked our way toward it.

You can still see those old corncribs standing lonely and empty on farms across Iowa. Why tear down a perfectly good structure I suppose, even if useless?

This is what I remember:

One Saturday morning in late spring Jackie Harlan, Rick Torgerson, and I were hired to clean out a long, wire crib at Ole Sorenson's place. Like all good farmers, Ole had been monitoring the market reports on the radio and decided it was high time to make some money and sell his crop from last fall.

Mel parked Shelly at the end of the crib and set up. As part of the service, he parked one of his trucks alongside to collect and haul the shelled corn to town. He swung one chute over the truck and the other over an open area for the soon-to-come cob pile for the farmer to use later for bedding in his animal pens.

Once the drag was in place along the crib, he fired up Shelly, making enough noise for us to shout to be heard.

When Ole swung open the first panel, a golden river of corn flowed out into the conveyor, pretty as you please. Initially, we raked the corn out with wooden-handled rakes with long metal tines or prongs bent at ninety degrees like a hoe. The tines were intentionally blunt to avoid impaling the corn.

In due time we cleaned out an area large enough for us to crawl up inside. We were old hands at this, and for a time, all we needed to do was kick or poke the mound of corn to create little avalanches that rolled neatly into the drag. This technique worked well most of the time, but occasionally, we worked a crib in which the corn had been harvested in the rain or snow. The result was corn packed hard enough to require a pickax to break up. This was thankfully not the case that day.

Eventually, we grabbed shovels and started scooping. This is what Ole was paying us for: bent-over work where, as he said, "All I wanna see are your asses and elbows."

We took a break when Mel brought the first load into town. When he returned, he got Shelly running and it was back to work.

Around the halfway point, things started to go south. A family of rats had discovered Nirvana and built themselves a home constructed entirely out of food. The location was perfect, being dry and surrounded with eats everywhere.

When Rick stuck his shovel into their happy home, it was bedlam, as rats began hightailing it in every direction. One panic-stricken member of the *Ratus ratus* family mistook Rick's open pant leg for an exit and scrambled in and up.

He grabbed his leg mid-calf screaming, "It's in my pants! It's in my pants!" And began stomping his foot and hopping around like a cornered jackrabbit.

Well, of course, we found this hysterically funny and were doubled over with laughter. Jackie wiped the tears from his eyes and shouted unneeded advice. "Don't let it get any higher, Rick!"

Rick, who had no intention whatsoever of letting it travel any farther north, was furiously punched at his leg. The rat finally gave up, ran back down onto his boots, and scurried off. After Jackie intercepted and dispatched it with his shovel, it was so much for the rat.

Rick was deeply embarrassed and wanted revenge, so he scooped up the now flat rodent and tossed it into the drag. Everyone, including Mel, stopped to see what Shelly was going to do with the deceased. Was it going to the corn or the cobs? It was the latter as it turned out. Shelly had come through with the correct decision. Mel grinned, shook his head, and Ole reminded us that time was wasting.

After the hilarity had settled, we found twine to tie off the bottoms of our pantlegs. There was no sense repeating Rick's experience. It was probably unnecessary as during the excitement, the other rats had escaped for parts unknown. Maybe the little fella had sacrificed himself for the good of his family? Who can say?

By noon we were cleaning up, as Mel packed up the drag and greased Shelly's gears for the next job. We handed Ole his tools, collected our pay, and drove for town in Dad's Ford station wagon. During the ride, Rick looked each of us firmly in the eye, shook his fist, and said, "Don't you guys EVER repeat this story. EVER!"

*

I never did until just now.

ROAD HUNT

Many of my friends went pheasant hunting. It was a good excuse to get together and do something out of the ordinary. Almost all activities were centered around the high school, so it was same old, same old. Loitering in the only restaurant in town got old fast and cost money, too. There was always farm work, but let's face it, there aren't a lot of yuks in scooping chicken poop or bailing hay. When we got our driver's licenses, a trip to a larger town offered more opportunities, but again, cost money.

Funny thing, we didn't watch TV at each other's houses, and computer games hadn't been invented yet. The only time I remember hanging around someone's house was when they had a pretty sister or if a good-looking cousin was visiting.

Pheasant hunting season is during the cold, snowy months from late October to early January. We looked forward to it each year, making plans for opening day, weeks in advance. Where to go, with whom, and who'd drive were important considerations. We certainly didn't trust those of questionable judgement near us with loaded shotguns. It wasn't a game, after all.

Several of our friends were farm kids, giving us the advantage of knowing where to hunt. Harvest time allowed farmers the opportunity to know where the pheasants were gathered. Farmers were very selective as to whom they allowed to hunt on their property. It wouldn't do for some knucklehead town kid to shoot one of their cows, break down a fence, or leave a gate open. An invitation to hunt on a farm was indeed an honor and a trust not to be squandered.

Gary and I hunted together as we trusted and looked out for each other. Both of us were carefully instructed by our uncles as to the use of firearms and had taken the NRA firearms safety course.

One Christmas, our uncles gave us joint ownership of a JC Higgins, 20 Ga., shotgun. We also had the use of Dad's single shot .410. The two of us worked out a system to decide who'd use which gun to avoid quarrels. Gary was a better shot with a shotgun than I while the rifle was my forte, but of no use for hunting pheasant.

Dad got his .410 shotgun as a youngster and hunted during the Great Depression when wild game made a welcomed cheap meal. He told us about a time when he went hunting with friends

190

on a bitter cold winter's day. While in the car scouting for a likely place to hunt, they saw a group of pheasants huddled in a ditch. They were puzzled when the birds didn't fly off and discovered they were frozen into immobility. Happy to have stumbled upon a pheasant bonanza, they picked up the half dozen birds and put them in the trunk of the car. When they returned to town and opened the trunk, they were stunned when the birds, now thawed, immediately flew to safety.

Pheasants glean the fields looking for corn spilled or missed during harvest. In addition, the bent and broken stalks offer protection and cover from predators like us. Their multicolored plumage allows them to blend in with their surroundings. They are so well hidden they could be underfoot before taking wing. The sudden explosion of a pheasant launching into the air gives hunters an exciting burst of adrenaline, so you must be alert.

Declines in the pheasant populations have been attributed to more efficient machinery. The new harvesters shell the corn from the cob, chop the cornstalks into small pieces, and spread it back on the ground. Consequently, there's not much of anything left for them to eat on a picked field. The return of coyotes to the area hasn't helped matters much either. Our area was fortunate to have a stable, abundant, ring-necked pheasant population making it a popular one for hunting.

We rural folks didn't take well to people from other towns hunting in our county, especially if they were Des Moines city slickers. A car with Polk County license plates was usually from Des Moines and never allowed on a farmer's field. We looked upon them with distain in their fancy hunting vests, expensive shotguns, and big city disrespectful ways. They didn't come up our way often but when they did, a BOLO was quickly sent... WARNING! DES MOINES HUNTERS SEEN!

An interesting note about pheasants: the smarter ones learn about hunters. Early in the season, they wait until you were near them before taking flight; later, they learn to lay low and sneak off to a safe distance before flying. I know it sounds incredible, but I saw it year after year.

Those with hunting dogs certainly have an advantage. A well-trained dog walks slightly ahead of its master, working back and forth, sniffing out birds. When detected, they hold their position with noses pointing to the prey. None of us had hunting dogs. The dogs we owned were the kind that lie around the house all day looking for belly rubs and handouts.

We did not hunt in groups larger than four or five, as big groups are hard to manage and tend to be loud and disorganized, inviting chaos. For safety, each hunter had to clearly know their zone of fire while walking abreast in a straight line. Birds could only be shot in the area directly in front or behind you. The rules protected those next to you from injury or shooting a bird that was someone else's to take.

Gary and I often hunted with friends, Jack, Rick, and Smitty. Rick was the son of a farmer and the rest of us were townies. His family had friendly neighbors that extended hunting privileges to their farms as well. Most often, I just went by myself after school along the railroad tracks to enjoy the solitude, fresh air, and exercise.

This is what I remember:

When a heavy December snow gave us a rare day off from school. Rick had chores to do so the rest of us decided to go road hunting. The snow was too deep for walking, so we drove the snow-packed country roads looking for pheasants sheltering in the weedy ditches. Dad let us take his '55 Ford station wagon that had seen better days.

The car burned oil like mad, so we carried extra oilcans in the space behind the backseat. The driver's door wouldn't stay closed but only a problem when making a left turn and it flew open. I'd grown accustomed to grabbing it by the door handle to pull it back before it swung out too far. Fortunately, the radio worked just fine, which was critical to teenagers.

We'd bagged a couple of birds, and I started to grouse about having to drive, so Smitty volunteered, and I moved to the backseat. When he stupidly gunned the motor to intentionally fishtail the car on packed snow, he lost control and put us in the ditch. The car's front end stayed up on the shoulder with the rearend at the bottom of a very steep, snowy slope.

I didn't say anything to Smitty about his stupidity, as he looked so pathetically sad and guilty; besides, I was the only one who was supposed to be driving. It was on me.

I was thankful there wasn't any damage, but we still had to get out of the ditch.

There was a farmhouse across the road, and I set off for it. As I neared, a kennel of beagles near the barn set up a real racket. *AROO! AROO!* I thought, *Wow*! *This place sure doesn't need an alarm system.*

I knocked on the front door and was greeted by a big, tall man with a long, full, dark beard, dressed in insulated overalls and stockinged feet.

"What can I do fer ya?"

192

I told him then he had me remain on the porch while he got his hat, coat, and boots. I climbed up behind him on his Farmall tractor and we rode back down the lane to the car.

He never asked how we came to be in the ditch. Instead, after assessing the situation, he quickly hooked a chain to his tractor and pulled us out in no time. I thanked him profusely offering to pay, but he refused. "Glad to help," was all he said. I looked for his name on the mailbox and read, Jack Thorn.

When we returned home safe and sound, I parked the car in the garage and promptly went into Dad's barbershop. "I'd better get this over with," I told my brother. Direct lies or those of omission were not appreciated by our father.

I told him about our ordeal leaving out the fact that I wasn't driving. (Yes, I know... an omission.). When I mentioned who'd helped us, he laughed and said, "I know the Thorns very well. I grew up with them in Rutland. Jack's a good customer." Then he added, "He raises huntin' dogs, ya know."

It may sound strange, but the four of us had a great time that day. Because I'd been honest (well... mostly) about ditching the car, we were able to joke openly about it for days. Even Dad thought it amusing. I'm sure he mentioned it when Mr. Thorn came in for a haircut, so it was a good thing I'd already confessed.

*

Covering your tracks is always worse than just admitting that you've made a mistake or had a momentary lapse of judgement. Some politicians never seem to have learned that.

As the oldest child, I blazed trails through uncharted territory on the way to adulthood. My parents initially encouraged me to reach life's milestones, but as I grew older other rites of passage were met with resistance. For example: learning to walk, talk, and potty-training are landmark achievements in every child's life. These are the events recorded in baby books and grounds for boasting. But dating, rock and roll, and learning to drive was another matter. I had to fight my parents for the advances my brother and sisters later took for granted.

On the other hand, parents better remember the firstborn's firsts better than of those arriving later. Just ask my mother when I walked or talked, and she'll tell you without hesitation. Now ask her about my siblings and you'll get a blank stare.

Iowa is practical about when you're allowed to drive. Farmers teach their children to operate a tractor as soon as they can reach the pedals. An extra hand can make the difference between getting a crop in before bad weather, literally making the difference between success and disaster. The miles and miles of lightly traveled roads in rural Iowa make driving a less harrowing experience than, say, cruising on an LA freeway.

As early as fourteen, Iowans may get a driver learner's permit. Over the next two years, the fledgling must drive with a licensed adult seated next to them and maintain a clean driving record.

Getting a driver's license was one of the most salient events in our lives, representing freedom and opportunity. The entire forbidden world suddenly became available. But for parents, it represented the first sign of a chick preparing to leave the nest ushering in higher insurance premiums, increased car maintenance, and the further proliferation of grey hair.

I studied hard for my learner's permit from the booklet published by the Iowa Department of Transportation. I knew by heart how many feet one must signal before turning, how to read the lines painted on roads, and the speed limits in various areas of town. The numbers and facts appeared on little road signs swirling around in my head.

At fourteen, my father took me to the townhall with its polished granite pillars and stone façade. Atop the building was the town's fire siren sounded daily by Ruthie, the town clerk. She blew the siren exactly at noon, letting it build to a howling crescendo. Everyone subconsciously held their breaths anticipating when Ruthie would release her terrible hold. She never abused her power and was rewarded with re-appointment year after year.

The firetrucks housed in townhall were kept clean, maintained, and polished by volunteer firefighters. Some volunteers, like my dad, couldn't take time from work to hang around the fire station, but did respond to fires. On several occasions, Dad's stunned barber customers were left sitting under the barber cloth with half a haircut as he dashed off with his fire-boots to attend a fire. His fire hat and turnout gear were kept ready for him at the station. When summoned, he had only to call the town's switchboard, manned by none other than Ruthie. "Fireman Christiansen," he'd say and be given the fire's location.

Street addresses weren't needed like bigger towns and cities. Instead, locations were given in relationship to landmarks like the water tower, the grain elevator, or some well-known farm. Most often, though, Ruthie only had to say whose property was on fire and everyone knew where it was anyway.

This is what I remember:

The townhall was where I aced my learners' permit written test.

Like most kids I'd only driven our car seated on my father's lap. It never seemed like a big deal to me. That is, until Dad tossed the car keys to me on the way out of the building that day. "You're drivin'… Ace."

I fumbled and dropped the keys. Not a good start.

Once behind the wheel, self-confidence seemed to ooze right out of me. I sat blinking in bewilderment at the dials, levers, switches, and do-dads on the dashboard. I turned on the motor, gripped the steering wheel, and pressed down on the accelerator of our 1955 Ford station wagon. I threw my right arm over the seat and turned my head to back out of the parking space.

The engine revved but nothing happened.

"Dontcha think ya ought a put 'er in gear?" my father said with a smirk.

"Oh, yeah," I said.

After I'd managed to back out, I pulled the gearshift into "D" for drive. I glanced over at my father and saw a bead of sweat on his forehead.

"Now eeeasy does it," he said. He held out his hand, palm down, emphasizing the word *easy*.

Never having used the accelerator before I had no idea what "easy" was, so I had to guess at the amount of pressure required. When the Ford bucked forward suddenly, I panicked and trounced on the brake throwing him forward and then jerking him back.

He shot me a nasty glance that started butterflies fluttering in my stomach.

"Sorry," I said meekly.

He took a deep breath and sighed wearily, "Try it again."

The five-block trip home seemed an eternity, but I was just beginning to get the hang of it by the time we'd pulled up in front of the house.

"Not as easy as it looks, huh?" Dad asked rhetorically and made a beeline for the cold sixpack in the refrigerator.

Over the following months, I was allowed to drive home after Dad had closed his barbershop and I'd finished my cleaning chores. I wasn't setting any speed records, but I was steadily improving and gaining confidence. Even Dad's sarcastic comments had tapered off.

One Sunday afternoon, our family was in the car headed for my grandmother's house for one of her pot-roast dinners (Dinner in the Midwest is the midday meal). It was springtime and the fields lay muddy and empty on each side of the blacktop.

Dad was never in a hurry to arrive, as Grandma Edwards' dinners were served in midafternoon and too formal for his taste.

He pulled abruptly to the side of the road and shifted into park. "Why don't you drive, kid?" he said, looking at me in the rearview mirror.

I'd never driven the car with the entire family before. My brother and father had been my only passengers.

Dad slid over to my mother's seat, ignoring the anxious look she gave him as she got out to sit in the back seat. I moved from the back on shaky legs and opened the driver's door. The moment I reached for the steering wheel; a terrible high-pitched wail emanated from the backseat. It was my oldest sister, Lee Ann, who did not share our father's confidence in my chauffeuring abilities. Her caterwauling didn't do wonders for my confidence, either.

"I don't know if this is the time for this," Mom said, placing a comforting arm around my weeping sister.

"Drive!" he commanded. Pop had a stubborn streak a mile wide.

I drove, Lee Ann wailed, and Mom comforted.

Later that day, after our roast beef, we said our goodbyes and walked to the car.

"You're drivin', not me," he said handing me the car keys.

After we'd settled in, I turned the key and started the car. Immediately, my poor sister started up, too. The long, high wail was once again an accompaniment to my driving.

"Aw, there she goes again, Dad." I moaned and rolled my eyes.

My father had just spent an entire afternoon somewhere he didn't want to be and in no mood for nonsense. He turned, fixed my sister with his best evil eye, and barked, "That'll be enough of that, little missy."

Mom mercifully covered Lee Ann's eyes with her hand and pulled her down into her lap where she remained for the entire ride home.

I'm ashamed to say…. I gloated. Fond of endlessly teasing my sister, I'd found a parent-sanctioned method of getting her goat. And so, it went for the remainder of my probationary two years. Each trip in the car was a command performance for me, but hell on earth for my poor, suffering, untrusting sister.

Finally came the day when I turned sixteen. Two days later, excused from school, Dad and I drove to the county courthouse for my driver's test. There were both written, and performance tests administered by a state trooper.

Once again, I aced the written portion.

The patrolman sauntered up, his leather belt creaking, and looked down at me from under his brown Smokey Bear hat. "You ready, sport?"

I gulped and nodded.

I was the oldest in my family, but the youngest in my high school class. Everyone had their driver's licenses by now, except me. It had been embarrassing to be seen driving around with one of my parents sitting next to me.

I assumed the position behind the steering wheel and the patrolman settled himself into the passenger side. I slid the bench seat forward, adjusting it to my short legs slamming his knees into the glove compartment. He winced and shifted slightly to make room for his long legs. I hoped he wouldn't be taking off points for personal injury.

He rubbed his knees and instructed me to make a right turn out of the parking lot and onto the street.

I glided out of the parking lot, smooth as silk. I remembered to use my turning signal and looked conscientiously in both directions. *Piece of cake*, I thought.

"Make a right at the corner," he said and scribbled on his clipboard. He seemed bored and I wondered how many tests he'd done that day.

In the center of the intersection was a beat-up, four-way stop sign with chipped and faded paint that listed hard to one side. It was a school zone stop sign, dragged out only during school hours. I'd been that way many times, but not during school, so I'd never seen it.

As I approached the intersection, I was convinced some mistake had been made and it was not a *real* stop sign. I decided to give it the kind of attention I thought it deserved, hesitating only briefly before making the right turn.

The trooper's head popped up from his clipboard and blinked his eyes with disbelief. He'd just been rescued from yet another routine, boring day.

"What the heck do you think you're doing?" he demanded.

A small voice in my head whispered, *Uh, oh!*

"You just flunked your driver's test, sport," he said with a wide grin. He seemed oddly happy.

"Wha, wha…what?" I stammered.

"You ran a stop sign! That's a moving violation, so you fail automatically. I can't give you a ticket because this is a test, but I can sure fail you." He grinned some more.

I'll bet you can't wait to get back to the courthouse to tell your buddies this one, I thought.

He had me turn into another entrance into the parking lot. We hadn't even gone around the block.

My father did not let me drive home refusing to even acknowledge my presence. I sat next to him on the front seat as far away as possible.

He kept muttering. "I don't believe it! I've never seen the like. I don't believe it!"

Well, I didn't believe it either. My friends at school knew I'd been excused from classes to take my test that morning. I mean, I'd practically announced it over the school intercom.

"Too late to go back to school, dontcha think?" I suggested.

But he just smiled a smile like the one on the patrolman's face. "Why... I think there's plenty of time for school," he said. It was payback for closing his barbershop for nothing.

Words can never express the embarrassment I felt that day as I slunk around the halls, hoping for invisibility. But word spread like wildfire after I'd secretly admitted my failure to a friend who turned out to have a very big mouth.

Between classes schoolmates couldn't wait to ask, "Is it true? Did you *really* flunk your driver's test?"

"Yeah, but..." I confessed and was never given the opportunity to fully explain.

The laughter rolled up and down the halls. My so-called friends pointed and hooted as I ducked into doorways. I wanted to die. I wanted the earth to open its craggy maw and swallow me right then and there. I wished for white-hot lightning to strike and smash me to atoms. I wanted... well, you get the idea.

That night, my family was merciful... at first. My brother never said a word. He just smirked and smirked some more. Mom, suppressing a smile of her own, patted my shoulder. "You can try again next month, dear," she said. Good ole Mom.

Later, relaxing in front of the TV, my terrible day nearing an end, I was recovering. *Ahh*, I thought, *it's bound to blow over eventually.*

Lee Ann arose, walked past me on the way to her bedroom, turned, and said loudly, "Hey, Mario Andretti! Can I have your autograph to bring to school tomorrow?"

I had it coming. It was the knockout punch that became a turning point in our relationship. She now had the power to pull this story out at will and with a few words, bring me to my knees. My teasing days were over.

*

The irony is that she claims to have no recollection of me failing my first driver's test and insists that using such knowledge to embarrass me would not have occurred to her. Yeah, sure...

Communities in small-town Iowa are islands in an ocean of farmland spreading as far as you can see. The reason many of the towns were established to begin with was to support the main industry... farming.

This is what I remember:

There weren't many jobs in town, so most of us did farm labor of one kind or another. Once my brother and I had established reputations for good dependable work, we were rarely without a job. We were in the fields during the growing season and found work related to livestock in the off-season. We preferred the fields over the animals as the latter tend to be very messy and malodorous, but we took whatever was available.

Land is expensive and every acre used to capacity. Confining cattle and hogs in feed lots is more economical than using good land for grazing. Feed lots allow farmers to prepare cattle more easily for market with vaccinations, tending, and feeding. In some locations, keeping predators away is an issue. Sadly, these lots often become a mud-manure morass that's unsanitary and cruel for animals that are herding, grazing creatures by nature.

Most farmers raised an assortment of animals, either for their own consumption or for market. It made sense not to buy animal feed when a portion of their corn, oats, and hay could be set aside for that purpose. The first crop harvested each year was hay. During the winter months, a supply of hay was very important, as it was cheaper than grain and easily stored.

Here's a little history for city folks: the old method of storing hay was a haystack. The crop was cut with a scythe then raked into piles around a central pole. A bed of brush or sticks placed under the stack provided for ventilation; then the top and sides of the stack were "combed" to help shed water. Later, the hay was loaded onto a wagon and brought to wherever needed.

A recent improvement is the rolling method where machinery tightly rolls the hay, wraps it in netting or plastic, and is left in the field.

Another method is to cut and auger it into a trailer to be blown into the barn. The wagon is tipped so the hay can be raked onto a conveyor feeding a blower and shot up into a dust-filled loft for another crew to spread with rakes. No one wore a mask, and I wonder sometimes just how much hay dust I've inhaled in my life.

Where I'm from, hay is mostly processed with a machine called a baler, used primarily on smaller farms.

The hay is cut and raked into rows for the baler to gather, compress into rectangles, and tie together with twine or wire. Wire isn't used anymore because it could end up in a cow's stomach or damage machinery, causing all manner of problems. Hence the phrase: something's gone haywire.

Baled hay is brought in from the field for storage, usually in a barn's hayloft, but sometimes it's stacked on the ground and covered with a tarp. The idea is to get it out of the weather to prevent it from molding and becoming toxic to animals.

On occasion, we were paid to cut and rake hay with a tractor, but the job for which we were most often hired was for the hayrack or the barn.

It's important to wait for hay to dry, as wet hay ferments and may release sufficient heat to burn down a barn. Consequently, all my memories of baling hay are of me being thirsty, hot, and dirty.

A tractor pulls the baler that's in turn hitched to a hayrack. Bales are pushed out of a chute onto the rack to be stacked into stable patterns. Bales ranged between 50 to 150 pounds, depending upon their moisture content. The faster the tractor goes, the faster the bales are made. It's important to establish a comfortable pace, as there's a rhythm to just about everything.

Two parallel lengths of twine holding it together were used for lifting and carrying. I learned to carry the scratchy things against my thigh and then use my leg to boost them up onto an ever-growing stack. At the end of the summer, the right thigh of my work jeans was worn so thin you could see through it. During haying season, I went through two pairs of leather gloves and my forearms were crosshatched with scratches in various stages of healing from the bristling hay.

Putting up baled hay is very different from the other methods. Most barns with a hayloft have a beak-like protrusion above the loft doors housing a lift mechanism. No one uses metal hayforks or tongs anymore. Instead, a flat metal grid with rows of hooks is set into several bales at once. A tractor rope pulls the load up to the peak where a trip mechanism converts the vertical lift onto a horizontal track into the barn. When the load reaches the desired location, the bales are released with a pull rope for the barn crew to stack.

Yet another method to move bales into a loft is via an elevator conveyor resembling a long-necked dinosaur. A tractor's spinning power train or power take off (PTO) provides the energy.

It was up to the farmer to decide who worked where... he was the boss. I preferred working on the hayrack where there was the chance of a breeze rather than a dusty, unventilated haymow.

Gary and I worked together in many barns and learned to hustle to keep up with the bales and stay out of the way as they fell.

The trick was to fill the back of the barn first and work toward the loft doors. It was important to keep the bales tightly together as you were essentially laying the floor for each new level. Lugging heavy bales on unsure footing was bad enough, but stepping into a hole from a stacking mistake could snap an ankle. I'll admit to a sense of satisfaction when tossing a bale so perfectly it needed no adjustment.

We did little things to break up the monotony. As we shuttled past each other, Gary would nod and say, "Hey." I'd nod back and reply, "Hey," and then he'd say, "It sure is." It was our secret little chuckle.

*

Those dirty jobs earned pocket money, taught me what hard work was, and put muscle on my skinny body. I appreciated those opportunities but working for $1.25 an hour in a hot, sweaty barn was a powerful incentive to take the college route instead.

CASTRATING CORN

Those of us from rural Iowa have a close relationship with corn. Iowa produces more of it than any other state hands down. In fact, Iowans proudly referred to their state as The Tall Corn State.

Here's some information you might find useful in reading this story: the corn plant is hermaphroditic, meaning it has both male and female parts. This is true of many plants, some animals, and on very rare occasions, humans. At the very top of the plant is the "male" tassel that releases copious amounts of pollen. The pollen settles upon the "female" silk hanging from the husk that protect what will become corn.

It may surprise you to learn that humans eat almost none of it. Sure, there are outliers like popcorn and sweet corn, but most of its used for things like ethanol, animal feed, corn starch, corn oil, corn syrup, etc.

Iowa has a song called *The Iowa Corn Song*. It goes like this:

"Oh, we're from Iowa, Iowa.
State of all the land
Joy on every hand.
We're from Iowa, Iowa.
That's where the tall corn grows!"

Kind of corny I know, but that's the whole idea.

Corn has been hybridized to the point that it could never survive as a species today. Instead, it requires planting specially selected seed corn every year.

The seed corn industry is alive and well in the Midwest, where new varieties are constantly tested to produce higher and higher yields. Different areas of the country, or regions within a state, use varieties better suited for each growing environment.

How is that done, you say? Well…

Some farmers are paid each year to devote part of their land to grow seed corn. Where I'm from the big seed corn company was DeKalb. Two rows of corn designated as pollinators or "bull rows" were allowed to keep their tassels. On each side of the bull rows were six rows to be pollinated, the "female rows." These rows must have their tassels removed so that they're pollinated only from the "males" with the desired genetic characteristics. The process of removing tassels is called detasseling (duh!) and carried out each summer during the hot humid months of July and August. The pattern of six and two is repeated across the field from fence to fence with some rows a mile long.

When the tassels begin emerging, it's all-hands-on-deck to remove them. We jokingly referred to this changing of the plant to all female as "castrating."

The trick is to pull off the tassel with as little damage to the plant as possible. Inspectors are constantly monitoring to ensure that a maximum of only three leaves are removed with the tassel. They also look for any tassels missed on the first pass. A field may need to be worked two or three times to insure none are left.

Detasseling crews at that time were either walking or machine crews. The machines were slow-moving, three-wheeled contraptions powered by gasoline engines. The crews stood on metal platforms suspended from extended "wings." Workers of mostly high school kids were segregated into girls' or boys' crews. I'm not sure what they do today with all the confusion about gender assignment but that's the way it was then.

For reasons unknown to me, most girls were on walking crews. Although slower, they were much more thorough. DeKalb must have figured out long ago that it was not wise to mix the sexes if any real work was to be done.

Gary and I and many of our friends did this quintessential work during our high school years.

This is what I remember:

On a typical day during detasseling season the alarm jangled, just as the sun began to light the horizon. We silently dressed, gobbled cereal, and grabbed our lunches from the refrigerator. The uniform of the day was sneakers, blue jeans, T-shirts, long-sleeved shirts (unbuttoned), and baseball caps. It never varied.

The crew's foreman, usually a farm kid home from college for the summer, gathered us at designated areas in a pickup truck covered with a tarp over a wooden frame. We sat on benches or on the floor, staring blankly, trying to wake up. It was like riding a cheap school bus.

Once at that day's field we stashed our lunches and unloaded.

Understand that an Iowa cornfield in mid-July on humid mornings at sunrise, is a steaming jungle dripping with dew. Each wet leaf deposits some moisture on you. Little by little, as you move through the corn, you get wetter and wetter. Even though it may be 80 degrees at 6:30 a.m., wet clothing still feels cold.

You must decide: do you plunge in to get wet right away, or let it soak you ever so slowly? The long-sleeved shirt allowed for body heat preservation until the sun was full up. I was not a plunger.

The corn waited tall, green, and dripping dew as the foreman started the Briggs and Stratton engine with a pull rope. The platform wings were swung out and we climbed aboard.

We shivered in the dew-wet coolness of the morning, eventually shedding our shirts as we picked the reluctant tassels. The squeaking sounds of the tassels as they were pulled mingled with the voices of the crew. We talked about what we'd done the night before, what we're going to do after work, and we talked about girls...

"We got any girl crews here today?" someone asks.

"I think I saw Loretta's truck with her girls' crew from Pitman," says another.

"Oh, great. The Pitman Pigs are all we got today?" from out on the right wing.

"Yah. They're the ugliest bunch, ain't they, though?" from the inside platform.

The foreman says, "Shuddup. You guys ain't no poster boys, ya know."

"Yah, but at least we ain't from that shithole, Pitman," someone says.

We all laugh and nod our heads in agreement that Pitman is a nowhere town, and that none of us are destined to be models.

Squeak. Squeak. The tassels drop to the ground, hour after hour.

The foreman notes, "Rick, you're missing too many. Each one you miss, I'm gonna stick in your pants."

Rick says, "Okay. Yer on. I'm the best detasseler on this crew and I'll prove it."

Thirty minutes later, Rick looks like a big-tailed, bantam rooster from all the tassels sticking out of the back of his jeans.

"Okay" he says, pulling the tassels out of his pants. "You can stop. I'll be more careful."

The foreman chuckles, "I told you so, meathead."

At the end of the row, we hop off to allow the foreman to turn the machine around and center it over the next section. We get a drink of water from the Igloo water jug strapped to the frame. It's getting hot now and we know we're going to fry. Our clothing is finally dry but will soon be wet again from sweat.

The motor drones and we work silently, lost in our thoughts. *Squeak.* *Squeak.*

Someone remembers to turn on the transistor radio tied to the frame. It's top 40 rock and roll. *A Hard Day's Night* by the Beatles plays over and over and over but nobody complains.

In the distance, other crews patrol the field. They seem to float above the corn in the shimmering heat. We race any crew going in the same direction at the same time. Only the hands and arms of the girl's crew are visible as they reach above their heads to work. Despite the low opinion of the Pitman crew, we all strain to see what they're wearing.

It's hot down there under the leaves out of reach of a breeze, so the girls strip to bathing suits, short-shorts, and skimpy tops. They wisely cover up when they finish a row and step out from the corn jungle.

It's lunchtime. All the crews working the field meet in the farmer's yard to rest and eat under the shade of trees. The inspectors appear to report how we're doing and then drive off in their DeKalb company cars to eat in town.

After we've eaten, it's time to refill the Igloos from the water pump. We've been waiting for this... The Water Fight.

Every available container is filled with the ice-cold water from the well. We sneak up on the unsuspecting and douse them, but the foremen, wise and experienced, stand with their backs to trees or farm buildings. Soon, we're all soaking wet again but laughing and smiling.

Back on the machines we resume: "Whaddya say we go swimmin' in the gravel pit over by West Bend after work?" Kirk says.

We all agree it's a wonderful idea. It's free, cool, and unsupervised.

My pal Jack says, "I'll see if I can get the car. My dad's driving truck today and I think the car's available.

"Maybe a girls' crew will be there!" says another.

We all think about this as hope springs eternal.

The foreman smokes cigarettes, the engine hums, the radio plays, and the sun beats down... hard.

At last, quitting time, and we leave our machine until morning. Back in the pickup truck, the conversation is animated and teasing. We're looking forward to our rendezvous at the gravel pit and the paycheck at the end of the week.

One by one we're dropped off for a quick supper. It's mid-summer and the sun will be up long enough for our plans.

The swim in the cool water of the gravel pit is refreshing and restores us. Sadly, no females arrive, but it allows us to shed our bathing suits... just... because... we can.

Later, Gary and I fall asleep on the floor watching TV in front of an electric fan. Eventually we get up and stumble off to bed. Another day awaits and there'll be no time off until the last cornstalk is castrated.

FLASH BURNED
(THE GARAGE)

Except for the most complicated repairs, my father handled most of the maintenance on our late-model, gas-guzzling cars. As we grew older, my brother and I were drafted into the roles of reluctant backyard mechanics. I rarely bucked my father when he assigned chores, but I truly hated this expectation.

These duties often fell to me as Gary, the family athlete, was often at practices or events. Dad was busy cutting hair except Sundays when, if the weather was right, he went fishing.

I don't mind getting my hands dirty. The dirt washes off at the end of the day and I consider physical labor a thing of honor, but it's there I draw the line. Grease and oil are a totally different matter, as you just never seem to be rid of it. The black stuff fills your pores, fingernails, and cuticles, resisting even the most vigorous scrubbing. If you're not careful, it can enter a cut or scrape creating an unwelcome tattoo.

Working in or under a car usually requires you to be a contortionist assuming positions simultaneously unnatural and uncomfortable... a position you must maintain until the job's done.

I was never interested in learning the workings of the internal combustion engine and its accompanying parts. Many of my friends, however, could quote the pros and cons of the various makes and models of a wide assortment of automobiles. Their statistical knowledge of horsepower, torque, wheel differentials, piston bore, the number of whizzbangs and doohickies could easily put the biggest baseball-stat geek to shame.

The decisions as to which size wrench, socket fitting, doodad, or toggle-fart required for a repair were a complete mystery. For me, there was no intuition involved and pretty much trial and error every time I extended my uncertain, trembling hand toward machinery.

It was a source of frustration for my father who was a natural and quite fearless when it came to all things mechanical. One summer he and our ancient neighbor, The Swede, replaced the engine in our 1955 Plymouth station wagon. Sixty years later, I'm still amazed by that.

This is what I remember:

When a small town, desperate for a barber, made my dad an offer he couldn't refuse, we relocated and took up residence above the shop. There was a large garage where, if not for the profusion of junk, there would have been room enough for three cars. We owned two used automobiles, and I mean *used* in every sense of the word. They were just one major breakdown away from the junkyard. There was always something breaking or wearing out on one or the other. Both cars burned oil badly requiring us to carry a supply in the trunk and learned to ignore the sounds of rolling oilcans.

One year, something called a heater core failed in one of our clunkers. Dad informed me that this was my repair project, and I'd best get cracking. I had no idea what or even where a heater core was and when I asked for a hint, he pointed vaguely to the area under the front passenger dashboard. "It's right there, for Pete's sake," he said and walked off to start his day.

It was a cold Saturday morning in mid-November. I was alone in our garage, with an assortment of gadgets with which I had only a fleeting acquaintance. On my back, under the dashboard, I was partially and painfully half in and half out of the car door. Debris kept falling into my eyes as I searched for the screws and clips securing the heater core.

Periodically, I went into the barbershop to warm up, ask for advice, and whine. "I can't get at some of the screws. The screwdrivers we have are too long," I grumbled.

Dad looked up from his customer, scissor in one hand, comb in the other. With a mixture of curiosity and disbelief, he squinted one eye and asked, "What do you use that head of yours for anyway, kid?"

I immediately recalled that my head quite adequately supported a baseball cap, but never got the chance to share the thought.

"There's a small screwdriver set in the glove compartment, if you'd just look," he growled and turned back to his customer. The customer shrugged in sympathy and Dad sighed, shaking his head in disgust. "Kids! What's this world coming to?"

I could never understand how my father remembered the various places he'd left his tools, but somehow couldn't bring himself to return them to a central, common location, like, say…. a toolbox.

Discussion over, I sulked back to the garage.

Sometime later that morning, I succeeded in removing the thing and discovered it resembled a miniature car radiator. I also discovered, much too late, that like a radiator, the heater core was filled with antifreeze. It's difficult to avoid a shower of sticky antifreeze lying on your back, stuffed under a dashboard. Lesson learned…

I proudly brought it into the shop and presented it to him for an atta boy. After a brief inspection, he pronounced it DOA. Thinking that was the end of it for me, I turned to leave for more pleasant Saturday afternoon pursuits.

"Where you think you're goin'?" he asked.

He didn't wait for an answer. "I want you to drive to the junkyard outside of West Bend and get a replacement. Make sure to ask if you can get a discount if you pull it out of the car yourself."

"But" I said, "it took me all morning just to do this. Can't we get a mechanic or something?"

He ignored me, reached for his wallet, and handed me a few dollars. "There. That should cover it. Now get a move on 'for it gets too late."

Getting the second heater core out of the junked car was admittedly easier because I already had practice. It was helpful, too, that the front seat of the junker was missing. I was pleased at how this phase of operations went quickly as it was cold in that desolate, prairie junkyard. I had to keep blowing on my fingers and shoving them under my armpits to warm them.

By late afternoon, I'd installed the new/used part, and all was well. Curiously, I had a screw, and a metal clip left over that I quickly made disappear.

When I announced completion, all he said was, "See?"

One of my chores was to keep a box filled with coal for the potbelly stove in the garage. When in use, a long stovepipe allowed the smoke to exit through the roof.

That same winter, my Uncle Dave announced he had to re-bore the cylinders of his car and needed a place out of the weather to work, so Dad offered our garage and my brother and me to assist him.

When I made a face of protest, he cut me off. "It'll be good for you. Maybe you'll even learn something?"

I defiantly stuck out my chin and announced, "Someday, I'm gonna hire a *real* mechanic to do my work for me."

"Someday," he said dryly, "you'll thank me for teaching you a few things."

Uncle Dave was to bring his car around late on a Sunday afternoon while my parents and two sisters were visiting our grandparents. Gary and I stayed home to get the garage stove going and be available to help.

The night was cold, and blowing snow muttered around the edges of the building. The thought of working in our freezing garage was daunting, so we dilly-dallied, stalling for when we'd have to tend to our task. When we'd run out of excuses, we put on our coats and went down to the garage.

The stove's heavy, cast-iron lid squealed open on a reluctant hinge, and we dumped in chunks of coal, pieces of scrap wood, and paper. One of us (I don't remember who.) came up with the bright idea of adding a splash or two of gasoline to speed things up.

When Gary struck a match and tossed it in... *WHOOOMMP!* The gasoline ignited with a shocking explosion. The force knocked the lid down onto the stove containing the explosion. The resulting release of energy blew the stovepipe connections apart, showering everything with soot. Flames shot out of the now open stovepipe hole and smoke was belching into the garage.

We looked at each other wide-eyed. We'd screwed up big time!

I ran to open the garage door, and Gary went for a bucket of water to douse the flames. It was too soon for the coal to have caught fire; a good thing, as that kind of fire isn't easily extinguished.

Once the fire was out, we fanned the smoke out with pieces of cardboard Dad used to catch oil leaks. The temperature in the garage dropped quickly, but we were too panicked to care.

If our uncle arrived then, he would most certainly rat us out and that was trouble. If Dad were to arrive early, well... that was trouble too horrible to imagine.

Once the smoke cleared, we turned to putting things right. After closing the garage door and reassembling the stovepipe, I fetched the stepladder for my taller brother to refit it into the ceiling. Next, we restarted the fire, slowly building it up enough to add coal. This time we wisely passed on the gasoline.

Things were looking up and we permitted ourselves wide congratulatory smiles. That's when we noticed the tiny particles of soot stuck to our teeth. Upon further inspection, Gary, who'd been closest to the explosion, had singed eyebrows, eyelashes, and hair. Even worse, every surface in the garage was speckled with sooty bits.

"We are so screwed!" Gary said through gritty teeth. That got us laughing hard enough for our laugh tears to wash little tracks through the grime.

We sobered fast. There was more to do.

"I'll get some rags," I said.

"I'll get the broom," Gary offered, and we launched into a cleaning frenzy.

Once the floor was swept, our attentions turned to the most obvious surfaces. There was no hope of meeting a formal inspection, but we hoped it would pass a quick scan.

The last things to clean were ourselves. We shook out our clothes, stuffed them beside the washing machine, and hit the shower. Once our soot-speckled teeth were brushed and Gary had trimmed his singed hair with Dad's barber scissors, we were ready to face what may come.

The family arrived, oblivious to our desperate two hours, just as we'd finished our tasks.

For the rest of the week, as Uncle Dave focused on his job under the hood of his car, we sneaked off to clean soot from windows, tools, benches, and shelves.

At the end of the week, we concluded that we'd indeed saved ourselves from the brink of disaster. It was a secret we were to keep between us for many years.

As much as I hate to admit it, my father was right. During the lean years of college, internship, residency, and getting established, I've used the mechanical knowledge he'd foisted upon me to save money doing routine maintenance on my aging automobiles. In turn, I applied those skills to other machinery, such as lawn mowers, snow blowers, chainsaws, and weed whackers. I came to realize that most jobs only require a few basic tools, WD 40, and a willingness to try

No, I haven't obtained any high levels of confidence in mechanical things, and still don't like getting my hands greasy, but at least I did the things I knew and knew the things I didn't.

Thank you, Pop.

A FARM PAINTING

This is what I remember:

The old gent squinted pale blue eyes from beneath the bill of his mattress-tick hat. "Get some paint on your brush, Carter," he said. The fact that he'd used my middle name told me everything... he was tired of repeating himself. Apparently, I was doing it wrong.

The summer I was sixteen my father volunteered me to help my grandfather paint a farm. Grandpa Agner had painted the very same buildings himself, thirty years ago. Now at seventy, it was thought he needed an assist. He quickly informed me that he'd be doing the high work and I'd be allowed only as high as a two-story ladder.

All the buildings, including a two-story house, corncrib, chicken house and garage, were to remain white.

Gramps didn't like the newfangled rollers, so it was brush-only to apply the oil-based paint. His metal paint buckets were so thickly coated with paint they seemed to be made of white rubber. A strand of wire stretched across the top of the buckets to scrape excess paint from the brush, had become so heavily coated it had doubled in size. There were stalactites of dried paint hanging from the wire.

Brushes were only partially flexible as the portion near the handles was as stiff as a board. The old man believed that an adequate cleaning was an overnight soak in a can of turpentine. After a quick wipe with a rag, away we went.

He started me out on the farmhouse where I quickly learned the old painter's trick of following the shade. Climbing up and down to move a ladder wastes time and energy, so with practice I learned to hop the ladder into a new position while standing on it.

Gramps was a pro at the ladder bounce. I watched in admiration as he jumped his ladder from place to place with his bandy bowed legs.

While he tackled the windowed cupola on the corncrib, I slapped paint on the house. Alone with no one to talk to, I quickly became bored. I decided to bring my transistor radio with me, tuned to my favorite rock-and-roll station, KIOA in Des Moines.

Everything went well for a time until disaster struck...

I stupidly set the radio on the second rung of the ladder and put the paint bucket in front of the ladder to refill. As I was pouring the paint I bumped the ladder and knocked the radio right into the bucket. That was that... no more tunes.

My next assignment was the chicken house. Let me say here and now that I do not like chickens. Having cleaned out many a henhouse, I'd formed very negative opinions of them. Sure, I like eating chicken and enjoy their eggs, but I find them to be intolerably stupid and very, very, dirty birds. They poop wherever and whenever they wish. They urinate and defecate at the same time which makes their droppings so rich in ammonia that it makes your eyes tear. It's chicken tear gas! They have no respect for each other and are constantly pecking and bullying members of their own flock.

Roosters are known to greet the first hint of sun in the morning with their loud crowing and then never shut up for the rest of the day. Wise farmers don't keep them around as they negatively affect egg production.

So, there I was, brush in hand, painting the chickens' house with no radio for diversion and left to listen to their incessant squawking, cackling, and clucking. Finally, unable to stand it a moment longer, I smacked the side of the low building with my brush. I was gratified to hear them flutter and squawk as they fled the sudden noise. For a few brief moments there was blessed silence, but all it took was for one of them to start up and soon they were all back at it. Chickens have very short memories.

This mindless game went on all day. The next morning, Gramps told me the farmer had complained that his hens had quit laying eggs, so I had to knock it off. I was nearly done anyway.

Mercifully, a summer job for which I'd applied came through with the DeKalb Seed Corn Company and I left the painting business. It was just as well, as my father informed me that I shouldn't expect to be paid.

I felt guilty about leaving Gramps to finish alone, but he never said anything one way or the other. Dad wasn't happy about my decision, but he ultimately understood that I needed to make money for college. We were not wealthy.

Much later that summer, a farmer for whom I'd worked in the past, hired me to do whatever needed to be done. He had a pretty daughter, so I readily agreed. In a few days he'd run out of fieldwork for me and, wouldn't you know, I was directed to paint the white, wooden-slat fence surrounding his large farmyard.

Once again, brush and bucket in hand, I was engrossed in the ultimate tedium of painting a fence. I would have pulled the old Tom Sawyer trick he'd used to paint his Aunt Polly's fence, but there weren't any available suckers. The rare appearance of the farmer's daughter did little to relieve my distress, and she never offered to help. It was just the hot sun, insects, weeds, and yours truly. After a while, I quit trying to keep the bugs and encroaching weeds out of the way and enshrined them in the next coat of paint. My sneakers, jeans, and T-shirt suffered the same fate and when I finished the job, I just threw everything away.

The fence turned out nicely, if you didn't look too closely.

The lessons I learned from my grandfather came to serve me well. My wife and I painted the interior of every house we've lived in. I did the big surfaces and she the trim. I've painted the exterior of our two-story home twice, remembering to hop the ladder and follow the shade like a pro. I was thankful that there were no chickens, and I remembered to keep the radio well away from the paint bucket.

I can still hear the old Dane, "Get some paint on your brush, Carter!"

AT THE HOP

This is what I remember:

"Aw, for the love 'a Pete, kid, what are you doin' mopin' around here on a Friday night? Why don't you go find somethin' fun to do?" Dad said from behind his white porcelain barber chair. The customer with half a haircut blinked at me, anticipating my answer.

"I went to the football game, but everybody was bummed out 'cause we got beat, so I came home," I said.

"Well, isn't there a dance at the high school after every home game?" he asked. He knew very well there was.

"Yeah, a sock hop in the gym," I said.

The half-shorn customer, Odin Oleson, cocked an eye and asked, "What the hell is a sock hop?"

Dad fired up his Oster clipper and went back to work. "It's what the kids call it. They hold the dances in the gym and can't wear shoes, so they dance in their socks," he explained.

"Makes sense," Odin shrugged.

Everything in our little town was within easy walking distance. The football field was five blocks away and the high school, three.

The gridiron on the edge of town was a desolate place surrounded by fields where the cold autumn winds swept beneath the bleachers of the faithfully gathered. Parents took turns selling snacks, soft drinks, and hot coffee at the concession stands to make money for the team.

I was the new kid, having moved there a couple weeks before the start of school. There were only thirty-two students in my sophomore class, so I knew everyone by now, but I still had the stink of the outsider on me. My tendency for shyness didn't help.

The walk to the barbershop after the game had been dark and lonely and I felt the need to be near my father.

Pop paused to take a drag from his constantly burning cigarette, squinted through the smoke and reached into his back pocket for his wallet. "Here," he said, "Take some money and go. Will ya'?"

Odin chuckled and shook his head as he got up from the chair, brushing hair clippings from his neck.

I shrugged. "Naw, Dad, I wouldn't know what to do."

"Just go. Just go and figure it out like everyone else," he said and stuck two bucks into my shirt pocket.

I looked around the shop at the farmers waiting their turns. Out on the street and sidewalks, people were gathering for the after-game analysis at the restaurant and tavern. The coach was in for a real tongue lashing after tonight's loss.

Maybe the dance wouldn't be so bad, I thought.

214

I shrugged, took the bills out of my shirt, and transferred them to my slacks. "Ok," I said, "I'll give it a shot." Hey, two dollars was two dollars.

"Congratulations, son," my dad said in mock exuberance, "welcome to the human race."

The farmers laughed and shifted in their seats, enjoying the floorshow.

There wasn't much more to add, so I left to join humans in their race. *Some race,* I thought, *I'm late off the starting blocks and wearing clown's shoes.*

The student council sponsored dances to make money for school projects. An unlucky teacher was always assigned chaperone duty to keep everyone on their best behavior. They weren't paid as it was considered part of their teaching duties.

As I neared the front door, my heart sped, and my palms felt greasy. I gave the kid at the door one of the dollars, got twenty-five cents change, took a deep breath and walked into the gym.

In a pathetic attempt to produce atmosphere, the lights over the two entrances of the gymnasium were lit as usual but turned off at the far end near the stage. Naturally, this was where everyone gathered. Music from a portable phonograph played over the gym's PA system. The 45rpm records were the property of members of the student council and whoever brought the most records oversaw the order of play.

The DJ was always the same girl who, although not the most attractive, was friendly and pleasant. They called her Whizzer for reasons not yet clear to me. She took her job seriously and looked dimly upon requests. This position, I was to discover, gave her a great deal of control over the pace of the evening.

A few brave souls were dancing in the new style (not touching) with each dancer moving as the music inspired them. Most of the dancers were small groups of girls while the boys sat watching on the bleachers.

In those days, everyone wore white socks making us look like big jack rabbits as we jittered and jumped around.

Students sat talking in clumps on the bleachers on either side of the gym. In the dim light I had trouble finding someone I recognized. Once I identified a familiar group of boys, I approached.

"Hey, it's the new barber's kid," one said.

It looked like my reputation had preceded me.

"It's Wayne," I said.

"Things are kinda borin' right now," a skinny freshman observed.

"Yeah, but it'll pick up when the football players finish showerin'," another boy assured me.

I looked around the gym as Whizzer spun another 45, a popular rock and roll tune.

One of the guys jumped up from his seat. "I love this song," he said. "I gotta dance with somebody." He scanned the gym's offerings and made a beeline for a tall girl with teased hair and a tight pink sweater. I watched the pantomime as he stood before her pleading his case. She nodded slightly and they walked together onto the floor. Her movements were smooth, controlled, and graceful; he flapped like a scarecrow in a stiff wind.

Oh man, I thought, *I hope I don't look like that*!

Heads turned to the doorway as Jake, a classmate of mine, sauntered into the gym moving our way.

Mr. Baird, the chaperone, who moments before had been nonchalantly speaking to a group of kids, shifted his focus to the new arrival. Jake had some sort of reputation, I gathered.

"Looky here, more losers," he said loudly. He punched a pimpled-face boy in the arm and blared, "Hey there, asshole." His loud voice carried over the gym, bringing quizzical glances.

"Hi, Jake," the boy said, rubbing his abused arm. "Whatcha been doin'?"

"Getting' messed up... that's what. Haw!" Jake said as he surveyed the crowd.

That's when I smelled the alcohol fog swirling around him.

"Want some?" He grinned, removing a small bottle from his inside jacket pocket. He unscrewed the cap and took a swig, then offered it to us.

"What are you drinkin'?" I asked, as if I was some connoisseur of fine alcoholic beverages.

He held out the bottle for us to read the label: Vanilla Extract 46% alcohol.

Jake smirked proudly, "It's all perfectly legal."

We didn't see Mr. Baird coming. He was a tall wiry man in his early 40s with a reputation for a low nonsense threshold. As coach of the track and baseball teams, he kept himself in good shape and knew how to deal with cocky out-of-line kids. During the Korean War he'd been an Army judo instructor. In short, he wasn't anyone to mess with.

Hey, I thought, *now this is getting interesting.*

"Whatcha got there, Jake?" Mr. Baird said, as if asking for the time of day.

"I'm just getting some stuff to bake cookies," Jake sneered. It was too late to put the bottle away, so he held it up and shook it gently between his fingers in Mr. Baird's face.

Quick as a flash, Mr. Baird snatched the bottle, read the label, and put two and two together. He inclined his head toward the door and said calmly, "Time you were leaving, Jakey Boy."

Jake grinned his best smart-ass grin. "Why? I didn't do nuthin' illegal."

Very slowly, Mr. Baird leaned in close to Jake and murmured, "You go now, or I'll throw you out in front of everybody."

Jake's face fell for a moment, but he quickly regained his composure. "Sure," he said, "I wasn't gonna stay at this lame dance anyway," and shuffled off for the exit with Mr. Baird dogging his path.

I decided to stick around.

A few minutes later the battered, bruised, and recently humiliated football team began arriving in twos and threes from the locker room. Hands stuffed deeply into the pockets of their letter jackets and heads hung low, they were the perfect pictures of defeat.

There was some milling around as players and their girlfriends found each other in the growing crowd. It was, I observed, the girlfriends' job to comfort the crestfallen jocks, who milked it for all it was worth.

Whizzer spun her magic with a slow Gene Pitney tune and a few of the football players were reluctantly pulled onto the floor. They danced in a subdued way with limited stiff movements, reflecting their lack of joy in the evening.

I watched the various tableaus around the gym. The players leaned back on the bleachers with their legs out straight, staring; their female comforters huddled next to them with their arms draped over their shoulders. It was a pathetic sight and not the infusion of liveliness I'd been led to expect.

I was beginning to think that this was how the rest of the night was going to go when there was a commotion at the door.

In strode six husky boys wearing the letter jackets of the school whose team had just soundly whipped ours. The contrast was remarkable. They were cocky, strutting, smiling, and… trouble.

There was a collective intake of breath and silence, save for Whizzer's phonograph playing a Roy Orbison tune.

Oh, yeah, now this was getting interesting.

Our football players were suddenly acutely attentive. I heard angry words. "Who do they think they are?" said one. "What a bunch of assholes!" hissed another.

The intruders took seats in a tight cluster on the opposite bleachers. They looked around defiantly, leering at "our" girls. I was surprised to see some of them posing and primping their hair.

Our team stood and swaggered across the floor to confront the new arrivals with clenched fists and defiant chins stuck out.

"You ain't welcome here," said the team's captain, stabbing the air with his finger to punctuate each word.

Everyone had ceased dancing when Whizzer stopped the music. It was beginning to resemble a scene from an old western movie when the sheriff walks into the saloon to confront the bad guys: the piano stops, the poker chips fall, and no one moves.

The intruders stood and one shaped like a fireplug stepped forward. "We paid our money at the door just like everybody else."

Mr. Baird shouldered his way through the gathering, placing himself directly between the two groups.

"Back off, fellas!" he said with clear ringing authority.

He addressed the out-of-towners. "If you came here to cause trouble, you most certainly have found it."

"We paid to come in here," the team's spokesman repeated.

"I guess you have the right to be here, but your reasons for being here are insulting. You'll have your money refunded if you leave now," Mr. Baird asserted.

The big linebacker stood his ground. "We're here for our victory dance and then we'll go."

Mr. Baird reached for the towering football player's left arm and said, "That's it. You're outta here."

The big guy jerked his arm free and launched a lazy roundhouse at Mr. Baird's head. Baird caught it with his left arm, wrapped it around the boy's extended elbow, twisted it tightly, stepped in close to grab the boy's belt, then threw him to the floor with a heavy thud. It happened so quickly I wasn't sure I'd even seen it.

We stood frozen in wide-eyed shock.

Mr. Baird seemed to awaken from a trance, released his hold, and slid into a defensive stance. "I'll take the rest of you on all at once or one at a time. It doesn't matter much to me," he said.

Whizzer kept her head and had called the town's police force, Carl Swanson. Carl was a sardonic, overweight, World War II veteran who'd lived in the town all his life except for his time in the Pacific. He normally spent his nights cruising the town in his late model police car, sipping thermos coffee, and gossiping with folks. He had a holstered .38 special, and a flashlight attached to a wide, black leather belt that sagged beneath his ample abdomen.

He burst into the gym with his belly preceding him and his gun belt creaking as he walked.

"What in the Sam Hill is goin' on here?" he demanded.

In short order he was appraised of the situation and took charge. Red-faced, he jerked his thumb toward the door and ordered, "You boys get the hell outta my town, now, or I'll run y'all in."

As I knew we didn't have a jail, I figured this was mostly bluff, but it worked.

The intruders slunk for the door closely escorted by Carl. "We'll call your admission fee a donation to our team," he said loudly, with a wink at Mr. Baird.

"Okay, let's call it a night, kids," Mr. Baird said, clapping his hands with finality.

The lights came on; we found our jackets and cleared out. Most piled into cars and drove off to find new adventures to round out the evening, while I walked back to the barbershop.

Dad was open late, still shearing shaggy farmers.

"Well, look who's back," he said as I entered. The cigarette smoke was thick by now and burned my eyes.

"How was the dance? Did you have a good time?" he asked.

"Yeah, Dad," I said, "it was kinda fun and I'm glad I went."

He smiled, "I told ya. You just gotta get out there."

I agreed that it was "out there" all right.

*

You'd be right to say it was a small drama in a small town of no real consequence… something I've reflected upon over the years.

I had the good fortune to have several teachers like Mr. Baird. They were World War II and Korean War veterans, who knew how to lead, were firmly grounded in principles, and relied upon their hard-acquired wisdom to guide them. Mr. Baird and his ilk are long gone from our schools, replaced by lawsuit-fearful schoolboards and timid administrators focused on the economic bottom line. Educators are not trusted to enforce even rules of common decency. Instead, they must follow protocols that strip them of authority and respect, leaving a void to be filled by the rude, the mean, the undisciplined, and ultimately… the ignorant.

No committee, no schoolboard, nor court of law would have sufficed in dealing with the showdowns of that evening. Instead, they were handled efficiently and effectively by a person of courage and integrity willing to step forward and face his responsibilities as he saw them.

Thank you, Mr. Baird. I miss you.

BENNY THE BELOVED

This is what I remember:

It was love at first sight. Our first look at the roly-poly little ball of puppy fur was all it took, and he was family.

There was none... well, not much, of the usual biting and chewing you see with most puppies; Benny was a licker. A little pink tongue darted out and licked my fingers the moment I reached for him. It was his greeting, but not carried to extremes the way that some dogs have of always licking, lapping, and slobbering until you're repulsed and made sorry you were introduced in the first place.

There was an abundance of long, soft black hair with a proud snow-white star on his chest, blazing a path up his throat and chin. His light-brown intelligent eyes had a kind of woeful look that compelled you to stroke and cup his perfectly round head. The hair growing long on his floppy ears curled slightly at the ends, matching the longer hair of a graceful eager tail.

Most dogs eventually avert their eyes when making eye contact, but not Benny. He matched you stare for stare with his mouth open and his tongue hanging off to one side in a goofy smile.

A friendly farmer had presented him as a gift at my father's barbershop. Dad, too, was charmed immediately, which was impressive. He hadn't been too keen on owning another dog after our old cocker, Spotty, had gone to the Big Kennel in the Sky. Parents view things in a very different way. All they see are the messy frantic baths, chewed shoes, shed dog hair, peed-on rugs, and surprise packages of dog doodoo. The unconditional loyal friendship and hours of romping fun with a dog are only distant memories of their own childhoods.

It was quite a surprise when my brother and I were called to the barber shop to see if we were interested. Naturally, we promised they would never have to so much as lift a finger to feed, water, walk, clean, or pick up after our dog. Truth be told, we would have promised anything to keep him. I'm certain Dad already knew this, and we knew that he knew, and so on.

We named him Benny.

Fortunately, during Benny's entire puppyhood, the extent of his transgression was the slightly chewed corner of an armchair. Our mother, like the rest of us, was captive of the warmth and sincerity that radiated like summer sunshine from Benny.

"Oh, what a handsome little dog!" was her first comment when we presented him to her. That summed up everyone's first response when they saw him.

My brother and two sisters adored Benny, but he was very careful not to let his attentions be given exclusively to any one of us for too long.

While playing with me, for example, he'd eye a nearby family member and, after what seemed like a polite interval, move off to be with them for a spell.

He also had respect for personal space. When we kids were lying on the living room carpet to watch TV, he'd walk up for a sniff, but not make it his business to plop down on top of you or start licking your face like some dogs. Instead, he found his own place to watch doggie TV… in his dreams.

You could tell he was dreaming when he started whimpering and yelping quietly. His upper lip curled, and his body jerked and shook. Then his feet began to move in rhythm as if running.

"He's dreaming he's chasing a rabbit," my mother told us in a hushed voice. How she knew what Benny had in his sights I don't know, but it truly seemed as if he were in hot pursuit of something.

When he grew into maturity, my brother and I took him with us on expeditions along the railroad tracks outside of town. Here he had the opportunity to chase real rabbits. Rooting around in the brush and briars he joyfully flushed pheasants, barking wildly as they beat their way into the sky.

Cows were his favorite quarry. Finding a hole in the fence, he'd race into fields barking playfully with ears flying. If they were smart, and believe me cows are far from that, they only had to stand still and wait until he became bored. Most often though, they trotted off to a far corner of the field, which was exactly what Benny wanted. The more they ran, the more he chased. He was oblivious to our calls and the game was over only when he tired and not before. He'd return covered in mud, his fur choked with cockleburs, sporting the demeanor of someone returning home from a day's work.

This lack of discipline would be revisited upon my brother...

My sisters had their turns with him, too. The sight of poor Benny in a frilly doll's dress and sunbonnet, stuffed into the bottom of a baby carriage, filled me with pity. He didn't seem to mind, though, and waited patiently. When an opportunity presented itself, he was up and out, shaking off clothing like water from a bath.

He had a real eagerness to learn. Besides many of the usual tricks like sit up, roll over, shake hands, stay, and jump the stick, he quickly mastered others. One of his best was to balance a piece of popcorn on his nose. He'd sit still as a statue looking cross-eyed at the white kernel until given the word 'okay'. Then, he'd toss it into the air with a quick movement of his head and catch it deftly on his tongue.

He consistently caught a rubber ball on the first bounce, chewed it briefly, and then dropped it at your feet for another throw, urging you to hurry with his baritone bark.

Between customers, Dad and Benny played find the glove. After making him leave the barbershop, Dad dragged an old leather glove across the floor, over furniture, around objects, and then hid it within dog reach. We were awed when Benny followed the scent trail exactly as planted and found the glove every time.

No, Benny was no saint. My brother Gary, shortly after getting his driver's license, found out the hard way one Sunday afternoon when he took him for a ride in the family station wagon. Benny loved to ride in the car and occupied the front passenger seat with his wet nose pressed against the glass.

Suddenly, out of the driver's side-window, Benny spotted a feedlot filled with cattle. In one leap, he landed with two front paws on the window ledge of the door, knocking Gary's hands off the steering wheel and pinning his arms to his sides. The car spun out of control, skidded sideways down the blacktop on two wheels, and settled in a shallow ditch.

Later, my brother related how the two of them sat for a moment looking at each other; then Benny emptied his bladder onto my brother's lap.

"Dumbbell!" he shouted. "What's the matter with you? You almost got us killed!"

As if in answer, Benny began to shake violently in a delayed stress reaction and proceeded to evacuate his bowels on the seat. Gary leaped out of the door to avoid further contamination, wondering if anyone would believe that a dog had not only caused the accident, but also wet his pants for him.

He was right. No one believed him.

The bond between my father and Benny grew steadily. In our town, dogs were allowed to run loose, provided they didn't annoy anyone. We saw no reason to keep him tied up and didn't have a fenced-in yard. He made it part of his daily routine to hang out in Dad's shop. There was always someone to rub his ears or play hide the glove.

Dad liked the company and looked forward to his daily visits. It got lonely in the middle of the day when there were fewer customers. He'd lie by the barber chair dozing, as my father read magazines and smoked.

Gradually, part of the routine included hitching a ride on a dairy truck as it made its rounds on Main Street. Dave, the driver, and Benny became good friends, as he too enjoyed the company. Benny sat in the open doorway of the van looking happy and important.

I was home alone one afternoon when my father walked in the back door. His ashen face and red-rimmed shocked eyes told me there was bad news waiting.

"What's the matter, Dad?" I asked.

"It's Benny, Son." He took a shuddering breath. "He was chasing the milk truck for a ride, and he must have misjudged the distance. Dave tried to brake, but it was too late and ran clean over him."

"Is he… is… he...?" I stammered.

"No, I got him in the car and called the vet. Doc's on his way. Help me move him, will ya?"

He was in the back seat, a tumble of black hair, with his rear legs grotesquely splayed frog-like. I peeked through the car window, and he looked up at me with those trusting eyes. I saw the pain.

"Oh, Benny, Benny," I whispered.

I opened the door and stroked his round head. He licked my hand.

"C'mon, Son, go easy and let's get him inside," Dad said.

Despite our careful movements, he yelped several times with pain. I felt his body tense and he once made a sudden move with his head as if to bite, but instead, the pink tongue rasped dryly on my hand.

I didn't see any blood and took it as an encouraging sign.

"Is he goin' to be all right, Dad?" I asked.

"I wish I knew," he said grimly, "I wish I knew."

We laid him on his blanket; he looked at us gratefully and bravely thumped his tail on the floor.

"Well, I got a shop full of customers, I have to get back," Dad said. I saw his hands shake as he lit a cigarette. "Doc should be here any minute. You two decide what's gotta be done."

"Me?" I sputtered.

He paused and looked into my eyes before turning away. In that moment I saw what he wanted: someone, *anyone*, to make this decision but him. He, this man who had tended the dead and horribly wounded as a Marine Hospital Corpsman during the Battle of Okinawa, couldn't do this. There was a deeper love here than I'd ever realized.

I sat on the floor next to my dog, stroking his head and rubbing his ears in that one spot I knew he liked. We waited together for the veterinarian and hoped he would never come.

An eternity of fifteen minutes passed when I saw the vet's salt-and-pepper hair through the screened door. I stood to let him in, my heart pounding.

Doc knelt and examined Benny with firm probing hands. He grunted when Benny yelped as he checked his hips. He finally stood and spoke softly, "Well, looks like your dog has a badly fractured pelvis, broken in at least two places, near as I can tell without x-rays.

"So, now what, Doc?" I asked. Deep in my jeans pockets I crossed my fingers.

"Surgery is the best way to fix this, but it's going to cost your folks a pretty penny." He understood the practicalities of his job quite well.

"Yeah, that's out," I said, mostly to myself. Now I knew another reason my father didn't want to make this decision. He knew we wouldn't be able to afford the expense of saving a dog over other family priorities.

"What if we just let him heal? Would that work?"

"Sure," Doc said, "eventually the bones will knit back together, but his pelvis will heal twisted and uneven. I'm not sure he would ever be able to walk, let alone run again. He'll be in pain for a long time."

Benny, not running, jumping, or walking? I choked back tears. My throat constricted to a dry straw. I bit my lip and stared at the floor. "Guess you better end it then, Doc," I heard myself say.

He laid an approving hand on my shoulder. "Will you help me? Benny would like it, I think, if someone was with him who he loves and trusts."

Through a thick gray fog I mumbled, "Just tell me what to do."

I held our beloved Benny's head to my chest, cradled him, and lied. "It's gonna be okay, pal. It's gonna be all right." I felt the hair of his soft head against my cheek and the warmth of his body. I felt like a Judas Iscariot.

He whimpered slightly as the needle flashed. I closed my eyes. Doc knelt beside me as Benny slipped away in a swiftly gathering drug haze. I said a quick prayer asking that there'd be plenty of rabbits and cows that liked to run where my dog was going, with milk trucks that floated over the road.

We buried him with full family honors by the rhubarb patch near the back steps and cried buckets of tears. Dad did not attend the funeral. "Customers..." he said.

That night as I lay feigning sleep, I heard for the first time the unconsolable sobbing of my father as he wept the tears of the little boy that lies deep within all men.

*

My oldest sister, Lee Ann, took Benny's death particularly hard. When a raffle was held in town for a purebred poodle pup, she bought a ticket. I was never prouder of our town, when everyone put my sister's name on their ticket. She won hands down and Pierre Mon Ami was hers. He was no Benny, but he quickly became a loved and longtime member of our family.

SNOWED IN

By mid-March in Iowa, signs of spring are already popping. Tulips send up hearty new leaves, crocuses emerge from the thawing ground, and early arriving birds search for food and call for mates. It's the time of year when thoughts turn to flying kites and making plans for the growing season. As prudent Midwesterners, no one has put away the snow shovels yet, but there's reason for optimism.

This is what I remember:

It was 1966 near the end of my high school senior year. People were still in an uproar over John Lennon's careless remark, "We (the Beatles) are more popular than Jesus." Army Staff Sargent Barry Sadler had a number one hit song called "The Ballad of the Green Berets."

I left for school as usual on a cloudy March morning. The weatherman had mentioned there would be snow later, but so what? We were busy planning our senior trip to St. Louis, typing term papers, rehearsing for the class play, and thinking about who to invite to the Senior prom.

After lunch, the snow arrived on a west wind. Not the usual few flakes that slowly thickened, but *WHAMO*! The white stuff blew in at a hard slant and quickly gained depth. Classes were let out early and the buses lined up in front of the school to take the farm kids home. There were happy shouts, but the drivers looked worried as they worked to keep snow and ice from the windows.

Older farm kids with cars usually drove to school, making them independent of the bus timetable. It was convenient for afterschool sports, school plays, and band practice. Engrossed in their activities, the time had slipped away before anyone noticed the snowstorm was now a blizzard and dangerous to travel the country roads.

The school's lovely homecoming queen, Julia, drove to school that day with her farm neighbor, my girlfriend, Anne. They made it four blocks to Main Street and wisely decided to pull over and park on the side street next to Dad's barbershop. As we lived in a large apartment above the shop, they knew they could find refuge and call their parents. My two sisters barely made it home on the school bus and my brother and I had walked home, holding books in front of our faces to block the wind-driven snow.

It was exciting! From the storefront windows in the barbershop, we watched the wind whip the snow around. At times it came down so heavily, you could barely see the other side of the street, turning buildings into blurred, dark shapes in the dusky light.

Mom went to make supper for eight while our two guests waited for instructions from their anxious parents.

As for me... I was thinking about the possibilities of two young ladies spending the night at La Casa Christiansen. I envisioned popping corn, listening to music, playing board games, laughing, talking, and... well... who knew? My seventeen-year-old brain was racing.

One of my high school teachers, Mr. V, was fresh out of college and only a few years older than us seniors. As a younger man he'd been a state football and basketball star and fancied himself a lady killer. His new Pontiac Bonneville convertible was the envy of every high school male.

From his rented apartment across the street, he'd noticed Julia arrive in her car. Always on the lookout for a pretty face, he braved the storm to join the party.

Julia seemed cautiously flattered by his flirtations. He had to have been aware of the taboo prohibiting personal relationships with students and was pushing the envelope. Things like that can sink a career.

My fantasies about a blizzard party were shattered when plans were finalized: we were to bring the two girls to Julia's aunt's house to ride out the storm. I think everyone was relieved but me.

Mr. V offered to drive them the three blocks, and I went with him. The snow was bumper deep as his Pontiac swerved and plowed through the streets, throwing clumps of snow over the windshield. He carried Julia and I carried Anne to the door through the drifts and bid them goodnight.

It snowed hard all night and most of the next day. The wind picked up tons of dirt from the open fields in the Dakotas, turning the snow dingy and making it pack into huge, hard drifts closing roads and streets. An overpass on a nearby highway was completely blocked for days. Snow had to be cleared with construction loaders, as the snowplows couldn't penetrate the drifts. It mattered little, as no one was going anywhere anyway. Some areas were scoured bare of snow while others were piled to the tops of telephone poles. Thankfully we never lost power, but others weren't so lucky, as repairmen had to wait days to get at the downed lines. Cattle died of starvation in the fields and were swallowed up in drifts. Folks were surprised to find dead birds in the snow, like nuts in a cookie.

As the storm wound down, Dad's barbershop became a gathering place. Customers and friends blew in the door to catch up on news, relieve boredom, and get out of the house. Someone suggested holding a cribbage tournament. The word quickly spread and soon there were about ten men, including the superintendent of schools, dealing cards on makeshift tables. They chipped in for prize money, brought cards and cribbage boards, and drank soda pop from the shop's cooler. The superintendent was the big winner.

School was suspended for the rest of the week while everyone dug out from their homes, farms, and businesses. The plowed snow was so high along the roads that it was impossible to safely see oncoming cars at intersections, resulting in several accidents.

My brother and our pals broke our backs helping the old widows in town by shoveling their walks. Even after the snow ended, the wind continued to blow it into drifts we'd cleared just hours before. The same was true for the surrounding county roads, requiring snowplows to run continually. It's what locals call a 'ground blizzard'.

We eventually cleared the snow from Julia's car and pushed her out. After she and Anne left, I'll admit to feeling letdown and cheated, but years later as the father of two daughters, I completely get it.

*

Because of that late winter blizzard, I still harbor a deep mistrust of March. When I see the brave tulips and crocuses first push out of the soil, I silently wish them luck.

FARMHAND

"See ya for supper, Mom," I shouted, as I bolted for the back door. I ran everywhere in those days, always in a hurry to be someplace else. In one move I tapped up the kickstand on my bike and jumped on, pony express style.

It was late spring in Iowa, and I was headed for a farm on the edge of town for the first day of my after-school job.

I'd always been able to find work. More accurately, it found me. My brother and I had earned reputations as conscientious, hardworking hired help even if we were "town kids."

Farmers tended to look upon town dwellers as soft lazy slackers, worthy of contempt. No one, we were told, worked as hard or as long for so little as those on the farm. Maybe they were right, but when they had some dirty job, they called us. The phone rang frequently with requests for our services. My father, the town barber, served as a job clearinghouse when farmers came in for haircuts and asked if we were available. Our friends looked out for each other, too. If one of us had a job and needed extra help, all it took was a phone call or two and we had a crew.

Together we'd done every dirty, stinking, sweaty drudgery found on a farm. We'd scooped tons of the fragrant remnants passing through the gastrointestinal tracts of cows, sheep, pigs, chickens, ducks, geese, and goats. Thousands of bales of hay had been stacked on wagons and in dusty haylofts throughout the county. We'd trudged up and down endless rows of corn and soybeans in the summer sun.

In the days before modern harvesters that pick and shell corn in one operation, it was stored in corncribs. After the corn had dried and the price was hopefully higher, farmers hired Big Mel to separate the corn from the cobs in the bowels of his huge, clanking, metal monster called a sheller. It was our job to shovel corn onto the long conveyor or drag feeding the beast. The work was dusty and back bending.

We mended fences, mowed and raked hay, helped castrate pigs, milked cows, painted farm buildings, and had fun in the process. When our crew was together there were always jokes, stories, gossip, and plenty of teasing. Everyone competed to see who could lift the heaviest load or shovel the fastest to make the time pass quickly. It put money in our pockets and muscle on our arms.

This is what I remember:

Pedaling along on the blacktop south of town, I reviewed how this job was going to differ from others. It wouldn't be for a single task; instead, I was to be a hired hand. There'd be no warm company of friends as the farmer, Thor Rolland, needed only me.

Thor summoned me from the barn door as I coasted to a stop in the farmyard. "Over here," he called. I saw him leaning over the lower half of a Dutch door, hands clasped in front of him. He made an obvious show of checking his watch, noting my arrival time. The meter, as they say, was running.

"Hi, Mr. Rolland," I answered as I pulled on my work gloves.

"What's the matter, 'fraid you're going to blister those dainty hands?" he sniffed. He held out his strong brown hands, palms up, for me to inspect the thick calluses.

With a low whistle I paid the proper homage to his badges of honor from years of labor. He had reason to be proud of his life as a toiler of the soil, but I didn't appreciate the inference that I was somehow less for being a town kid. I was used to this by now and had long ago learned to ignore it; after all, I had my share of calluses, too.

"Well, let's get to it, then," he said and swung the door open for me.

I followed him through the barn to a large area used as winter shelter for the few head of cattle he owned. Manure mixed with straw lay wall to wall in a wet, foul mat a foot thick.

"Tractor loader's broke down so gotta do it by hand, I guess," he explained absently, more to himself than me.

He pointed to a collection of pitchforks leaning in a cobwebbed corner. The larger the fork, the more prongs or tines; more tines mean larger loads. I noticed there was an assortment from three to ten-tine forks. I selected the ten-tine-job with a well-worn handle. From the corner of my eye, I saw him nod his head slightly. I'd passed the first test.

He picked out the other large fork and we began working side-by-side pitching forkfuls onto a manure spreader parked outside the double door. Later, it would be spread on fields for fertilizer.

We worked for two hours before taking a break. Thor pumped cold, clear well water into a metal cup looped on a wire near the pump. After a swirling rinse he handed the first cupful to me. The familiar taste of the iron-hard water bit my tongue, and I gulped it down eagerly. I drank too fast for water that cold, giving me the sudden icepick-of-a-headache you can get from eating ice cream too quickly.

Thor saw my eyes narrow and tear, "Colder 'n your town water, isn't it?"

I nodded.

"Never freezes though, same temperature all year 'round."

I nodded again.

After we'd refreshed ourselves, he gestured to the barn and said, "Well, guess it won't clean itself."

An hour later we quit for the day and washed up at the pump.

"See ya tomorrow after school then?" he asked with a quizzical look.

"I'll be here," I said, with little enthusiasm.

"That was three dollars an hour, wasn't it?" he asked carelessly.

"You can pay me at the end of the week," I said, "and it was three twenty-five."

Thor shook his head sadly, "Didn't remember you bein' that high. Okay. That's okay, I guess."

On the way home I recalled what I knew about Thor. He was my father's age, around forty-two or so. He'd served in Europe in the army during WWII and was active in the local American Legion Post. It was through this connection and as a customer of my dad's that they'd become friendly.

Thor inherited his two-hundred-acre farm after his father's death six years before. He lived in a rambling farmhouse with his schoolteacher wife, six-year-old son, and two daughters ten and twelve.

They were prominent members of the Saint Olaf Lutheran Church and involved in many of its activities. Thor ushered, sat on the church council, and led many of the fundraisers. Julia, his wife, organized social events, sang in the choir, and was always there to help a neighbor. They were good people, though Julia liked to gossip, and Thor had a reputation for being a penny pincher.

He was a wiry five-feet-nine with dark brown, graying hair that my father clipped into a short flattop every other Saturday afternoon. His Scandinavian blue eyes were held in a perpetual squint from a lifetime in the sun. Even though it was early in the year, his leathery skin had the farmer's tan confined to the areas exposed by a short-sleeved shirt and a Dekalb seed-corn cap. When he removed the hat, there was a pale stripe on his forehead.

I took stock of my feelings about working all spring on Rolland's farm. If my first day was any measure, I was sure it wasn't going to be any treat.

For the next two afternoons, we cleaned out the barn. I was determined to match Thor scoop for scoop, stopping only when he did. At times I sped up the pace just to show him I was no slouch.

I worked all day on Saturdays, eating lunch in the kitchen with his family. The meals were hearty, and Mrs. Rolland made me feel at home as she was much more talkative than her husband.

When the daily farm market reports were announced on the radio, there was a pause in conversation. Farmers pay close attention to fluctuations in farm market prices. It helps them decide the best time to sell livestock or stored crops. It was serious business, as a misjudgment could make the difference between profit and loss for the entire year. Thor had a reputation for being shrewd with his timing.

For obvious reasons, farmers are hesitant to allow just anyone to operate their tractors and expensive machinery. My employer was no different. He started me out on the tractor raking the hay he'd cut the day before into windrows. It was an easy chore; one usually reserved for the farmer's children. I'd raked hay many times before and knew what I was doing, but Thor treated me like a beginner, and I played along. When I failed to live up to his expectations of not being able to distinguish the clutch from the brake, he graduated me to other tasks.

Abruptly one Saturday after lunch he asked, "You ever operate a disc?"

I said I hadn't.

"Wanna learn?"

"Sure," I answered eagerly. I was anxious to do something different.

A disc is a series of thin metal plates arranged vertically in rows and pulled behind a tractor to slice and break up large dirt clods made during plowing.

He made a few passes with me on his International Harvester showing me how and when to turn. Each step in preparing the soil for planting required a particular piece of equipment with its own special pattern of turns and method of attack.

I enjoyed the process of making rough fields into smooth patches of rich, black earth. Each turn at the end of a pass brought the challenge of judging the distance from the fence. To keep a straight line, I learned to steer for a distant point of reference. Easier said than done...

By six in the afternoon, I'd been sitting on the bouncing seat of Thor's tractor for five hours. At first, I'd been bored. The steady drone of the tractor's motor drowned out all other sounds, but to my surprise I found the isolation in that far-off field comforting. There was time to think. Sometimes I entertained myself by singing, reciting snatches of poetry, or talking to the birds that were searching the newly broken ground.

The interlude between late afternoon and early evening was my favorite time of day. The sun slowly retired from a deepening blue sky dotted with billowing clouds. Each west-facing pass presented a view of the horizon and the gentle curvature of the Earth, a perspective familiar to sailors and the folk of the Great Plains. As distant farmhouses caught the waning sunlight, their windows were lit as if by fire. The low clouds changed colors and shape in a slow kaleidoscope, with rose pink bottoms and violet peaks. Here and there the sun pierced them with shafts of gold in a finale that promised a fond return tomorrow.

Birds darted over the field engaged in a last meal before settling for the night in some farmer's grove. The scent of the newly turned earth and freshly cut hay wafted on the soft evening breeze.

I ate it up, feasting on the beauty of the Iowa farmland around me. *How lucky I am to live here!* I thought. People chose to spend their lives in such work for moments like this, when the Earth seems to smile and the sun blesses your good fortune. You are the caretaker of a sacred gift, the guardian of life... a farmer.

I was jarred from my reverie when I made a disturbing discovery. I'd been watching the sunset and not paying proper attention to my guide points. The result had been an erosion of my straight line across the field; it had become a huge arc.

I pushed in the clutch, shifted into neutral, set the idle, and stood up on the seat to assess the problem. If I kept the present course, the bow would only become larger and larger with each pass. This was a problem, as the field was a rectangle.

I decided to correct my mistake by overlapping already covered ground. That way the bend would be absorbed and corrected. I hoped Thor wouldn't notice before I was done.

It was getting dark, so I switched on the tractor's lights. I thought my employer would see that I just wanted to stick with it until finished. I was sure he'd approve.

At the end of the field, I spun the steering wheel to make a turn when I heard a ringing sound and felt the tractor shudder, heave, and lurch.

I stomped on the brake and turned in the seat to inspect the disc, thinking I'd struck a rock. Instead, I'd sent the disc through Thor's barbed wire fence, snapping the wire strands into coils like New Year's Eve streamers, shearing off an iron fence post, and bending two others to the ground.

Wow! I thought. *Thor will kill me! I'm finished! I'll never be allowed tractor work again.* Word would spread from farmer to farmer, and I wouldn't get a job gathering eggs.

Thankfully, the disc was undamaged, so I decided to finish. When done, I parked the tractor in the machine shed and walked like a man to the gallows to the Rolland's house.

At the back door, Thor turned on the porch light and motioned me inside. He stood in his stockinged feet with a cigarette clamped in his teeth. He squinted and asked, "Putin' in a little overtime, huh?"

I shifted my weight self-consciously from foot to foot with my eyes on the braided rug under his feet.

"Had a little accident Mr. Rolland, I put the disc smack through the southwest fence; took out three, maybe four posts. I'm sorry, sir." I rushed on. "The disc's okay, and I promise to fix the fence soon as I can." I'd prepared the speech while in my lonely field.

Thor's expression never changed. He nodded several times and said finally, "Well, we'll see ya Monday, then."

That was it? No comments about my being a good-for-nothing-town-kid? I was stunned.

For the remainder of the weekend, I stewed and fretted over what Thor was *really* thinking... or worse, *saying* about me.

I saw him briefly at church when he shot me a nod of recognition and nothing more.

Monday was a miserable, rainy, windswept day.

My mother drove me out to the farm after school. "You're not working outside on a day like this, are you?" she asked.

I shrugged and said nothing; my silence would do the lying for me.

From Thor's machine shed, I selected the needed equipment: a length of barbed wire, tools, three metal fence posts, and a post driver. After loading everything onto a cart, I trudged off to the scene of the crime.

Thankfully, Thor was nowhere to be seen.

It was hard work pushing the cart across the soggy field. The ground was muddy and pockmarked with puddles.

The damaged fence was waiting. No fairy godmother had mended it for me. I could hear the mean barbed wire snickering.

First, the broken and twisted posts had to be extracted from the ground, like rotted teeth. Next, I pounded the new posts into the ground with the fencepost driver.

The rain continued to fall in a steady drizzle. It wasn't long before my jacket was soaked, and rain trickled down my neck. I could feel the water squishing between my toes.

The trickiest job was splicing the wire and keeping it taut. Time and again, I had to start over when the wire slacked. I swore with words I never thought I'd use.

When it was done, I stood back to survey my work and was satisfied the damage had been put right.

I returned the tools, rung out my soaked clothes, and removed a list of the hours I'd worked that week from under my hat. I'd carefully written "No Charge" for that day. It was only fair; I'd made the mistake, and Thor shouldn't have to pay.

I was sliding the damp paper under the door when Thor himself stepped out onto the porch and took it from my hand. After reading it he asked stiffly, "Need a lift to town?"

"I'd appreciate it," I said.

We drove to Dad's shop as we'd worked… in silence.

"Won't be needin' you any further, Wayne, he said. "I can handle the rest myself. Only got the planting to do, anyways."

I nodded. I was being let go. I'd screwed up.

He parked his car in front of the barbershop and surprised me by getting out with me.

My father was sitting on his white, porcelain barber chair reading the newspaper and smoking a cigarette. No one, it seemed, was out and about on a rainy afternoon.

Dad looked up, "Hello, Thor, how's that kid of mine workin' out for you?"

Thor smiled and motioned at me with his head. "That's what I came in to talk to you about, Leo," he said.

Here it comes, I thought, and bit my lip. *He's firing me.*

233

"When your son here came out, I figured, here's another darned town kid with only one thing on his mind: make some money doin' as little as possible. Well, I was dead wrong. He's done everything I asked, kept up with me and then some." He jerked his thumb at me for emphasis.

"I've been watchin' him. He's a hard worker and a good kid. I'd already made up my mind 'bout that, but the frostin' on the cake was today.

"Out he comes on a day like this, desperate to fix an ol' fence I was planning to tear down anyways. So, I says to the wife, 'Julia, if that don't just beat all! Look at that kid out there in the rain!' We watched him from the window, see? Then he never even charged me for it."

I looked at my muddy boots.

My father nodded silently but his expression said, *"Nothing special... he's my son, what did you expect?"*

"Thanks, Thor, he's a pretty good kid," he said finally.

Thor listened and said, "Oh, I'm not finished. Now, I know you and your family is strugglin' and I know that Wayne here wants to go to college next year. So, I figure, hell, I got more 'n I need right now. What I'm tryin' to say is... if he needs some help with money for college, come talk to me first afore you go off to the bank. Okay?"

The two men looked at each other for a moment, then Dad stood and stuck out his hand that Thor shook firmly.

"Thank you, Thor, I really appreciate it, and I know Wayne does too," he said.

The farmer turned and gave me a wink on his way out the door.

"Go get cleaned up, Son," Dad said. "You look like a wet pup."

I moved to go when he added, "I'm proud of you, Son."

He was not one to lavish praise and when offered, it was usually a memorable occasion. This was one of them.

*

Of course, we never took Thor's offer, even though we knew it was genuine. Our family would not... could not do such a thing. We would do it ourselves or it wouldn't be done, that's all.

I did go to college and found myself educated out of jobs like the one on Thor's farm. I tell myself I'm better off for it, and I know I'm right. Just the same, I can't help missing those days in my beautiful Iowa as a toiler of the soil.

In May 1966 at the ripe old age of 17, I graduated from high school. It was a proud moment, as I was the first child in our family to become a high school graduate.

This is what I remember:

My parents threw a little party inviting aunts, uncles, grandparents, and close friends for punch and cake. I still have a few of the graduation gifts from that night, like two sets of monogramed handkerchiefs I've never used... ever. In addition, there were three sets of Cross pens, including mechanical pencils that still work. There were cards aplenty with inspirational messages and poems meant to set my feet on the right path.

College was still months away in the hazy future and I was going to need money. My father made certain I'd not be idling away my time that summer and had secured a job for me without so much as a "Whaddya think, Son?"

Up until then, most of my jobs had been farm labor. I was used to the tasks, the rhythms of the work, and dealing with farmers. Farmers have personalities that are as varied as any cross section of America, but they have many things in common: a sense of fairness, a deep commitment to the land, an independent spirit, and a firm belief that rewards are commensurate with the work.

The new job was all day Monday through Friday with half-days on Saturdays, providing steadier income compared to day labor.

My employer was not a farmer, nor had he ever been. He was a town-dwelling, general contractor named Harold who'd been a Navy Seabee in the Pacific during WWII.

Harold was a regular customer in Dad's barbershop and apparently during a haircut the conversation got around to work. Harold admitted that he needed help; I, it seemed, needed immediate employment.

My first day in the building trade came the morning after my graduation party. As my Grandma Christiansen used to say, "There's no rest for the wicked." The old expression puzzled me, as I'd never thought of myself as particularly wicked, but did, however, understand the "no rest" part.

I met Harold at his garage at seven a.m. the next morning to help load his pickup. He said little; instead, he just passed me tools, lumber, bags of cement, and so on. I didn't feel much like talking anyway, as I didn't know him from a hill of beans, but I'd expected at least a short introduction and information as to the day's destination.

I didn't know it then, but it set the pattern for the entire time I worked for him.

The first job was the construction of a small house along the Des Moines River in Humboldt, a town not far from ours.

In the time before poured concrete foundations, cement blocks were used. My job was to mix the "mud" (mortar), scoop it onto the masons' mortarboards, set up the blocks, and then "strike" the still moist mortar joints with a steel tool. The striker was shaped so when pressed into the wet cement, a concave depression was made to dress up the appearance and strengthen the joint.

Harold had hired three masons for this part of the job. I'd never met a mason and quickly surmised that they were the spoiled brats of the construction trades, but I was certainly in no position to say so.

These men just wanted to lay block or brick and not be bothered with anything else. It was my responsibility to keep their mortarboards full and the cement tempered to just the right texture by periodically adding water. They insisted that the blocks be set precisely so they only had to bend ever so slightly to retrieve them.

They almost never spoke except to say "mud" when they needed more mortar. I became familiar with the sounds of their trowels scraping off excess mortar and the *tink, tink, tink* as they tapped blocks into place with their trowels. They didn't even speak to each other!

For days, I frantically tended the cement mixer, the masons, and my striker duties. While attending one task, another was surely being neglected. One tall, burly mason named Demetri asked me sarcastically, "What do I have to do to get more mud? Get on my knees and beg?" He constantly criticized the readiness of my cement mixtures that quickly dried in the sun.

Out of frustration one hot day, I screwed up my courage and asked him, "So, how do you want the next batch? Too wet or too dry?" He put his hands on his hips, threw his head back and loudly announced, "Harold! I didn't know you'd hired a fucking comedian!"

Harold glared at me, shook his head sadly, and returned to studying his blueprints.

I tried to remedy the problem by leaving a can of water on each mortarboard for the pampered pricks to use as they saw fit. Demetri scowled and scornfully knocked his water over with his trowel, but the others thought it a reasonable idea.

Once the foundation was laid, it was good riddance to the masons and enter the carpenters.

There were two in addition to Harold, now banging and sawing away like mad. Here was a job I knew something about, as I already had a familiarity with hammer and nails.

The carpenters measured and cut the wood I brought them and instructed me where to pound in nails. They were an easygoing lot compared to the masons and razzed me good-naturedly. The men were happy to show me tricks of the trade and sent me to find a left-handed saw or a board stretcher. Yah, I was gullible.

Side jobs were saved for Saturdays, when I wheelbarrowed cement to make floors in old farmhouse basements.

I learned a lot that summer. In addition to making money, I picked up bits of knowledge I've later used. Harold never did warm up to me and I grew to believe he wanted me gone when his usual helper became available. He got the chance to ditch me in mid-July.

I'd made it clear from the start that I needed to be gone for a week on a canoe camping/fishing trip to northern Minnesota with my Boy Scout troop. Members of our troop, my brother, Scoutmaster father, and two assistant Scoutmasters were going. It would be the last time with my beloved Boy Scouts of America.

We used an outfitting company in Minnesota located at the point of embarkation. All we had to bring were our clothing, toiletries, and fishing gear, as the backpacks, food, tents, canoes, axes, and paddles were part of the package.

The weather was perfect when we set off. The warm sun beat down on our backs as we paddled blissfully away from the dock and into the Great North Woods. Our looped route was to take us up into Canada's Lake of the Woods and back. I had visions of freshly caught fish frying over campfires in piney woods on quiet lakeshores.

Our assistant Scoutmaster, Arly, was a great guy who was also the town's postmaster and fire chief. A decorated combat veteran of the Korean War at the Chosin Reservoir, he took no lip.

Arly took charge of the map and compass and led the way. Our route required making a certain distance each day to stay on schedule. If we were late returning, we were told searching parties would be sent, which would be too embarrassing to imagine.

Now, when I say, "canoe trip," I imagine you think of lots of paddling. Right? Well, yes, the route was via a series of lakes, but the lakes were connected by a piece of land called a portage. Portage is derived from the French word porter, meaning "to carry." We came to believe it was another word for torture.

After spending a few hours paddling, usually into a stiff breeze, we were ready for a break, but no. The break was always one of those damned portages.

The routine was: beach the canoes, unload, pack up all the gear you could carry, and lug the whole works to the next lake. Dad, my canoeing partner, had made it clear that he had no intention of carrying ours. By default, I became the designated canoe carrier, in addition to a heavy backpack.

The two-man canoes were equipped with cushions amidship to carry overhead on your shoulders. To avoid wondering off the trail, the canoe had to be tipped back slightly to see the path. If tipped too far, the stern or back of the canoe dragged and bounced on the rocks. For balance, I placed my arms inside the canoe along the gunnels. My bare arms were easy targets.

It's *always* mosquito season in Minnesota, as far as I know. Little squadrons of them gathered inside the canoe to dive-bomb my arms and hands. There was nothing to do but watch the little vampires suck my blood to anemia.

Even the most carefully laid plans miss details, and no one had thought to bring insect repellent. By the third day everyone's arms were a mass of lumps, bumps, and scabby welts that itched incessantly.

The portages were of various lengths and elevations, but all were muddy, rocky, and miserable. Some of the trails had poles lashed perpendicular to trees to park the bow of the canoe for a rest. They were rare.

It usually required two trips to move all the gear to the next lake, but at least the second trip was without a hot, mosquito-plagued canoe overhead.

Did I mention the flies? They were thick. Fortunately, they weren't biters and merely happy to land on every square inch of exposed skin to lick our salty sweat. They climbed over the food and explored every opening in our heads. The only respite was out on the lake or after sunset. The mosquitoes, however, had absolutely no regard for the sunset rule.

Due to the tight schedule, we paddled past huge northern pikes, walleyes, bass, and trout. I saw them swimming nonchalantly beside the canoe looking for a handout, or just out of curiosity. My father, a die-hard fisherman, became frustrated as we passed by the many fishing opportunities. He shouted to Arly, "Hey! Isn't this a fishin' trip? Here's the fish, for Pete's sake!" But Arly just shrugged and paddled on, a slave to the schedule.

In desperation, I unreeled a lure to troll behind the canoe. It was bad timing, as it became snagged on a long dead moose afloat on the lake. After paddling back to retrieve my favorite lure from the rotting carcass... it was so much for trolling.

But there were good times, too. After supper and a campfire, we retreated to our tents. No radios were allowed so we sang songs, with each tent trying to outdo the other. Our repertoire included songs from Frankie Valli and the Four Seasons, the Beach Boys, and the Beatles. The songs reminded us of the comforts we'd happily and naïvely left just a few days ago. The sessions were short-lived due to the exertions of the day and Arly being an early riser.

One day the wind was strong enough to keep us off the lake, so we spent the day in camp doing as we pleased. Most of us grabbed fishing poles and headed out to try our luck.

The fish weren't biting, so I decided to see what I could find among the rocks and trees. In a little clearing, I watched as a beautifully plumaged duck flew into a hole about twenty feet up a tree. *Hmmm,* I wondered, *ducks livin' in trees*? That was new to me, so I decided to shinny up the trunk and see for myself.

When level with the hole, I peeked inside to see a beautiful wood duck who was as surprised as I was. He immediately launched right at my head, knocking my cap off in a desperate effort to escape. *Who would believe that I had to duck a duck?*

When our week in the woods finally came to an end and we were back at the dock, we celebrated by throwing each other into the lake. A hot shower later and we were on the road to Iowa and civilization.

*

Not surprisingly, we caught few fish, with most of our energies devoted to paddling and portaging. The not-so-fun times became part of the stories we told and retold. It was an unforgettable experience that I've grown to appreciate even more with the passing years.

Back home, I found that Harold had indeed not welcomed me back into his employ. Instead, I quickly found steady work for the rest of the summer with the seed corn company DeKalb, tending the endless rows of corn that are the hallmark of Iowa.

CEMENTING MY FUTURE

This is what I remember:

I'd finished my first year of college in 1967 and needed money for the coming fall semester.

My first experience in the construction trade had been a dismal failure. I blame it on my immaturity and a boss who was terrible at giving instruction.... that and my leaving on a week's fishing trip in the middle the summer.

I decided to take another stab at it and went to work for Concrete Products, a company just outside of Humboldt, Iowa. Some of my friends had worked there and our neighbor, Mort, had been there for years.

He was a customer in my father's barbershop, and I suspect that the two of them had colluded in one way or another. Dad considered it one of his missions in life to keep me employed and out of the trouble stemming from idleness.

Mort and I alternated driving the fifteen miles every other week and became friends despite a ten-year age difference. We passed the travel time insulting each other and swapping stories. At other times we just rode in the silence induced by a 5 a.m. alarm clock.

Mort was a welder and the operator of the company's crane. With a reputation as a dependable hard worker and in possession of good common sense, he was often sought out for advice.

The company's stock and trade was the production of concrete drainage pipes. In the center of the sprawling property was a large building where they were made and "cured" to hardness overnight in steam jackets. Propane-powered forklifts constantly zipped around, moving the pipe to and from storage and onto delivery trucks.

There were also cement trucks that briought fresh cement to constructions sites around the county.

The summer I worked there they'd received a big contract to build underground chambers for electrical and telephone equipment. Iowa's power and telephone companies had decided to move their wires from traditional poles and get them underground, away from the grip of midwestern winters and summer storms. The entrances to these chambers are the manholes you see in and along roadways.

The company had to hire a cadre of money-hungry college kids to turn out as many as possible before the resumption of classes in the fall. I worked directly under Mort's supervision, assembling steel rebar cages to reinforce the concrete boxes. The entire crew worked outdoors on a long walkway.

Mort, an older man named Shulty, and Ted, a kid my age, made up the team. Shulty entertained us with stories about working on the wheat thrashing circuit as a young man in bygone days. Now in his late fifties, he had a pronounced limp and stooped shoulders from his many years of hard work. Despite coming from rival towns, Ted and I became friends and often double dated that summer.

A steel factory that produced the rebar bent it into prescribed shapes, corresponding to its location on wooden assembly jigs. Once in position, we tied the steel together with twist wires, then Mort welded it at strategic points to increase strength. When each cage was completed, Mort fired up the crane, lifted them off the jig, and stacked them nearby.

Further down the line were four sets of metal forms, each with specific dimensions. Every morning, they were taken apart and the finished concrete boxes lifted out with the crane. Our rebar cages were then placed into the forms to be covered with cement.

Crews attending the wet concrete used long, heavy vibrators they dipped into the pour to ensure it went into every nook and cranny. At quitting time, the forms were covered with heavy tarps to cure overnight with piped-in steam.

Each completed box had a sample of the cement set aside for strength testing. The contract stipulated that any structure failing testing had to be destroyed, costing the company money. Foremen made certain that didn't happen.

Work began at 6:00 AM and ended around 5:00 PM, with a thirty-minute midmorning break and an hour for lunch.

The lunchroom turned out to be an interesting educational experience for us college boys.

Lunch boxes and insulated bags were stashed under the benches lining the lunchroom. There were no tables, so everyone sat around the room facing a small trash barrel.

One of the older fellas amused us with a little routine: after eating an apple, he'd do an elaborate wind up and then throw the core with all his might into the trashcan. Pieces of apple flew as it hit the inside of the barrel and he'd shout, "hot damn!" then chuckle to himself. The novelty wore off quickly, but he continued undeterred every day without fail.

We were considerably younger than the rank-and-file employees. Many had been there all their working lives and would be until they retired or died. I got the sense that some were envious of the opportunities our educations presented us or thought that maybe we looked down on them. A few went out of their way to ensure we felt unwelcome and knew our place. Some were talkative, while others ate in sullen silence.

In time, we became more comfortable with each other and the razing and teasing began. Woe be to anyone who let slip a pet peeve, foible, or an embarrassing bit of information as it quickly became fodder for ridicule.

When one of the summer workers decided to grow a goatee, it started....

Old Timer: "So, I wanna know, College Boy, just what part of the human body are ya tryin' to look like with what's growin' on yer face?"

(General snickering)

College Boy: "For your information, it's called a goatee."

Old Timer: "Well, ya sure fooled me. Come to think of it, though, you do look like a damned goat at that."

All: "Har! Har! Har!"

(Another time)

Old Timer: "So whatcha studyin' at that college o' yours?"

College Boy: "Mathematics."

Old Timer: "Is that so you can learn to figure?"

College Boy (cautiously): "I… I guess so."

Old Timer: "Well, do ya *figure* you'll ever amount to a fuckin' thing?"

All: "Har! Har! Har!"

I learned to keep my mouth shut and volunteer little. Better to remain silent and have you thought a fool, than to open your mouth and prove it, the saying goes.

The weather was strange that summer. For two weeks in July, it rained hard once or twice every day. The downpours drove us into buildings to wait it out, which adversely affected productivity. Something had to be done, so the company bought everyone raincoats. The coats retained body heat and made us feel like we were being cured along with the cement.

After the rains ended, it got steaming hot. One morning at 5:30, as Mort and I drove through town on our way to work, the First National Bank's thermometer read 98 degrees. All we could do was look at each other and sigh. It was going to be miserable.

One scorched day, Ted and I decided to gobble our lunches and go for a swim in an abandoned limestone quarry on the property. Soon, others joined us, and it became a daily event until the killjoy supervisors shut it down due to liability concerns.

By summer's end I'd made friends with many of the workers both old and new and found it sad to say goodbye. Promises of weekend work never developed, so I found regular Saturday work elsewhere.

That summer cemented my understanding of my grandfather's admonishment that it was better to work with your head than your back. I knew then I'd finish my education, come hell or high water. I didn't want to be worn down and used up by fifty with few options. Labor is a necessary and honorable thing, but there's a price to be paid. I'd seen it for myself.

On visits with my family in Iowa, I occasionally drive by the old plant. The place where we'd labored in the sun and rain so many years ago is abandoned now and gone to weeds. It's a surprisingly bittersweet ride as I remember those men who spent their lives working there.

I'll always be thankful and grateful for the many things I learned from so many good people in those little Iowa towns and farms of my youth.

The Rutland Dam
Rutland, Iowa
Present day

www.ingramcontent.com/pod-product-compliance
Lightning Source LLC
Chambersburg PA
CBHW080417270326
41929CB00018B/3055